THE SCULPTURE MACHINE

To Scott
(the Bambino)
my own, who
makes all things
possible —
you are my
co-author in
life as well as
in this book,

with love
and devotion

Michael

The Sculpture Machine

Physical Culture and Body Politics in the Age of Empire

Michael Anton Budd
Department of History
Bradford College
Massachusetts

NEW YORK UNIVERSITY PRESS
Washington Square, New York

First published in the U.S.A. in 1997 by
NEW YORK UNIVERSITY PRESS
Washington Square
New York, N.Y. 10003

Library of Congress Cataloging-in-Publication Data
Budd, Michael Anton, 1955–
The sculpture machine : physical culture and body politics in the
age of Empire / Michael Anton Budd.
p.   cm.
Includes bibliographical references (p.   ) and index.
ISBN 0–8147–1266–5
1. Bodybuilding—Great Britain.   2. Masculinity (Psychology)–
–Great Britain.   3. Body, Human—Social aspects.   I. Title.
GV546.5.B8   1996
646.7'5—dc20   96–15168
                                                      CIP

Printed in Great Britain

For Mabel and
for Scott

and

in memory of
Kevin Jon (1959–94)

The first duty in life is to assume a pose . . .
Oscar Wilde

A constant attitude of repose is a pose that
always leads to failure.
Eugen Sandow

Civilization has done much for our country . . .
but, as a nation, we are still, thank God, savages
in one thing – we admire bodily strength.
C. B. Irwin (ex-Amateur Champion)

Always they must see these things and hear them,
Batter of guns and shatter of flying muscles . . .
Wilfred Owen, 'Mental Cases'

Contents

List of Plates

Preface

This book examines the aspiration towards representing and perfecting primarily male bodies in the consummate age of industry and empire. Its centrepiece is *fin-de-siècle* physical culture commerce. The premodern or mythopoetic masculine ideal sold by physical culturists on stage and later in magazines was a central image in nineteenth-century popular culture and political discourse. If there was a truly representative male body in the period, it was the clichéd figure of the European strongman in leopard skin and sandals. The photographed strength performer posed like a statue from antiquity and as a mass-produced image was just as bloodless and unreal. Other competing body images, some more clearly connected to everyday work and life, suffered by comparison. The image of the physical culture strongman supported claims of European superiority and pointed to the complexity of bodily desires that fuelled capitalist consumerism. Physical culture discourse and iconography thus vividly evoke the body politics of industry and empire in their articulation of the possibility of actual physical transformation and their embodiment of the fantasies that denied the many industrial and social changes of the age.

The initial research for this book began with a traditional focus on the nineteenth-century military as a central mechanism in the control and training of men's bodies. My early research included an examination of turn-of-the-century British military magazines and publications with the First World War as a provisional endpoint. As I paged through *Hart's Military Register* and other like publications I gradually began to notice changes in the advertisements. Soon, I was looking almost solely at the end pages in such volumes. In those back sections I spied my first physical culture advertisement. It was for 'Physical Culture at home', and was composed of an illustration of a nude male body segmented by measuring tapes and sporting a fig-leaf. It included an application for instruction by post for two shillings and six pence, a health questionnaire and a handy place for filling in one's own measurements. The body in the illustration was that of German émigré, Ernst Müller, also known on the stage as strongman Eugen Sandow. From that point, I began to shift from my earlier institutional and state focus to an emphasis

ix

on the field of popular media. Soon thereafter I discovered the collection of physical culture magazines, including *Sandow's Magazine of Physical Culture*, kept in the special restricted cupboards of the British Library.

One of the first questions that occurred to me regarding that first physical culture advertisement was its obvious emphasis on a normal body: its standardized anthropometric chart and the idealized figure of Sandow. In whose interests were the bodies of physical culture clients being normalized and made ideal? I began a content analysis of physical culture publications focusing on their approach to the physique and their potential customers. I wanted to know more about what motivated both its buyers and sellers and the contexts in which they acted. My thematic concerns were shaped by the organization of the journals themselves: the particular subject matter of their editorials, letter columns, illustrations and features. By placing popular culture practices and meanings in direct juxtaposition to efforts aimed at social change, one of my aims was to search for traces of our own present understandings of the body.

Physical culture media and products relied on the modern perception that the body could be shaped and repaired. Such perceptions paralleled the growth of mass society and the West's increasing ability to manipulate nature in the context of a dominant imperial-corporeal framework. Relationships between ideas about bodies and constructs such as nations and machines formed ideologies in which worldly and bodily knowledge reinforced one another.[1] As Baron Pierre de Coubertin argued in the first modern Olympiad's programme in 1896, the many new inventions and technologies of the age prompted the peoples of the world to know more about one another and inevitably to construct comparisons between nations.[2] In making comparisons, nations were frequently described as if they were physical bodies with the same organic properties as human beings. As Coubertin's belief in British sporting superiority implied, communication and technological integration did not do away with international hierarchy. Indeed, the tendency to envision nations as bodies helped to support notions that societies not only were dangerously susceptible to the forces of degeneration from within but also were organic entities that battled one another for survival on the outside. At the same time, it became commonplace for individual bodies themselves to be discussed as if they were political systems, fighting off their own 'insidious' foreign enemies.[3]

The subject of physical culture and related issues addressed below are by no means established historical topics.[4] To search through current economic history concerning male labourers in the nineteenth century for references to changes in cultural expectation, ideas about the individual male body or concepts of the 'self' will net little. Within the field of British history alone, a perusal of book indexes, card catalogues and databases still reveals infrequent mention of the history of the body in general or physical culture in particular. Considering these gaps in the literature, the following pages aim to present an evocative history of the body and the media that helps us to think about how bodies and lives were experienced and represented, and who benefited from particular forms of representation and bodily activity.

The mass of men as individuals or workers with real bodies have most often been studied as pawns within the narrow confines of social econometrics or as flat symbols of patriarchal dominance.[5] The drama of the world marketplace has been characterized as the 'puberty of nations, the passage that separates the men from the boys'. The connotation being that judgements of 'success and virility' naturally adhere to such processes.[6] Common and deeply held assumptions relating to an embodied gender order link physical power and material prosperity with embodied masculinity. The subject of male physicality might seem overworked but it remains important. For example, 'muscularity' has been taken as fundamentally masculine, just as boundaries of landscape and language have acted as markers of national character or spirit.[7] Thus, countries grow economically according to the rules of a vague tribal initiatory competition that separates the men from the un-men.[8] In this sense, investigating the idea and experience of the male body is crucial to understanding the topics of empire and industry.

The epoch in which physical culture developed roughly covers the period 1850–1918. In terms of larger historical context, I have also found the periodization 1829–1929 useful in thinking about physicality as a modern social production. One of my major premises is that several significant shifts took place in the 1820s and 1830s. What had once been defined by dynastic politics and religious orthodoxies began to be understood in terms of industry and political reform, medicine and science.[9] The bodily notions found in evolving industrial practices and consequent utilitarian ideas displaced many older views of the body. For example, the passage of the Catholic Emancipation Act in 1829 provided significant proof that the centuries-old importance of the moral-spiritual body was on the wane in Britain. At the same moment, Louis J. M. Daguerre and J. N. Niepce formed a partnership for developing new means of capturing the human image.

With regard to the production of images, my choice of the years 1829–1929 depends upon my larger argument that the modern history of the body is divided into three or perhaps four parts. The first is the epoch of the glorified body, a kind of prehistory of the modern body that stretches from early modern perspective painting, neo-classical sculpture and Renaissance individualism to the era of the American and French revolutions at the end of the eighteenth century. The second epoch is the one focused on here. I have called it the age of the sculpture machine, an era marked by better and better means of mechanical reproduction that was also witness to the zenith of old world empires. It spans the age of photography or that of the graphic revolution, and the rise of democratic and national popular cultures.[10]

In the modern era, body-oriented consumerism expanded and the power of the state grew considerably. As the image of the physical self became more pronounced as a focal point for communities, nations and individuals, the world also became one through steam power, print, wire, cinema and radio wave. In the twentieth century the masses were able to witness almost firsthand the sweep of revolutionary change, the destruction of indigenous cultures by colonial powers, the blood bath of the First World War, and the dramatic beginnings of communism and fascism. Apart from these events and their individual records of bodily waste, the era saw huge numbers of people understanding the body as something marginally more pleasurable than burdensome.

By the beginning of the First World War, commercial sellers of fitness and the body beautiful had brought earlier aspirations toward the medical and aesthetic rationalization of bodies to fruition within a growing consumer culture. In the process, notions of European progress, scientific racism and the imperatives of imperial ambition were hitched to the carts of strongmen entrepreneurs and physical culture hucksters. Incongruously, their mechanisms for sculpting new races of men and women were then overshadowed by the gargantuan slaughtering machines of the the First World War.

The age of the sculpture machine did not end in 1914. The numbing discipline of wartime horror and ennui stood in stark contrast to the pleasures of self-transformation promised by physical culturists. But the spectre of a healthy invigorating national battle always loomed large in fitness media rhetoric. Which is not to say that commercial sellers of fitness intended to encourage a war. Certainly, the First World War was a devastating and shocking example of how uncontrollable the forces of nationalism and industrial capital could become. In peace and in war, however, individuals counted more than has sometimes been acknowledged. The response to hostilities in 1914 echoed fears and desires that were foreshadowed repeatedly in popular fitness media. The war did not end those fears and desires. Indeed in some ways, its shattering experience contributed to a resurgence of new forms of body culture in the postwar era.

Not long after the deliberations at Versailles, resurgent militarist elements were already seeking to harness the proven bodily power of the masses. As Hollywood became the world's dominant image maker, National Socialists in Germany began to dramatically employ new radio and film technology in spreading their body-oriented propaganda. From the depression and industrialization of mass killing in Germany, to forced collectivization and purges under Stalin and massive war efforts made between 1939 and 1945, the decline of older European empires and the shifting battles between fascism, socialism and democracy provided a new context for body politics in global terms. In the subsequent Cold War era, the domination of American advertising and consumerism and the rise of more elaborate world networks further encouraged a new and radically different body consciousness.

Remnants of the mentality behind the sculpture machine persist today, but other crucial shifts and events distinguish our own era from the age of industry and empire. The third epoch of body politics embraces the polarized and totalitarian 1930s, the Second World War and the Holocaust, new heights in planetary destruction, the rise of the electronic global village and the phenomenon of the robot-cyborg. This last period, which we still inhabit, might in fact be divided into two: an age of war technology and modernism from 1929 to 1960; and a subsequent postmodern era of political and sexual rebellion occurring alongside the final dissolution of Eurocentric colonialism. The latter might be called the age of holographic reality. Together or separately, they form a new and distinct stage in the history of body politics.

All history is about bodies and nothing can be written or understood outside of bodily experience. In this sense, a literal history of the body is vast and nearly unthinkable. Histories of body politics, such as that attempted here concerning physical culture, provide a more focused area of study and offer a useful ground for coming to grips with elusive constructs such as the 'self' and 'power'.

Nonetheless analyses and studies of the body have often tended towards opacity. In many cases, largely ahistorical theories of the body have veered back and forth between the rocks of particularity and the shoals of ungrounded generalization. From craniology and the measuring sticks of nineteenth-century scientific racism to the latest sociobiology and new age theories, the body multiplies itself across our range of perceptual frames and continually escapes precise definition. One of my central arguments is that the body requires more than repeated analytical fragmentation. Instead, it needs to be addressed as we find it: as something that is present and yet elusive, that defies type and categorization and yet is routinely and sensibly a meeting place for our many different understandings of what a body is. The recognition and experience of varied body types, spectacles, disciplines, pleasures and desires help to constitute the equally elusive conscious self. Merely listing the varieties of bodies and bodily manifestations of sentience brings us no closer to understanding the significance of the body as the vehicle and ground of social, cultural and political action. In this sense, however, we need to be careful not to let the universality of bodily experience propel its study toward the meaningless study of everything.[11]

Every age has its characteristic body politics. Their historical study charts changes in the way that a multitude of bodies – from the 'natural' to the symbolic – have been perceived and interpreted. We cannot think our way out of our bodies. Nor can we use the idea of a natural or more real body as a vehicle to escape from discourse and culture. What we can do is locate ourselves in relation to other bodies – historically and in the present – and to the institutions and discourses that seek to define and cater to them.

The body politics focused on here include the assemblage of representation, communication, expression, spectacle and direct force that have tended to focus more explicitly on the physical body in the modern era. The term 'body politic', as used by Hobbes in the seventeenth century, took on new significance with the arrival of industrialization. The idea of the nation as a unified body became more complex as the boundaries of individual citizen bodies began to be as intensely contested as national frontiers. In the nineteenth century, several such forces converged on the bodies of male soldiers, clerks and labourers among others with the lead taken first by early-nineteenth-century reformers and government and later by the commercial physical culture media.

The chapters that follow are organized chronologically and thematically. The introduction describes James Watt's sculpture machine and serves as a prologue to physical culture and the body politics of the Victorian era. It spans the shift from early industrial and Enlightenment liberty and libertinage to the anti-industrial responses of Regency Romanticism. It juxtaposes the representative bodies of the monarch, workers, the middle classes and popular culture figures as a way of better understanding the political, symbolic and economic shifts that created the age of the sculpture machine. Chapter 1 describes the specific institutional contexts in which the century of the sculpture machine emerged. It examines early Victorian constructions of the body as a site of physical and spiritual reform. Schools and slums are discussed in concert with concerns over worker revolt, military preparedness and rising worries over national degeneracy. Chapter 2 summarizes the popular culture predecessors of physical culture and describes the spread of body-oriented spectacle and media in the music hall and in popular literature and the early physical culture press. Its central focus is the 'heroic' strongman poseur as a new type of representative body. Chapter 3 addresses the impact of new image technologies, body performance and consumer approaches to the body that tacitly recognized the importance of individual desires and wants. It explores how the heroic and erotic were separated and diffused within one another in the physical culture press, and attempts to explain how the capitalist mass media both encouraged a mono-sexual identity and opened resistances to it. Chapter 4 focuses on imperial concerns in physical culture media. It describes how the rhetoric of empire acted as a mirror for physical culture and as a rationale behind fitness appeals. In addition, it examines the ways that the emphasis on the body both supported and undercut typical imperial and racial assumptions. Chapter 5 views the workings of physical culture and the sculpture machine in the First World War and its aftermath, reflecting upon the irony of building bodies only to destroy them. Chapter 6, the Conclusion, addresses the changes characterizing the coming body politics of the 1920s and 1930s with reference to cinema, improvements in body alteration such as plastic surgery, the rise of fascism and 'robopathology'.[12]

In our own bodily obsessed culture, the discussion of the sexual and political body retains a radical and almost dangerous cast. This introduces the problem of examining residues of something from the past that we have profound difficulty discussing in the present. As the vehicle of our very existence, the experience of the body will always be a complex subject to address. It allows us to make connections and to cut ourselves off from one another. Consciousness may be something different from the organs and limbs, but we still do not know of any thinking selves that do not have some kind of physical body. This means, among other things, that writing any history of the body requires questioning ideas about the nature of the self and corporeality that historians often take for granted. This book offers the historical contrivance of the 'sculpture machine' as a metaphor for thinking about an evolving constellation of institutions, material objects and social relations.

The conceptual frame of the sculpture machine allows us to encompass the intersecting discussions and representations, technologies, knowledges and systems for influencing bodies that appeared between the 1820s and 1930s. Its principal devices were the camera and the printing press; its output the enormous debris of early consumer culture and the modern mass media. As a temporary refuge for many living bodies, its forces and workings were never controlled by a single group or class. Although its component parts were utilized by elites seeking control over a changing language of bodily symbols, as well as the actual bodies of the masses, its systems and mechanisms were also employed by countless workers and others in their own search for individual autonomy.

Today's world is characterized by the daily distribution of a virtual avalanche of images and representations in which the possibility of bodily pleasure and perfection shimmer more enticingly than ever. The promise of a perfected physical body was first asserted with the emergence of a modern mentality supported by the mechanisms of industrial technology. Combining the market and industrial techniques with a search for a moral centre, the consumerist state created during the age of industry and empire promoted desire only to quash it or, rather, encourage its rechannelling into perpetual acts of consumer purchasing. The relentless pursuit of bodily improvement and enjoyment by an expanding world population remains at the heart of today's global consumer economy.

The greater sculpture machine of this book's title was never built. Like many of the symbolic bodies examined below, it is an imaginary device. But its apparatus, the bodies it referred to, and its associated products were none the less tangible and real. As a shorthand for such processes, techniques and changes, the image and idea of the sculpture machine addresses the modern manifestation of the desire to step beyond the confines of conventional bodily limits – to reshape, reform and perfect the body and the self. It is not a structural theory in the strict empirical sense, nor is it meant to be yet another 'master narrative' of the unifying body. In the end, its success depends on the extent to which it helps us think about the sublime and ineluctable experience of our own bodies and those we move with together and apart in our own present world.

In this regard, the following investigation of our common bodily past is offered as an invitation to reinvent the dialogue concerning what we have created historically and will continue to revise and rebuild in the realm of bodily discourse and representation. As the Russian semiotician Mikhail Bahktin noted, we cannot actually live in the house that theory builds. I hope, none the less, that the sculpture machine might provide a conceptual structure to inhabit while examining traces of bodily experience from a past that is long gone. To rephrase Corbusier, it is a machine and refuge for rethinking our shared past and our own corporeal selves.

MAB
Wooster, Ohio

Acknowledgements

I first articulated the ideas in this book during my graduate studies at Rutgers University. I owe a tremendous debt to Philip Greven for his readings course on masculinity and heroism and the series of seminars conducted by Traian Stoianovich in which the ideas found here were first elaborated and refined. My greatest gratitude is owed to my father whose love of history and athletics started me on the path to this study. I wish he could be here to read it. The writing of this book would not have been possible without the support of a Marion Johnson fellowship from Rutgers University and a faculty development grant and research funds from the College of Wooster. I would also like to extend my appreciation to the British Library, the Institute for Historical Research and King's College Military Archives, University of London, the Center for Research Libraries in Chicago, the Providence Athenaeum, Rockefeller Library at Brown University, the Sager Symposium at Swarthmore College, the Yale Center for British Art, the Center for the Critical Analysis of Contemporary Culture at Rutgers and the Faculty Colloquium Series at Rhode Island School of Design. I thank Michael Adas, Scott Cook, Antje Harnsiche, Jennifer Hayward, Alphine Jefferson, Beth Irwin Lewis, Peter Pozefsky, Joan Wallach Scott, Karen Taylor, Pamela Walker, Simon Watney and Susan Whitney for reading portions of my work in various finished and unfinished forms. Special thanks go to Marta L. Budd for her insights as an art historian. I am also indebted to my students, especially the members of my 'Knight to the Cyborg' and 'People and Machines' courses. I owe a great debt to my teaching assistants and researchers, especially Matthew Mariola, Thomas Teper, Tracy Cubbal, Sara Passino and David Arthur at the College of Wooster and Russell Bigelman and Claudien Durocher at Bradford College. Special thanks to Dale Catteau for her administrative talents and to John Hondros for the use of his library. Appreciations go to Niko Pfund and Jennifer Hammer at New York University Press and to Tim Farmiloe Sunder Katwala and John M. Smith at Macmillan. Thanks also to David Chapman for assistance with photo illustrations, to Henry Abelove for mentioning me to publishers, and to Robert Krusynski of the Natural History Museum in London for leading me through the labyrinth of the anthropology skeletal stores in search of Sandow's cast. In thanking those who have assisted me and others that I may have forgotten, I must add, of course, that all errors and omissions are my own.

Introduction

> making a cutting or gnawing point ... with next to mathematical precision ... so as to search for beautiful Forms, into the heart of marble and bring them out into full day light, is no mean instance of human sagacity.
>
> Dr Patrick Wilson to James Watt[1]

As political agitation and bodily repression grew in Regency Britain, James Watt occupied his final years developing a mechanical system for copying human sculpture. Watt's work on such a device was emblematic of the many activities aimed at improving, rationalizing and objectifying bodies in the period defined here as the century of the sculpture machine. Between 1829 and 1929, the upsets and turmoil of industrialization made reproduced images from the past more common and desirable as buffers against accelerating social and political changes. In this sense, Watt's desire for a sculpture machine was evidence of a hope that industrial processes might do more than amass profits and speed production. More specifically, Watt may have seen the industrial manufacture and proliferation of classical forms as a means of righting the seeming imbalance brought about by his own inventions.

Almost fifty years earlier, as Watt worked towards perfecting his version of Newcomen's steam engine, Joseph Wright unveiled his neo-classical painting *The Gladiator* in London. Although the imitation of the symmetrical physique from antiquity stood in stark contrast to the dirty and battered bodies of workers and the poor, such ideals offered a comforting link with the past. Indeed, the use of bodily forms from antiquity as architectural decoration and in expanding political contexts increased significantly as a direct consequence of industrialism.[2] In Wright's day, the present routinely met the past in idealized eighteenth-century portraits of contemporary figures; in works by Johann Zoffany, Jacques-Louis David, Jean-Antoine Houdon, Antonio Canova and A.-L. Girodet.[3]

The juxtaposition of Watt and Wright is instructive because it underscores the dynamic character of technological change and the repicturing of the past in the period. Although executed in the classical tradition, Wright's painting betrayed a different bodily sensibility from

1

that represented by the nymphs and satyrs of rococo classicism. A lesser Caravaggio of the Enlightenment, the Derbyshire-born Wright was a friend of Erasmus Darwin and others in the Lunar Society of which Watt was also a member.[4] As an amateur scientist, Wright sought to paint scientifically and record the world in accordance with nature's laws. His paintings demonstrated the continuing importance of depicting the heroic physique and the search for new contemporary bodily ideals. Physiological models could be traced back to the earliest documented forays into philosophy when the body was distinguished from the mind. Certainly, sculpting the physique was already a time-worn cliché.[5] But the authority of bodily metaphors increased during the Enlightenment as the regimentation of the physical body became ever more aggressively articulated in war and industry. In the eighteenth century, the realms of art, manufacturing and politics began to offer different opportunities for representing, controlling and freeing bodies. This was the age of well-drilled standing armies led in a gentlemanly manner by officer-aristocrats who prided themselves on their fashionable military finery. The 'grotesque body' of the worker or peasant soldier and that of the idealized noble represented only two poles among many in a widening gambit of Enlightenment bodily objectification that included both old and new corporeal experiences.[6] The desire to control people on a large scale was certainly not a unique characteristic of the eighteenth century. Neither was the idea of freeing the body through activity. The body at play had been an established counterweight to the experience of labouring long before the industrial revolution.[7] Dancing, cockfighting, ball games, boxing and wrestling had long been popular and remained local in character well into the industrial period. What made the late-eighteenth-century experience of the body unique and different was its emerging range of possibilities for using new systems and technologies to control and enjoy bodies – to represent and reshape them as timeless.[8]

By the second decade of the nineteenth century, when Watt began working on his sculpture machine, the body of the common worker had become enormously more profitable as an input in industrial capitalism. Watt's observations of the natural world had improved the partnership between people and machines, making himself and others rich in the bargain. At the same time, consumerism based on body improvement and the experience of the self as pleasurable spectacle began to come to the forefront. Increasing worker demand for cotton clothing promoted mechanization and, as Watt noted, more pumping engines were also needed because 'People now have such a rage for washing their b—ms'.[9] Machine begat machine and a growing number of bodily desires helped feed the growth of a consumer economy. Such developments were exemplified by Britain's Regent, later George IV, who regularly spent over £20 a week on various creams, colognes, pomades, powders and oils.[10] In his consumption patterns and desire to remake himself, the Regent personified the emerging consumer trends of his age. From the 1820s many began to expect that the monarch and aristocracy should also embody the emerging values of middle-class domestic life. The reaction to George IV's barring of his hated Queen-Consort Caroline from the coronation at Westminster Abbey in 1821 revealed the growing importance of public opinion and the spread of the idea of a respectable middle-class representative body.[11] But George IV's habits and interests followed those of the 'fancy' more than that of the sober middle class. His reputed knighting of the Irish boxer Dan Donnelly in a house of ill-fame brought the artifice of the modernizing Prince together with the self-made body of the common man.[12] A symbol of Irish pride, Donnelly beat the English champion George Cooper in 1815 and took a hard-drinking tour of Britain where he was said to have met the Prince of Wales. Donnelly was a product of the Dublin docks and, like most prizefighters of the day, his rise to fame and success was brief and ill-fated. His subsequent ownership of several public houses ended in failure. Eventually, the fighter's life of hard knocks, carousing and heavy drinking exacted its price. In 1820, the champion collapsed in his Greek Street pub in Dublin and died at the age of 32. Whether it was from a bad liver, a sexually transmitted disease or too much ice water following a game of racquets, 'Sir Dan's' life and death typified that of the successful boxer whose bodily prowess might only momentarily pull him up from the lower rungs of society. As a member of a 'lesser race' who had beaten his English superior, Donnelly did nothing to change the British domination of Ireland. His double value as just another working-class corpse and as a cultural symbol, however, was proven in a ghastly fashion when grave-diggers attempted to sell his corpse to a physician. They brought the boxer to a Dr Hall, who was a fan of the prizefight. Hall recognized Donnelly immediately and sent him back to his tomb, but not without first sawing off the champion's good right arm. The relic eventually found its way to Edinburgh where it was used to teach anatomy to medical students, and was later a popular attraction in Victorian travelling circuses.

Donnelly's association with the monarchy, and his treatment in the contemporary press and later popular memory, indicated the continued cultural importance of the physically powerful male and a desire for alternative symbols of national and class identity based on the body. Long before the nineteenth century, boxing had been hailed as the British national sport, a pastime whose 'lessons helped English armies prevail'.[13] The majority of clubs that Lord Byron or Regency bucks such as Scrope Davies might have attended for physical training were the boxing gyms found during the golden age of bare-knuckle fighting. The decline of boxing as a legitimate sport began not long after Donnelly's death. The middle-class rejection of the sport was based upon a religious view of the body emphasizing human sinfulness and renouncing pleasures of the flesh. The reassertion of bodily sin within the ethos of an economic and social class did not completely displace cross-class glorifications of violence.[14] There were building scientific, philosophical and commercial pressures that began to push against that same middle-class religious/moral economy. Indeed, the very interest in controlling boxing in the first place was itself indicative of a growing obsession with corporeal matters in general.[15]

The period in which boxing was driven underground revealed a range of bodies that bore the damaging marks of industrial progress. That the bodily 'liberation' brought about by industrialization was uneven and frequently offset by reverses can be seen in workers' response to government's unwillingness to protect them from the advances of early-nineteenth-century technology. In 1811, Luddites lashed back at new ways of manufacturing that undercut their incomes and rendered their skills superfluous. As Lord Byron feared, Britain's elite was all too willing to place a value on the representative worker's body of 'something less than the price of a stocking-frame'. The injury of industrial property was put on a par with murder as Parliament passed a law against the breaking of frames in 1812, adding to the considerable list of hanging offences that still included sodomy, poaching and the theft of a single sheep.

Workers suffered the brunt of changes engendered by the machine, but non-labouring bodies also ran foul of state and industry's combined mechanisms. As seen in the example of George III's long and torturous illness, the bodies of the elite as well those of workers were being discussed and experienced in thoroughly new ways.[16] Apart from the king's treatment at the hands of his physician-gaolers, another significant example of the pervasive impact of the mechanical across the class spectrum occurred on the occasion of the opening of Britain's first commercial railway.

On 15 September 1830 eight special trains inaugurated the line between Liverpool and Manchester. But the celebratory mood was darkened by the collision of the former Tory Member of Parliament (MP) for Liverpool, William Huskisson, with George Stephenson's prizewinning engine the *Rocket*.[17] Just 17 miles out of Liverpool, as the *Northumbrian*, *Phoenix* and *North Star* took on water and fuel, the hapless victim was trapped between the open door of the Duke of Wellington's carriage and the oncoming *Rocket*, which crushed his leg and thigh 'in so dreadful a manner as to produce death before the lapse of many hours'.[18] The fact that the victim was not a common worker but the 'first financial statesman of the country' did not prevent the commemoration of such an important event in the history of industrial progress from proceeding.[19] After some discussion it was decided that the train would continue to Manchester where the official group would 'refrain from all festivity'.[20] Upon arriving at their destination the carriage containing the Duke and his party was booed and hissed by a 'grimy' crowd of 'scowling' artisans and mechanics dissatisfied by the current government's policies. Word of Huskisson's probable demise had spread quickly. His death later that evening was doubtless viewed as a bad omen, but most of those waiting to greet the train in Manchester were certainly more concerned with their own personal collisions with the machine age than with the unfortunate end of Huskisson. The presence of a 'representative man' and his weaving frame high above the jeering crowd attested to their concerns. As one observer described the scene, the 'tattered, starved looking weaver' stood as a 'protest against this triumph of machinery, and the gain and glory which the wealthy Liverpool and Manchester men were likely to derive from it'.[21] Surely, the weaver was more representative in a numerical sense than Huskisson. But whether Huskisson's damaged body or the figure of the tattered weaver is taken as the 'representative man', the message is similar. Machines were having a huge bodily impact on society and sometimes a murderous one.

Earlier in 1830, a decade after the death of his father, George IV lay similarly trapped at Windsor. The living bodily symbol of a still expanding British empire, the one time Regent was an impressive John Bull towards the end of his reign, weighing some 325 lb.[22] Like the dandy, Beau Brummell, the royal vibrancy of youth and artifice finally gave way to the inevitable ravages of time and excess.[23] In his final hours, the representative body of the monarch presented a sobering story of inevitable physical decline and the chimerical promises of consumerism. In the description of his funeral as well, images of industrial process were joined with the realities of death and physical decay.

> The coffin was very fine and a most enormous size. They were very near having a frightful accident for, when the body was in the leaden coffin, the lead was observed to have bulged very considerably & in fact was in great danger of bursting. They were obliged to puncture the lead to let out the air & then to fresh cover it with lead. Rather an unpleasant operation, I shd think, but the embalming must have been very ill done.[24]

In post-Regency London the initial move began towards the Victorian project of literally and figuratively covering up the performance of the self that immense technological and social change had uncomfortably laid bare. A new and more complex attitude toward bodily propriety and display was evidenced in Thomas Carlyle's critical treatise on clothes published near the time of George IV's death.[25] A eulogy for both the king and the dandy, Carlyle attacked the artifice of modern kingship and pointless consumer fashion.[26] Thackeray conveyed a similar message in his *Four Georges*. Noting that Madame Tussaud's had obtained George IV's coronation robes, he inquired after the missing royal body:

> I look through all his life and recognize but a bow and a grin. I try to take him to pieces, and find silk stockings, padding, stays, a coat with frogs and fur collar, and star and blue ribbon, a pocket-handkerchief prodigiously scented, one of Truefitt's best nutty-brown wigs reeking with oil, a set of teeth and a huge black stock, underwaistcoats, more underwaistcoats, and then nothing.

Even the King's body was becoming what a consuming industrial society made it and nothing else. Such 'empty' bodily artifice persisted in more than the memory of Queen Victoria, who recalled that as a child she did not like kissing the King because of his greasepaint make-up. Indeed, body consumerism was assimilated within modes of Victorian respectability. Even the concealing and sombre attire of the period was part of the regime of consumerism.

And in Victoria's own life and that of her vast range of subjects, the theatre and performance of the modern self continued to expand in myriad and unexpected ways.

From the spread of photographic images and reorganization of sport, to varied legislation concerning disease control and the creation of new associations for working men, the decades following the 1830s saw significant shifts in mass cultural activities and discussions touching upon body. The predecessors of the commercial phenomenon of physical culture included a broad range of state and reform society efforts that began before the middle of the century. The determining preconditions and ideas that furthered the proliferation of mass fitness in the 1890s and the early twentieth century first appeared in the 1820s and 1830s as competing views concerning the rights of individual bodies became more apparent. As workers combined to demand rights and the slave trade began to be dismantled, new forms of bodily oppression associated with colonialism and capitalism grew more powerful. As soon as workers thought to organize, trade unions were outlawed in Britain. Ironically, in an increasingly secularized society, growing dependency upon excessive, almost pagan, consumption, indebtedness, sexual liberty and poverty continued to be punished in Old Testament style. Debtors' prisons, increased executions for sodomy, and horribly run poorhouses were all examples of continuing contradictions in body politics as basic social and economic conditions changed. Indeed, the gross bodily exploitation of the European masses and subaltern peoples remained the rule well into the nineteenth century as breaking a frame or having same-sex physical relations continued to result in imprisonment or execution.

Watt never perfected his sculpture machine. And yet, the dialectic between heroic perfection and the rough realities of technological change implied by his project continued to characterize the remainder of the nineteenth century. Watt's death in 1819 coincided with the marching of some 50 000–100 000 workers, weavers, shoemakers, artisans and agricultural labourers to amass at St Peter's Fields near Manchester. When the yeomanry of manufacturers, merchants and shopkeepers charged into the crowd eleven were killed and over four hundred wounded. It was instantly dubbed the Peterloo Massacre, a biting reference to Wellington's triumph at Waterloo. The viciousness of the response to peaceful protest polarized Britain. Percy Bysshe Shelley put the tenor of the times into poetic verse:

An old mad, blind, despised, and dying king –
Princes, the dregs of their dull race, who flow
Through public scorn – mud from a muddy spring –
Rulers who neither see, nor feel, nor know,
But leechlike to their fainting country cling,
Till they drop, blind in blood, without a blow –
A people starved and stabbed in the untilled field –
An army, which liberticide and prey
Makes as a two-edged sword . . .

Where her husband depicted in graphic bodily terms the meld-
ing of new industrial systems with the decaying structures of the
ancien régime, Mary Godwin Shelley horrified her audience with
the spectre of a manufactured body and a lesson in the costs of
human pride and technological ambition. Published in the same year
as Peterloo, *Frankenstein* was a commentary on the impossibility of
either knowing or controlling bodies. Her novel illustrated a dis-
comfort with the body politics created by science and industrialization. As the personification of technology out of control or as the
embodiment of abused workers coming to consciousness, the crea-
ture illustrated the same moral: knowledge of the world and the
body were dangerous, unfathomable and better left unexplored.
Watt's machine for copying statues was clearly less ambitious than
Victor Frankenstein's reanimating mechanism and was certainly a
more comforting technology of bodily representation.[27] But his earlier steam engine had already created as much havoc if not more
than the 'hideous progeny' of Shelley's anti-hero.

In the greater scheme of things, Watt's system for copying statues was the harbinger of a solidifying web of desires, institutions
and techniques for improving bodies. The dramatic proximity of
heroic statuary and massive engines displayed at the Great Exhibition in 1851 illustrated a central dialectic of the age that combined
the revisioning of the past with the confrontation of the modern.
In this regard, late-eighteenth-century moral views and standards
of bodily representation, alongside the period's many jarring social
and economic changes, set the stage for the emergence of a bodily oriented mass society. The era of the sculpture machine was
largely synonymous with the Victorian Age and the shift toward
an industrial consumer society. Political economists from Smith to
Marx argued that bodily labour was the single source of wealth. The
industrial revolution supplied abundant support for their claim.[28] New

systems of mechanization, organization and discipline increased the value of the labouring body. It was, after all, mechanization's initial ability to regiment and amplify human production that made it so valuable. In turn, the needs and desires of individual bodies enabled consumer society to develop. Individuals' relationship to themselves and to the bodies of others seemed to become, as it were, more naked facts. And yet, like soldiers who were termed 'units of fire', the mass of workers' bodies were often described in disembodied terms as 'hands', or orifices of consumption.[29]

Even though the empowered and disciplined physique was increasingly recognized as a social good, the assertion that bodies were a key source of wealth and productivity was countered by a palpable fear of bodies as dangerous and uncontrollable. The overdeveloped and strongly willed body posed a grave threat – whether it appeared in the guise of the revolutionary mob, marauding Luddites, or social 'deviants' and the filthy poor. New systems for disciplining and categorizing bodies on a larger scale became the plausible remedy for the many problems associated with what was perceived to be an increasingly unstable social body. Gradually, various physical ideals were incorporated into developing political, racial and scientific hierarchies. As the modern nation emerged, images associated with a national body were thus linked with new notions of health, moral good and the practical imperatives of defence.

The paradigms of reformism, and the technological and ideological tools of physical culture were already being shaped by the 1850s. At the same time, the complex relationship between the competing representative bodies of kings and boxers, workers and middle-class capitalists, was also evolving as the mechanisms of celebrity and mass culture expanded and developed. In this context, Victorian reform and degeneracy debates began to coincide with early recreation and fitness discourse in a world increasingly defined by the funhouse mirrors of consumerism.

By mid-century, the majority of European urban dwellers continued to subsist on a poor diet, lived in inadequate housing and had little opportunity for leisure or recreation. In the half-century that followed, people in cities and many outlying areas increasingly satisfied a host of newly created desires with a growing abundance of consumer goods. Even those with negligible resources at least wanted to buy new clothes, took trouble to clean what they did own, began bathing more regularly, and indulged in new forms of leisure and recreation. The harnessing of the masses to the needs of new industry was gradually if only partially balanced by the creation of forms of mass consumerism that gave some degree of autonomy to individuals. Within a web of other social constraints, people made choices about products and leisure that demonstrated a consistent resistance to didactic attempts to improve their health or cultivate particular beliefs. The political ramifications of all consumerism in this period were considerable. But body-oriented consumerism – that directly concerned with the improvement of health and physical well-being – was perhaps more important than any other in responding to and shaping the political temper of the times.

1

Bridging Reform and Consumerism

By the time of the Great Exhibition in 1851, Watt's attempt at constructing a sculpture machine had already been made somewhat redundant by photography. But the desire for 'beautiful forms' had not lessened. In the physiques of their young men as well as their architecture, Victorians desired a solidity, a firm 'muscularity' that belied the increasing uncertainty characterizing a nascent mass society.[1] Bedevilled by the ominous presence of the machine, they were comforted by the past's pantheon of virtuous heroes and statuesque bodies. After a visit to the Great Exhibition, a middle-class visitor named Gideon Mantell expressed particular dismay in his diary at having seen 'many dirty women' breastfeeding their children just beneath the 'lovely . . . figures of the sculptor'.[2] His comparison of real bodies to statues was not unusual, but Mantell wanted something beyond a mere imitation of the forms found in stone. He wrote of his fervent wish for 'the power to petrify the living, and animate the marble: perhaps the time will come when this fantasy will become realized and the human breed be succeeded by finer forms and lovelier features'.[3]

The more complex female form, moulded by the surface of fashion, was at odds with the desire to create a naturally erotic and uncomplicated feminine body. Mantell's wish was predicated on the march of scientific progress demonstrated by the technologies and products displayed at the exhibition. In the end, he seemed to hope that the messy reproductive role of women might somehow be usurped by men of science. Importantly, the representative bodies of the sculpture machine were by and large masculine, and to possess the heroic body was to be the very opposite of the feminine.[4]

The decades after 1851 witnessed the highwater mark of British industrial and scientific achievement. The 1860s were the decade of 'muscular Christianity' and the 'Cult of Manliness' first espoused by Carlyle, Charles Kingsley and Thomas Hughes.[5] Religion remained a successful mediator of the rocky relationship between the body

11

and the crass material world. The bodies of elites mimicking the poses of the ancient world also remained important, but new technologies – in transport, printing and manufacturing – radically changed attitudes towards the body, and the larger contexts in which bodily issues could be debated and discussed. Physical environment, the body, character and morality were progressively linked.[6] Class position, from wealth to poverty, was inscribed upon the body through new codes of dress, cleanliness and markers of good health.[7] Soldiers' bodies were regularly measured according to standard recruitment ideals. Phrenology or the reading of the skull and other body parts as a key to character came into vogue. Empires, rationalized by scientific racism, became the model for the expansion of industrial states. At the same time, women's bodies were at once more completely concealed by clothing and more intimately probed by science than at any other time in history. Technologies such as photography aided state authorities as well by 'exposing' the salient features of the deviant and criminal type and helping to keep track of a seeming growing number of offenders. Identifying criminals and the abnormal developed first. The use of photographs to present ideal physical types and sell body-improving devices followed. Although reformers reversed the emphasis in the relationship between moral and hygienic improvement,[8] a moral Christian perspective did not entirely disappear. But improving the physical body and its environment began to take precedence over changing morals.[9] Certainly by mid-century the view of society as a product of changing social and medical perspectives was increasingly seen in literary and critical works. From Marx to Dickens, body metaphors were central.[10] As epitomized in the philosophy of health reformer George Henry Lewes, however, the concept of the corporeal was still resolutely tied to some higher idea of the soul or spirit.[11] In any event, the very possibility of sustaining the health of the soul's implement beyond youth, even for the middle classes, was not great. Lewes was thus stating a sad reality of the mid-Victorian age when he noted that 'few of us, after thirty, can boast of robust health'.[12]

Rather than a central template, as it would become later in the century, the body was a collateral part of the model, a form upon which a spiritual structure was imposed. Such a body was interpreted as being at risk to disease in terms similar to bodily sin even before the paradigm of the germ theory was adopted in the 1880s.[13] In partial result, a new type of literary and practical heroism focusing upon the body began to be articulated. Dickens' works were particularly crucial in establishing a more sociological and scientific linkage between the urban community and the dying body as a metaphorical literary and social standard. Here, we cannot underemphasize the sustained threat and palpably greater presence of deadly disease in daily life. Dickens' special use of the organic was part of the growth of the 'humanitarian narrative', which developed as the industrialized city steadily encroached on its rural hinterlands.[14] Whether as an organism or as a machine, the body increasingly became a separate thing, a *corpus* subject to dissection and reconstruction. The description of such a metaphorical and real body was necessary before legislators and reformers could use it as a marker of the ability to exercise power, or as a symbol of national weakness. This was increasingly being done through the collection and dissemination of statistical analyses of crime, disease, fitness for military service, and the like. Such issues were all the more easily discussed and understood by way of their common reliance upon an idea of the body as reified through such statistical data collection. This new statistical idea of the body was actually a void, a space around which activities and languages formed. In many instances it was almost a trick of language itself, an ever-expanding numerical abstraction or approximation of actual living bodies. In this sense, nineteenth-century journalistic and fictional discourse related the body within the larger paradigm of humanitarian narrative, which was linked to the evolution of medical description in the process of the autopsy. Such a discursive evolution was indicative of a shift away from thinking of the body in terms of its 'being' to a conception of what it 'ought to be'.[15]

Carlyle's clear and rhapsodical worship of English bodily force, linked inextricably as it was to the 'fearful symmetry' of the urban industrial machine, was part of a common Victorian vision that was imbued with the Romantics' idea of a combined physical and spiritual power.[16] In his reformed-Byronic social vision the emphasis fell upon the need for a manly heroic temperament more than it did upon the value of a pointedly individual healthy body. At the same time, popular, commercial and professional interests in health began to shift away from patent nostrums to preventive approaches such as hydropathy and to an increasing number of books and 'scientific' pamphlets focused upon individual bodies.[17]

By the second half of the century, Matthew Arnold's bodily metaphor of the 'strange disease of modern life', with its 'sick hurry' and 'divided aims', had become a handy commonplace.[18] It was present throughout social and literary discourse, and even the cautious liberalism of Tennyson betrayed traces of the industrial, scientific and cultural changes that influenced Dickens, George Eliot and others.[19] In Eliot's work, we can see the dramatic change from a spiritualized to a new organic and scientific bodily model.[20] *Middlemarch* (1872) was the very reverse of Carlyle's heroic notion of life seen from the summit of history, with its intense social historical focus on those to whom no monuments would ever be erected. But Eliot's last novel, *Daniel Deronda* (1876), was a severe departure from the kind of realism seen in her earlier works. Although not well received in its day, its story of two ethnically and class-contrasted women, and a young man who discovers that he is Jewish, revealed a world conceived not as a spiritual design but as marked and determined by the bodily and material circumstances of race and class. It was characterized early in the twentieth century, along with her other late writings, as 'almost choked by science and psychology'.[21] In this sense, the increasing intrusion of the analytical if not the avowedly scientific continued as the social novel's method of commentary on real bodies and the corporeal entity of the nation became ever more self-conscious if not more stylistically sophisticated.

Victorian social critics, reformers and novelists such as Dickens and Eliot helped frame the body within a scientific-literary discourse based upon decay. Notwithstanding continued reference to traditional Christian approaches to the salvation of the soul or spirit, the individual and national body were increasingly viewed in terms of health and illness. Carlyle and Arnold, among many others, also responded to a cultural climate which associated societal ills with biological causes, and healthy bodies with national prosperity. But Carlyle's vision of historical epochs, as seen in terms of the life of the body and soul moving together towards death, was complimented by a new biological and generational model.

The growth of nineteenth-century industry, nationalism and imperialism relied heavily on the regular use of evolutionary bodily metaphors in the articulation of the ideal roles of its citizen-soldiers and citizen-mothers.[22] The categories of bodily sin and grace were redeployed within the new opposition of health and degeneracy.[23] The secularized body that emerged after mid-century was connected to changing cultural practices and the development of a new medico-scientific paradigm.[24] A significant part of its basis was found not only in pathology and in photography, but also in changing ideas about disease progression and control. For example, the move toward ever smaller microscopic levels of biological research helped to foster a growing discourse of bodily health centred on the individual organism. A more secular view was prompted by the specific epidemiological advances of scientists such as Koch and Pasteur, who by the 1880s had contributed to the isolation of the agents responsible for some of the major diseases of the day.[25] The medical model encouraged by such discoveries helped reify bodies as sites of biological study and control. This helped make them more manageable units for cultural and political discussion as well.

With the advent of industrialization, factory regimes and urbanization seemed to have supplanted formerly 'healthful' forms of agricultural labouring. But even though such developments were consistently bemoaned it was not to bucolic toil that reformers turned for their models.[26] The repetitions of agricultural labour, like those of the factory, were often deemed harmful and asymmetrical in their effects on the physique. Instead, throughout the century, the most easily referenced models of robust physicality were military in character.[27]

Armies and navies had for centuries been the prime example of male association and bodily training. They continued to be important as models of bodily reform in the nineteenth century.[28] By the end of the century, the actual bodies of workers, soldiers or sailors were of less practical value than they had been in the first flush of industrialization and the era of the Napoleonic mass army. Wars between 1856 and 1899 were relatively quick and cheap, but Britain's triumphs in the era between the Crimean and Boer wars were almost always accompanied by dogged assertions of national physical decline. At mid-century, industrial technology had already begun to make the nationalized citizen more important as a consumer than as a producer or warrior. But war remained a palpable threat, and the fear of a moral and physical virus devouring Britain's martial and economic sinew became current within an atmosphere darkened by the débâcle in the Crimea and the first great recruitment scare of the century. A subsequent government investigation into the quality of army recruits was further fuelled by the invasion scare of 1859.[29]

The measurement of military recruits had long been a continental European practice. In the nineteenth century the ideal warrior, marked by signs of a 'bodily rhetoric of honour' according to certain postures and physical properties, was replaced by the standardized soldier, as height and chest size became the barometers of health for recruiters.[30] New systems of measurement helped inspire fears of social decay and new methods of bodily training.[31] The focus upon reforming the *volk* through exercise was pioneered in the German states as a response to military defeat at the hands of the modern French mass army under Napoleon. Unlike the popular and raucous spectacle of the prizefight in Regency England, the post-Napoleonic German states gave rise to the more orderly and rationalist phenomena of the Fraternal and Gymnastic movements. Friedrich L. Jahn was a pioneer in the movement.[32] His one-time residence in a cave and sporting a bearskin on the streets of Berlin were later used to link him to various 'primitivist' body culture movements in Germany.[33] German gymnastics' more important long-term role was found in its emphasis upon bodily beauty tightly connected to physical prowess.[34] Largely through Jahn and others, greater Germany and the Scandinavian nations were viewed throughout Europe and North America as the home of a functional if not a protomilitary gymnastics which aimed to develop a pool of efficient soldiers with classically symmetrical bodies.[35] It was also in the German states and in Austria that the occupation of the weightlifter was most firmly embedded as a part of popular entertainment.[36] Other proponents of gymnastics, such as Dr Moritz Schreber, tried to employ similar mechanical and engineering principles in changing actual bodies. Alongside developing surgical means for fixing limbs shattered by nineteenth-century firepower, Schreber was active in advancing orthopaedic methods for treating children with malformations of the spine. During 1844–52, Schreber treated 252 cases and invented the 'straightener', or *Geradehalter*, a painful device which he used on his own children as a means of preventing curvatures of the spine.[37]

Systematic approaches to physical training and education did not catch on as quickly in Britain. For example, like many poorhouses, the Regency public school was run to suit its masters. For the most part, boys were left to their own devices in arranging their recreational pursuits.[38] In the late eighteenth and early nineteenth centuries, the original seven ancient schools along with the English universities reached their nadir. At that time, games and sporting pastimes were in a state of dangerous anarchy by comparison to public schools later in the century. The routine of brutality and corruption amidst crowded filth resembled Bentham's unreformed prison more than it did an educational establishment.[39] And it was not until the 1870s and 1880s that such chaotic tribalism disappeared as the public school institutionalization of sports as a primary symbol of social sucess was made complete.[40] The gradual rationalization of military training proceeded along similar lines.

Britain first began to be influenced in the 1830s and 1840s by athletic and gymnastic movements begun in the continental nations.[41] It was thought as early as the 1820s that something apart from formal drill and team sports was needed in the British armed forces and in 1822 Britain hired a Swiss army officer, Phokion Clias.[42] Clias was placed in charge of all naval and army physical training and also taught at Charterhouse, one of the prestigious public schools. He relied upon the theories of gymnastic leaders like Jahn but his efforts did not prove long-lasting.[43] It was not until 1865 that the first official British army physical training regulations were published and an examination of the recruiting returns and the structure of the overall system of military intake was undertaken.[44] Two years later, in 1867, the Commission Inquiring into the Recruiting of the Army made its report to the House of Commons. The commission report focused not only on what the army did with its recruits once it got them but also on the problem of why recruits were inadequate in the first place.[45] In the end, however, nothing very dramatic or useful was done to revamp the training of the common soldier.[46]

The more important efforts at reforming bodies in the period were made in schools and among the working class. With the 1860s came the 'New Athleticism' and its society-wide organization and codification of games and sports. As some reformers attempted to improve the military, others sought a more practical application of Muscular Christianity in the rationalization of sports in education. The aims of the New Athleticism were those of instilling character and bridging class differences, emphasizing teamwork, manliness and modesty.[47] Notwithstanding the success of athleticism in the public schools, the majority of recreationally oriented self-help activities and related reform efforts occurring in this same period were aimed not at the elite but at workers or the lower middle classes. In this sense, the New Athleticism was part of a movement that was not solely an elite phenomenon in either its causes or effects. Rather than percolating downward from the elite school into broader society, the ethos for bodily reform developed within different classes at the same time. It was implicit in the public school's very structure that middle- and upper-class boys would lead, but there was a creeping belief inherent in the training emphasis of the

Arnoldian school that even members of the elite were 'made' rather than born.

As freshly enfranchised working-class men began to exercise their political muscle between 1867 and 1884–5, a new world of leisure and recreation was also developing. Sports, exercise, health policies, popular entertainment, and military and moral concerns for the nation's 'physical' well-being began to converge within a jumble of attempts to salvage the physical body of the 'degenerate' British worker. Across Europe there was a greater emphasis on the body, leisure and fitness as social reformers became more concerned with the threat of national and individual physical decline.[48]

In Britain, the middle-class building of parks, art galleries, swimming baths, museums, exhibitions, adult schools, libraries and gymnasia was in some way tied to fears that the lower orders would swamp bourgeois leisure spaces, as indeed they did at the seashore.[49] Whatever the intentions of the middle class, the ultimate form which mass leisure tended towards created numerous opportunities for the various members of a developing mass society to shape their experience of leisure apart from the control of a single dominant class. Greater infusions of capital and a tendency towards vertical integration meant that sport, music and the theatre in general were transformed along with publishing into an integrated mass entertainment network dependent upon high volume sales and quick-changing spectacle.[50] Indeed, the awareness that individual consumer desires were significant was not lost on some reformers.

The recognition that worker desires were important was seen in the activities of 'early closing' proponents' arguments for worker-directed leisure.[51] John Lilwall was an activist during the middle of the nineteenth century who emphasized the necessity of recreation for the worker: 'Persons may moralize and talk as they will, but men are so constituted that social intercourse and recreation are amongst the *necessities* of our common nature'.[52] Lilwall foresaw the importance of individual agency not only in creating systems of beneficial recreation but also in restructuring greater society. His larger argument was that excessive labour was both demoralizing in the literal sense as well as counterproductive to economic efficiency. Lilwall argued for the necessity of 'sinew-bracing recreation for the young men of the city'.[53] He suggested that the area of Smithfield in London be used as a spot not only for manly pursuits and games but also for gravelled walks and gardens for the convenience of 'females, invalids, elderly persons, and children'.[54] In making his case for working-class leisure and the half-holiday, Lilwall had exact models in mind. He made mention of an early public gymnasium begun by the Earl of Carlisle in 1849 at London's Primrose Hill where 'A considerable number of young persons, principally young men, avail themselves of this means of pleasing stalwart exercise, especially during the summer mornings and evenings, often in the presence of a large concourse of spectators.'[55]

In the middle of the century, the opportunity for activities such as those promoted by Lord Carlisle was the exception rather than the rule. None the less, in Lilwall's arguments for reducing the hours of commerce we can see the early articulation of exercise as a consumable spectacle and potential product, and some inkling of its significance as a political and social issue. Lilwall's approach was different from that of many others within the early closing movement. Rather than focusing strictly upon the dangers to health posed by an industrial urban working environment, his analysis had a mass cultural dimension. Its fundamental basis was not only that too much work was unhealthy, but also that the space opened up by shorter hours needed to be filled with something purposeful although not overdetermined by middle-class desires for controlling working persons. Needless to say there were already numerous examples of middle-class failures in the attempt to provide edifying and beneficial social activities for the working classes. Initially such failures often resulted from the bourgeoisie's assumption that workers and the poor could be educated like their own middle-class children. This was apparent in the many examples of workers' outright refusals to be treated as such. One earlier example was that of reformer Charles Bray's failed Coventry Labourers and Artizans' Co-operative Society which offered weavers the dubious opportunity to practise healthful gardening after a long hard week of work.[56]

Lilwall seems to have been particularly cognizant of this pitfall. He believed that recreation was something needed by the working man above all others, and cautioned against the typical moralist's concern with what such 'men *ought* to do'. He offered instead that it was better to begin by inquiring into 'their real condition'.[57] Of course, such inquiry was the responsibility of middle-class reformers like Lilwall himself. But even this was an improvement on more paternalistic approaches in which workers' desires were deemed to be unformed or even unimportant.

Lilwall had been preceded in this pragmatic view by the reformer

James Hole of Leeds, who argued that the principle of supply and demand was the key to effectively engaging the working man.[58] According to Hole, reformers needed to let the market or what workers collectively decided to take up decide the question of what kind of recreation ought to be supplied. Both views gave agency to working people in the realm of leisure and recognized the limits of the middle classes' ability to 'surgically' influence other classes.

Another example of the recognition of workers' desires was the initiation of the working-men's clubs movement in 1862. The assumptions of the club movement were not dissimilar to public school athleticism. A major question was one of what leisure or recreation for the labouring classes ought to entail. If the working man had to have leisure it was presumed by middle-class patrons that it might at least be of an edifying nature. The clubs movement, like the preceding London Working Men's College, began as a middle-class endeavour to introduce workers to temperance and intellectual pursuits. And yet, by gradually admitting to the operative principle of letting workers choose their own leisure activities, middle-class reformers undercut their ability to control them.

Such approaches to Victorian reform developed within an atmosphere of rising nationalism, and a mass fascination with the club or society as an adjunct to or replacement for more traditional social identities based in locality or as alternatives to the home. Following upon the public school and reformers such as Lilwall and Hole, the Young Men's Christian Association (YMCA) was the first organization to enter into the practice of systematically providing recreational sites and activities for the working man.[59] The YMCA's first efforts were in the drapery trade. Ultimately pragmatic in its engagement of the working classes, its presumptions about the urban environment echoed Thomas Arnold's view that the grouping together of undisciplined male bodies created a combustible situation. In both the public school and the slum, the energies of young men needed to be channelled.

The British YMCA's provision of recreation in the 1860s resulted more from a demand for such activities by workers and lower-middle-class patrons than from any clear plan on the part of its central leadership.[60] Originating under the leadership of George Williams and 12 of his co-workers, the YMCA was founded in 1844 as a charitable mission run by workers for fellow employees aiming to improve the spiritual condition of young men in the drapery and other trades. At the same time, Samuel Smiles began delivering the lectures included in the enormous bestseller, *Self-Help* (published in 1859). Interestingly, Smiles' first book was a treatise entitled *Physical Education*. He frequently contributed articles on health to newspapers and periodicals, and as seen in the YMCA *Lectures to Young Men* (1849–50), the association's philosophy was similar to the gospel preached by Smiles: that physical steadfastness and bodily health were both supports and results of self-reliance.[61] Lilwall, Hole and the YMCA illustrated the development of a new notion of the embodied self – one emphasizing the possibility of improving the body and character – to make changes in the temporal as well as in the spiritual sphere.

By the 1870s, a more turbulent period of socialism and trades unionism had also begun. The first socialist rhetoric for more than a generation resurfaced as the all-encompassing mass press began to assume a new position of importance. As workers banded together, governments responded with limited social reforms that were tied to nationalistic and imperialist aims. At the same time, the 1870s and 1880s were marked by continuing economic depression and increasing unemployment, and an upsurge in concerns over race suicide and degeneracy in Europe and North America.[62] In 1883, the British Fabian Society – an important support of a social-imperial ethos during the following decade – was founded. Increasingly, appeals to fitness were made with an explicit view towards improving Britain's military efficiency.

With the extension of the British franchise in 1867 and in 1884–5, working-class men acquired a new importance as political consumers and voters. Views of society as highly susceptible to decay were further animated by the emergence of an enfranchised 'able-bodied' citizenry, and yet the social role of adult males continued to be couched in productive terms linked with assertions of military necessity.[63] The goal of electoral reforms was to enable what William Gladstone called the 'capable citizen' (an adult employed male holding a regular domicile) to register to vote.[64] The bodily implications of the term 'capable' were reinforced by provisions of the Poor Law which required the automatic disenfranchisement of any registrant who applied for relief. The aim of the latter's authors had been 'the depauperizing of the able-bodied'.[65] But up until 1885 the seeking of simple medical assistance alone meant the loss of the vote. Increases in the franchise were thus significant in terms of the clear linkage of voting to bodily health, or, at the very least, one's demonstrable fitness for work. It was also a connection that put the privilege of voting in direct relation to the responsibility for national military service.

Despite the widening of the franchise and growing importance of sophisticated military and other industrial technologies, raw manpower and land continued to be viewed as the most important quantities that defined a nation. Indeed, geographical predictions of an imminent world order dominated by the territorial and demographic giants of the United States and Russia troubled British leaders for most of the late Victorian era.[66] Even improving the health of children could be reduced to nationally oriented military terms. For example, Lord Brabazon (later the 15th Earl of Meath), a popular writer and speaker on the subject of national competitiveness and social decay in the 1880s and 1890s, isolated England as the one country among the 'civilized' that failed to consider the improvement of children's health and strength as carefully as that of their mental condition.[67] Rehearsing the fears of many others, Brabazon believed that the lives of the masses were already leading 'towards degeneration and the wholesale decay of the race'.[68] He sweepingly argued that the rapid flow of population from rural areas to the cities was the prime factor contributing to Britain's supposed degeneracy. Brabazon's comments were part of a steady critique following the Crimean war, which linked social unrest with working-class diseases and immoral practices.[69] Like most of his contemporaries, Brabazon's arguments for improving the health of children were based upon impressionistic data, such as comparisons between the people one might see at a given market day in the country and those at a comparable event in the city. In addition, he used the most impressive statistical example of his day: the alarming upswing in the number of men rejected for military service between the periods 1860–64 and 1882–6.

Such discourse assumed that individual bodies and the *corpus* of the nation – land, not production in and of itself – represented the true wealth of the state. A broader conception emerged of the community or nation as a body liable to infection or vulnerable to virally caused decay. The British record of state activity in promoting a fit male population was frequently seen as lacking by comparison with almost any other country. In an editorial entitled 'Are We Decaying?', which referred to the contemporary folktale of the modern Englishman trying on a suit of old armour and finding himself too big for it, Brabazon warned against the easy assumption that such anecdotes provided any substantial proof of the nation's progress in terms of bodily improvement.[70] In spite of the developments in science and other arts, Brabazon asserted that the 'national physique is by no means all that it should be'.[71] In an address given at the Liverpool Gymnasium, he used the example of Germany and the importance of gymnastics in maintaining the modern nation.[72] Referring to Jahn's *Turner-Vereine* or gymnastic associations, he linked martial muscle with freedom in his identification of gymnastics as the practical beginnings of the march to Paris which culminated in Germany's 1870 victory in the Franco-Prussian war.

It was within this climate and at a time of confusion and political setback for the Liberal party (divided and defeated over the issue of Home Rule in 1886) that Herbert Gladstone began to apply some of his political acumen to the task of encouraging physical fitness for the common man. Gladstone may have been led in the direction of promoting fitness for the working-class male through his own exerience with physical training in a non-military context (he had trained in a gymnasium as a young man).[73] The result was the establishment of the National Physical Recreation Society. The fact that the younger Gladstone took an avid interest in promoting exercise for working men at precisely the same time as his party's defeat highlighted the growing appreciation of the working population's potential power.[74]

The founders of the National Physical Recreation Society (NPRS) were all active in creating a more explicit linkage between imperial rhetoric and social reform. Instituted during a watershed decade in the transformation of British popular culture and the development of mass leisure, the society formed crucial links between old-style rational recreation, military concerns and the coming wave of commercial fitness. In the context of the developing mass press, particular issues concerning national well-being were highlighted more than others. The Home Rule issue, which had brought down the government, for example, was an especially volatile issue which was thought to threaten the stability if not the very shape of the United Kingdom. General Gordon's martyrdom in 1885 was yet another event that added fuel to popular fears of national and imperial decline.[75] 'Chinese' Gordon's death at the hands of rebellious colonial subjects put the capstone on his career as the quintessential Victorian bachelor hero. Both his death and the debate over Home Rule helped encourage national discussions on the topics of sovereignty and colonial conquest that viewed the nation in organic bodily terms.[76]

During the decade preceding the founding of the NPRS, social critics often portrayed working men as timid. At the same time, fears of outright worker revolt were voiced. The passage of the Trades Union Act 1871 had indeed allowed for the development of a new and more threatening type of worker organization composed of semi-skilled and unskilled workers. These were the unions that eventually used the strike most effectively. In part they had been encouraged by the renewed spread of socialist ideas. The models and rhetoric of both American and European socialists were more and more finding fertile ground in Britain. For the first time in over thirty years the fervour of the Chartists began to be matched. Over the next two decades unions grew more militant and, by the late 1890s, everyone from match girls to dockers were combining successfully.[77]

Ironically, increasing worker interest in political action was partially the consequence of marginally improved conditions rather than degenerating ones. The period between 1875 and 1900 saw few reforming measures passed by Parliament. This was due in part to the preponderance of successful legislation that had already been enacted in the previous decades. According to earlier assumptions and from an elite point of view, the important items on the social reform agenda had been all but completed by the 1880s with the improvement of urban hygiene and sanitation, the creation of a system of elementary education, and the bettering of working hours and conditions in many occupations. But the zeal for and habit of reformism on the part of the middle and upper classes did not entirely fade as a result. The formation of the NPRS in this same fallow period of reform legislation demonstrated a search for new objects of social improvement and a re-evaluation of old reformist goals.

During the spring of 1886, several worthies and notables apart from the younger Gladstone were recruited for the NPRS's founding honour roll. They included Gladstone's father, then Prime Minister; Sir Charles Beresford; Lord Randolph Churchill, later Conservative Foreign Secretary; Lord Rosebery, later Prime Minister; Cardinal Manning; the Revd Edward Lyttleton, headmaster of Eton; Col. Onslow of the Army Gymnastic Staff; and General Lord Wolseley, the man who arrived two days too late to rescue Gordon at Khartoum. Preparations for the first public meeting at Exeter Hall continued through the summer elections in which the Liberals were decidedly rejected at the polls. At the same time a brochure publicizing the coming public gathering was prepared for Gladstone's approval.[78] In addition, months before the society's official début, its journal was already being organized.

The founders were not unaware of the value of marketing their new organization. From the very beginning, they engaged in the business of promoting their cause through publicity and the production of a quasi-commercial magazine.[79] In a letter to Gladstone dated 21 June, fellow organizer A. Alexander listed the contents of the NPRS's first journal issue, including 'planted' leading articles to be republished from mass newspapers. In articles from the *Daily News*, *Globe* and *Telegraph*, the society was lauded for its concern with improving the quality of the national racial stock.[80] Though not a mass circulation publication, the NPRS journal was an intermediary between earlier magazines with hundreds or a thousand or so readers (like the radical *Westminster Review*) and later popular fitness magazines which sold in the tens and sometimes hundreds of thousands.[81]

As publishers of a journal, Gladstone's NPRS provided a rubric under which emerging commercial fitness entrepreneurs could begin to discuss their activities and advertise their products and services. Although it effectively sheltered those with professional and pecuniary interests in the promotion of fitness, the NPRS's aim was a charitable one meant to remedy the perceived problem of a degraded British workforce through the organized encouragement of exercise among the masses. The organization pursued its goals through the most familiar Victorian version of panopticism, in which social problems were made real and visible by the formation of a reform society. That entailed, among other things, obtaining aristocratic patronage and electing an 'honorable president' like the younger Gladstone. At the same time the society entered new territory and went beyond simple panopticism. Although they would be eclipsed in the developing golden age of the small periodical by their more dynamic commercial rivals, the NPRS's publication enterprises, *Recreation*, and the later *Gymnasium News* and *Physical Education* were ground breaking. The society's publication efforts provided some of the only successful models for subsequent commercial appropriators of reforming fitness and bodily rhetoric in the period before the 1890s.

The founding of the NPRS was pivotal in the transition from the particular uses of fitness by Victorian reformers to its general turn-of-the-century burgeoning as a health and strength subeconomy. In this, there was a shift away from middle- and upper-class views of workers as passive political variables, towards an acceptance of their growing power as both voters and buyers of products. Still, the example of the NPRS is not simply the story of the middle classes learning how to better manipulate workers. Nor was it the tale of labour's triumph over its betters within an increasingly consumer-ruled economy. In a greater sense, the NPRS was the result of a long-standing growth in concern with training and shaping the human body.

The formation of the NPRS did in fact represent an attempt to influence workers in their use of leisure time, but its real successes arose only in those areas where ideological conflict was most easily masked.[82] Its formation can be viewed in one way as a response to growing worker agitation. However, the longer range causes behind the creation of the NPRS and of such labour activity itself were largely determined by a complex of other structural and ideo-logical changes that dealt specifically with the articulation and salva-tion of a social body.

Many of new bodily pursuits, like the expression of nationalism itself, relied upon a desire for individual identity anchored by group association. From the 1860s onwards the rising value of participa-tion in non-traditional groups was demonstrated by the growth of political and oratorical societies among the middle class in Britain.[83] The same can be said of the working classes, in terms of both eco-nomic necessity and social inclination in trades union organizing and working-men's clubs. Another important step in promoting male physicality as a legitimate public spectacle in the 1870s and 1880s was the founding of the Royal Tournments by Major Gildea in 1878, with the first 'assault-at-arms' presented at the Royal Albert Hall. It was followed with a combination display with the volun-teer forces at Wimbledon in the next year. In 1880, the perform-ance was moved to the larger Agricultural Hall in London. It later became known as the Royal Naval and Military Tournament and was viewed as an effective advertisement for the military in times of peace. It was, in addition, a promoter of the linkage between phys-ical training and the spectacle of strength performance within wider society.

In 1885 the Army Gymnastic Staff (AGS) was officially recog-nized under the rubric of 'schools of instruction' as a part of the Army. Col. Fox, also a founder of the NPRS, became its new head in 1890. The military was finally beginning to catch up with reform rhetoric.[84] Discussions on the subject of bodily training in its precise military context and in terms of the larger population continued to develop throughout the 1880s and 1890s. The underlying organic reconceptualization of the nation as a body liable to decay remained important. As subsequent attempts to sell the improved body as a commodity demonstrated, a heavy reliance upon medical and ideological articulations of social problems impinging upon the self and the body continued to be valuable well into the next century. And yet, the emphasis upon decay and its connection with bodies was not simply determined by vague fears of invasion and the scaremongering use of military statistics.

Before the coming of the mass newspaper and magazine, the typical reform society's presence – the actualization of its power – was dependent upon its physical contact with the bodies of prisoners, the afflicted and poor as seen in the early YMCA. In the physical fitness reform discourse encouraged by the NPRS, the individual in the gym class became the personification of both pleasurable spectacle and panoptic surveillance. Fitness readers became the primary proselytizers and representations of fitness reform: sending in photographs, writing letters describing their experiences and the conversion of their friends, and informing their fellow fitness advocates of the 'data' resulting from their observations of physical decay on the streets of their own towns. In the example of the NPRS journal, creating such initial linkages among the subscribing readership was as important as the formation of competitive leagues and awarding of trophies. Although not ideally positioned to physically survey and influence the bodies of the population, the NPRS hoped to disseminate a common social vision through uniting middle-class reformers in physical training efforts and in coaxing the lower classes to actually take up sport and exercise.[85]

The Physical Recreation Society was part of a long line of formalistic attempts to control working-class leisure.[86] In the end, it was never as important in promoting a patriotic working-class fitness ethic as it was in providing a workable model for the selling of health, beauty and strength as commodities in subsequent decades. While not without their notable successes in attaining their original goals, earlier middle-class reformers such as Lilwall and the originators of the working-men's clubs movement had, by the time of the NPRS's founding, been effectively replaced by working men themselves, who had abandoned the latter movement's temperance and intellectual objectives.

By the 1880s working men as well as lower-middle-class clerks and others interested in sport could meet in YMCAs, working-men's clubs, pubs or at work in order to form social organizations or athletic teams.[87] While athletic activity itself and the interest of the NPRS in channelling working men's leisure time in 'proper' directions were not new, all the talk of rational recreation in the previous decades had not resulted in a system which gave the middle class or elite any real ability to direct working-class leisure activities.[88] Like Lilwall, the NPRS emphasized the 'want of open spaces' in the urban environment, and proposed the establishment of a system of recreational sites to remedy this problem. The YMCA and working-men's clubs notwithstanding, organizing of teams and exercising in public spaces was still largely limited in the 1880s to organizations or places that were not solely intended for such activities.

According to its 'Gymnasium Intelligence', the society did not make much progress in promoting new sites for healthful pursuits in its first year.[89] The NPRS membership retained its hopes, and an excerpt reflecting upon the future of fitness was culled from a publication of the YMCA in far away St Joseph, Missouri. An anonymous writer opined that

a new era is dawning in the science of physical culture . . . a higher class of instructors are coming into the field – men who have made physical culture a profession, and who seek, by proper use of suitable apparatus and the baths, to build up every part of the physical system equally.[90]

If the NPRS can be said to have influenced or even controlled worker choices as regards leisure, it did so at the price of any real ideological specificity in protecting its own class interests. The term 'physical efficiency' as used earlier in the nineteenth century with reference to the quality of military recruits, or by Rowntree in his study of poverty in York, took on new meanings in the hybrid world of Victorian reform and consumerism.[91] The acquisition of an efficient body was not yet understood as an affordable luxury good by many working-class and petit-bourgeois men. Rowntree's bare notion of physical efficiency was equivalent with the meanest standard of a healthful diet and lifestyle for an average family at the poverty line.[92] Far from allowing for physical fitness instruction or equipment, adhering to such a standard meant that the families of either craftsmen or regularly employed labourers must never purchase a halfpenny newspaper or spend a penny to buy a ticket for a popular concert. They must write no letters to absent children, for they cannot afford to pay the postage. . . . They cannot save, nor can they join a sick club or Trade Union, because they cannot pay the necessary subscriptions. [Their] children must have no pocket money . . . [they] must smoke no tobacco, and must drink no beer . . . must never buy any pretty clothes. . . . Nothing must be bought but that which is absolutely necessary for the maintenance of physical health. . . . If any of these conditions are broken, the extra expenditure involved is met, *and can only be met*, by limiting the diet . . . by sacrificing physical efficiency.[93]

Of course, Rowntree's analysis of incomes and expenses for the working poor and his implied sumptuary regulations were broken frequently as families scrimped and shifted their purchasing to accommodate for emergencies such as illness, as well as other desires: from the simple pleasures to be found in sweets, drink and tobacco, to the respectability associated with other more durable consumer goods. Which is not to say that family men might not have been tempted to sacrifice these other purchases in favour of the promises of a better life through physical exercise. The appearance of being able-bodied was of no mean importance in a strictly practical sense. However, without the precious time to consider issues of personal vanity, patriotism or bodily desires, many men stood beyond the reach of fitness appeals.

In the following decades, the contest over the control of worker recreation took a new turn as its rhetoric grew more vague and leisure began to be more firmly established as an issue in discussions of political economy.[94] By the late 1890s, the NPRS and other bodily oriented reformers had helped to create a mentality and a language well suited toward what later fitness entrepreneurs sought to market. Like the 'New Athleticism', the society offered the language of sport and the playing field as a means of crossing class boundaries.

In July 1887, the NPRS journal changed its name from *Recreation* to the *Gymnasium News*. This indicated a move away from the earlier pursuit of rational recreation. Within the next decade, others made a cleaner break, and the Physical Recreation Society's altruistic goal of exercise for the working man was effectively displaced by a rush to exploit the masses' potential demand for amusement and physical improvement. Still, by 1890, British publications aimed at professional physical educators and a broad audience of physically minded folk had little hope of success. In 1891, a journal entitled *Physique* published two issues and folded.[95] Its full title included 'physical education, domestic, school and personal hygiene, gymnastics, athletics, games and sports'. *Physique* tried to include all physical activities and it presaged the typical physical culture connection of fitness training with the military in articles on the national physique and the training of soldiers and sailors.[96] Its pages included treatments of games in public schools, historical articles on sport in the ancient world, and even an editorial concerning the danger of physical education falling too much into the hands of the drill sergeant and professional gymnast alone. The experience of *Physique* was not atypical. The magazines that followed it trafficked in similar fare, but other developments were necessary apart from changes in content to make them successful.

There were successes, such as an Anglo-American effort, the *American Referee*, renamed the *Cycle Referee*, which followed the same trend as other US technical and trade journals such as the *American Machinist* that published European editions.[97] More common were protoprofessional examples such as *Dancing*, which began in the same year as *Physique*. Like the latter, it sought to legitimize and aid its practitioners in the move towards professionalization (in this case those teaching the 'terpsichorean' art).[98] Employing the term 'physical culture' in its official title, *Dancing* enjoyed a longer run than *Physique* but it too ceased publishing after a stint of about two years.[99] Both publications illustrated the still limited appeal of magazines too closely focused on a particular social agenda or group.

The NPRS evolved from the convergence of several contradictory notions regarding social good and changing treatments of the body, many of which had been fomented by the new urban and industrial experience. Sometimes, these had a clear class dimension. Rising fears of both societal decay and labor unrest were examples of class-based explanations of social problems that were somewhat at cross purposes. On the one hand, workers were a strong force that needed to be channelled. On the other, they were conceived of as a source of potential contagion. Eventually, within consumer culture these contradictory views of the simultaneously weak and vibrant male citizen were happily subsumed within the lively play of fitness marketing rhetoric.

2
Picturing Physical Culture Consumers

Alongside the tradition of reform, the development of different forms of popular and political bodily spectacle were important to the emergence of late-nineteenth-century physical culture. Before industrialization, images of saints, the nobility and idealized common men were the major representative figures in Christian Europe. It was against their images that depictions of the debauched and supernatural, the heretical and foreign, and even women were opposed. By the end of the eighteenth century, the idealized deity, prince and commoner were challenged by a variety of new representative figures and opposing images. Although still officially idealized, royal bodies were increasingly liable to satirical and other less serious treatments. In the case of the early Hanovers, the first two Georges inspired little in the way of awe and respect. During their reigns, the power of the actual royal body became less important than that of the represented royal body. When George I died while visiting his German domain in 1727, no one seemed concerned about the disposition of the royal remains.[1] Later, however, newspapers were eager to report that George II died in the lavatory and the *Gentleman's Magazine* even went so far as to publish a coloured illustration of his dissected heart.[2] In both cases, the interest in the British monarchy and its degradation in the press signalled not only changing political realities but also important shifts in the mechanisms of bodily representation.

In the British pleasure gardens of the same period, nationalist evocations and unusual bodily spectacles were combined with the staple fare of more elevated musical offerings. The role that royal figures played in such popular activities illustrated the dynamic interchange between conventional images of power and changing social circumstances. By taking an interest in popular entertainments, monarchs and aristocrats satisfied their own tastes and helped reproduce a sense of common nationality that crossed the boundaries of class. Political discussions of bodily control and liberty were

31

also paralleled by a growing number of printed body images. Cranial and facial typologies were asserted alongside the didactic classicism of academic painters and popular depictions of heroic royalty such as those displayed at London's Vauxhall Gardens. Beautiful chandeliers and large mirrors added to the charm and spectacle for audiences unused to seeing pictures of the famous or even images of themselves. The archetype of Louis XIV's panopticon at Versailles was thus translated into the realm of popular culture at the same time that sacred and mythical bodies began to be juxtaposed with more realistic depictions and caricatures of politicians and kings.

Of course, depictions of idealized or elite bodies were not the only examples of changing bodily representation found in the eighteenth century. Images of the unusual or grotesque remained important as well. One of the 'best known performers in the world' near the beginning of the century was Matthew Buchinger, remarkable not only for his renowned abilities as a conjurer, marksman and musician but also by virtue of his 'lacking feet, thighs, or arms'.[3] Using his mouth to hold pen and brush he was also noteworthy as a portraitist and calligrapher. Buchinger demonstrated a long-standing interest on the part of audiences with the odd and incredible. As with jesters with bodily deformities from the Spanish court, he was considered a wonder of creation. The ideal body and Buchinger the oddity both defied the boundaries of conventional bodily expectation. Much like the timeless classical statue, his popular appeal illustrated a desire to step byond the typical limitations of physical life.

Freakish, royal and common bodies seldom existed in isolation from one another and, in this respect, the eighteenth century was no exception. Images of less respectfully treated monarchs were counterposed by new images of everyday citizen-subjects. As a precursor to later popular culture figures, Thomas Topham, the son of a joiner who ran the Red Lion Inn near the Moorfield's Green boxing ring in the 1740s, was an early example of the commoner as an ideal of bodily perfection. Born in 1710, Topham was known for performing a variety of weightlifting feats.[4] A common citizen with an extraordinary body, his defiance of body limits foreshadowed the idealization of the ordinary man's physique later articulated by the mechanisms of the Victorian sculpture machine.

Although Topham's feats found their way into the press, the eighteenth-century strongman remained an oddity on a par with Buchinger. His own torso fell somewhere in between the category of the ideal aristocratic or classical body and the grotesque. Topham and other strength performers of the eighteenth century such as 'stone-eaters' Battalia and Reeves Williams had long been popular in circuses and fairs or between acts in the legitimate theatre in Britain and on the continent.[5] Further industrialization and the development of new technologies for the mass production of images were required before strength performers could become more significant figures within a mass commodity culture. Monarchs and re-empowered nobles in their roles as officers in new standing armies remained more likely representative figures.

An early-nineteenth-century successor of Topham and a contemporary of Dan Donnelly was Charles Rouselle. Known in the European press for his feats of strength, Rouselle was the first model of the Royal Academy of Painting and Sculpture in Paris. He posed for the statue of Hercules by Bosio in the Tuileries garden, and for several other artists at academies in Lyons and London. When Rouselle was commanded to appear before Napoleon, the emperor proposed that his sister be married to Roussel in order to raise a 'race of titans'. Doctors dissuaded the emperor from his ill-conceived and early effort at eugenics.[6] But the linkage of the strong-man and Bonaparte, like that of Donnelly and the Prince Regent, pointed to the growing importance of the image of physical strength and vitality in the realms of politics, style and popular culture. As the realm of popular culture expanded, figures such as Rouselle came into contact with major actors in a changing political arena.[7] New types of disciplined figures that were connected to long-standing traditions of manly behaviour emerged in the forms of the opposing brute force and fashionable comportment personified by Regency boxers such as Donnelly and the dandy Beau Brummell.[8] As suggested by meetings between Rouselle and Napoleon, George IV and Brummell or Donnelly, new types of representative bodies were interacting with monarchs as each played a part in 'making' the other.[9]

In effect, popular and royal bodies became peers in a commercial order that treated all bodies as commodities. The relationship between monarchs and figures like strongmen and dandies foregrounded changes in the shape of society and the development of new understandings of the body. Popular culture figures such as Rouselle, boxers, circus performers and gentlemen dandies referenced themselves to old and new bodily ideals and in some ways began to compete with monarchs and nobles as society's more representative bodies. Certainly, by the beginning of George IV's reign, the British monarch was neither the physically strongest nor the most fashionable figure in society.

The popular culture successors of Topham and Rouselle gained in popularity as boxing went underground in the 1820s and 1830s. Within the realm of nineteenth-century bodily display the first significant example of 'rational' posing, weightlifting and selling fitness was that demonstrated by another Frenchman, Hippolyte Triat. Born at St Chaptes near Nîmes in 1813, the young Triat joined an athletic act in a circus which travelled to Italy, Austria, France and Spain. During the 1840s he established a physical training school in Brussels. The success of this venture was sufficient to prompt him upon his return to France to open another gym, which was said to have been frequented by the Emperor Louis Napoleon.[10] Like Charles Rouselle, Triat was also an example of the strongman associated with a more familiar wielder of political authority. The links between physical prowess and political power, long a critical part of the royal image, were thus reaffirmed, in the connection between a minor celebrity and a dynast with a less than impeccable pedigree.

Triat complemented his display of the body with other activities more specifically in line with reproducing the body as an object of knowledge and site of reform. As a strongman-cum-author he balanced his gymnastic publications with calls for the introduction of public education in France.[11] His combination of performance with entrepreneurship and his more catholic interest in social reform was a rare exception in the days before a mass consumer culture proper. Another figure whose career was of interest to elite patrons, and whose image was more in line with normalized images of power as were found later in the century, was the American lion tamer, Isaac Van Amburgh, who had his portrait painted by Edwin Landseer (*c*. 1830s). The picture, which was purchased by the Queen in 1839, shows a muscular Van Amburgh as he appeared at the London Theatre in that year, dressed in a biblical tunic and belt, and wearing leather sandals.[12] A similar painting was commissioned by the Duke of Wellington, *Isaac Van Amburgh and his animals*, and was completed by Landseer in 1847. The Duke himself chose the inscription which is incorporated into the elaborate gilt frame: 'And God said let us make man in our image . . . [and give him] dominion over every living thing . . . , Genesis, 26th verse'.[13] The potential popularity of a figure like Van Amburgh, as a Daniel in the lion's den, or as an icon of European progress and domination, was enhanced by improvements in printing technology and entertainment networks.[14] He was especially interesting in his display of male prowess over nature within a historicized popular culture or theatrical setting rather than a more typical royal or military one. Like Rouselle and Triat, he was not an aristocratic soldier or a monarch but an entertainer. Wrestlers and lion tamers were hardly representative bodily images in the first half of the century of progress and liberal reform that Victorian intellectuals sought to understand and define. But the body of the popular culture figure was growing in importance as the mirror of mass media and consumerism developed.

The body that captivated reformers early in the century was not yet a popular or a mass body. In Carlyle's case, for example, the truly representative body remained a physical manifestation of spirit, a kind of clothing for the soul that projected its wearer's essential qualities. Despite all the renovated discourse on corporeality, the tendency to look toward traditional representative bodies such as monarchs continued. But a confusion of bodies with needs and complaints and new means for voicing them increased the tension between the heroic and the popular, the classical and mechanical, the religious and the medical, that characterized the century of the sculpture machine.

Although the exemplary prototypes of physical fitness in Britain remained military ones, the society-wide emphasis upon physical training was increasingly influenced by changing tastes and mechanisms in spectacle and entertainment.[15] The fear of large gatherings exhibited by the banning of horse race meetings in the London suburbs in the early 1870s 'as a threat to law and order' lessened by the 1880s and 1890s as mass spectatorship became institutionalized in Britain.[16] The elite's fear of 'outsiders, artisans, mechanics, and such like troublesome persons' in amateur sports were reduced as sport and fitness were professionalized within a commercial framework.[17]

From the 1860s to the 1890s there was an increasing synthesis of the languages of science and bodily reform with profit-making. The conversion in 1864 of the Panopticon of Science and Art in Leicester Square into the Alhambra Music Hall was an early indication of the growing importance of spectacle in mass society.[18] As the press expanded and attempts were made to rationalize the military and the public school, music halls were also developing. British working-class society was increasingly characterized by the 'pub, sporting paper, the race-course and the music-hall', rather than the friendly society or evening class.[19] In Britain alone by the end of the century, the *Era Almanack* listed 226 'Empires, Palaces of Variety, and Hippodromes' outside London, alongside the Alhambra, the Albert, Sadler's Wells, the Parthenon and 38 others in the capital.[20] Moreover, the vaudeville palace and music hall provided advertising and fodder for the expanding mass press. At the end of an age in which a book might cost one-tenth of a middling servant's yearly income, the expansion of the reading populace provided numerous opportunities for profit-making, and many new publications were tied to sports, entertainment and the performing arts.

The changing spectacle of the popular body was presaged in the early 1880s in the United States, when boxers John L. Sullivan and William Muldoon took advantage of the rage for 'living statuary' that had just arrived on the American popular stage. An imitation of the French *poses plastiques*, the acts consisted of living tableaux of one or several figures embodying some aesthetic or historical representation. More practically, it was a device for displaying the body as undraped as convention would allow.[21] In 1885, Sullivan signed on to do living statuary with the Lester and Allen Minstrel Show for the 1885–6 season at the exceptional price of $500 a week for 20 weeks. Sullivan was also photographed in June of that year at John Wood's Broadway photo gallery in New York City.[22] In December 1885, Sullivan was still posing with the minstrel show, and his friend, the slightly more lithe William Muldoon, joined him. The show was then playing at the Third Avenue Theater in New York City, where Sullivan was billed as 'the best formed man in the world'.[23] Advertised as portraying 'the biggest undressed heroes of antiquity', the master of ceremonies introduced the boxer as the curtain opened briefly to reveal 'a scantily clad Sullivan, ill at ease in white tights and wig', acting the part of a Gladiator in Combat.[24] Doubtless, many of the spectators might have been happier with a ringside seat at a Sullivan match-up.

The relegitimized sport of prizefighting was much less brutal in the 1880s than in its Regency heyday, and even more popular as an international phenomenon. Before paying his respects to the memory of Donnelly in Ireland in 1887, Sullivan visited Britain where he was fêted by aristocrats and delegations of working men.[25] The *Pall Mall Gazette* was alone perhaps in its view that 'this worship of brutality and muscle is merely an unhealthy sign of the age'.[26] Sullivan's tour followed on the success of William F. Cody's Wild West Show during the earlier jubilee summer. The champion's visit was certainly less exciting as performance, since it was largely composed of public appearances rather than fights, but he drew huge crowds anyway. It was noted that recent Prime Minister William Gladstone might bring thousands to provincial railway stations, but only Sullivan could create mob scenes in 'blasé London'.[27] Over nineteen thousand came to see him during two nights in Birmingham, where he was given 'a welcome scarcely accorded to a royal prince'.[28] Indeed, the Prince of Wales – who was fond of all occasions for wagering and no less so of boxing – made a point of meeting Sullivan privately.[29] Middle-class papers other than the *Pall Mall Gazette* paid little attention to Sullivan's visit, but the avid interest of working-class men and the penny press showed that figures like him had grown in importance as representations of national and class identity since the days of Donnelly.

Sullivan's tour foreshadowed the arrival on the scene of the most important successor of Rouselle, Donnelly and Triat. Unlike American boxers who moonlighted on stage, Sullivan's contemporary Eugen Sandow began as a circus and music hall performer.[30] Born Ernst Müller in Königsberg, East Prussia, his initial fame and commercial success rested on the spectacle of his own well-developed and smartly displayed physique. A few years after Sullivan's British tour, he was described in the London *Daily Telegraph* as

a short but perfectly built young man of twenty-two years of age, with the face of a somewhat ancient Greek type, but with the clear blue eyes and curling fair hair of the Teuton. When in evening dress there is nothing specially remarkable about this quiet mannered, good natured youth; but when he takes off his coat. . . .[31]

Along with the many imitators who followed him, Sandow capitalized on the long-standing working-class appeal of sporting figures and strength performers. One of the first to join body performance with magazine publishing, he began *Sandow's Magazine of Physical Culture* in 1898.[32] Advancing beyond stage-posing and the fitness/boxing postcard, he positioned his own body and those of his consumer clients as a central focus in the advertising and marketing of fitness goods and services.[33] Sandow's success in publishing was remarkable by comparison to *Recreation* and *Physique*, as well as earlier American attempts at fitness magazines. His achievements in this respect resulted from the increased currency of degeneracy rhetoric at the century's end and the ongoing expansion of the market for smaller publications and fitness products. His ability to capitalize on these developments, however, depended on his initial popularity as a performer.

Sandow's mentor, Oscard Atilla, built on the tradition of Rouselle and Triat by marketing the connection between strength performance and kingship.[34] Among other notables and European heads of state Atilla claimed to have instructed the British heir apparent.[35] He was the only strongman invited to perform at Victoria's 1887 jubilee at which time the Prince of Wales (later Edward VII) gave him a diamond stickpin.[36] It was Atilla that Sandow visited on his first visit to London after touring Italy in 1889. In London, their talents as performers and fitness instructors placed them in the large category labelled teachers that included everything from 'governessing to university lecturing'.[37]

On his first visit to London, an appropriately dramatic display of Sandow's talents was arranged by Atilla.[38] Dressed in full evening attire, he was to attend a performance given by the strongman team of 'Samson and Cyclops' at the London Aquarium. Franz Bienkowski, or Cyclops, offered a standard £100 to anyone who could lift as much as he could. At an appropriate moment the young German leapt on to the stage to take up the challenge. The smaller and more compact 'Herr Sandow' removed his evening clothes to reveal his well-developed physique and, according to the next day's *Sportsman*, easily bested the Cyclops. On the following Saturday, Sandow forced his way through the crowds that had come to see the follow-up challenge to Cyclops' partner, Samson.[39]

Sandow claimed that his initial inspiration for building his body was a result of seeing statues from antiquity in Italy as a young man. His more immediate success was directly tied to the models provided by professional boxers and wrestlers in the United States.[40] Americans learned in turn from Sandow. Bernarr Macfadden was an American contemporary who also grafted a successful publishing career on to an earlier vocation as a strength performer.[41] Beginning as a body performer on the American wrestling circuit and as a young 'roustabout' at Chicago's Columbian Exposition, he learned the tricks of strength performance firsthand from watching Sandow's act.[42] Not unlike the young Müller in Italy, he was seduced by the sinuous properties of the numerous neo-classical sculptures littering the exposition, which he glowingly characterized as 'perfect specimens of human life carried out in stone'.[43]

Like Dan Donnelly, Sullivan and Atilla, Sandow was also a recipient of royal favours. As a subject of the 'Kaiser Frederich Wilhelm' [*sic*], he visited the imperial refuge at the Villa Zirio in San Remo in 1889. During the audience, the emperor tore a pack of cards in two. His young guest responded by tearing two packs in half at once. Ripping packs of cards in half and other similar feats of stage strength trickery were of course Sandow's stock in trade. It was as much as a token of admiration for the young man's growing renown as a music-hall personality as it was a payment for his private performance, that the Kaiser gave his guest a ring from his own finger.[44] Like the legend of earlier meetings between Rouselle and Napoleon, Donnelly and the Prince Regent, and the example of Triat's supposed training of Louis Napoleon, Sandow's meeting with the Kaiser illustrated an effective reinfusion of the monarchy with an element of actual personal and physical power. It was not an uncommon assumption of the day that the modern monarchy itself was a decadent remnant of an earlier more 'natural' or vibrant form of leadership. Presaging Weber's theories of charisma and atavism, social critic and degeneracy theorist Max Nordau argued that ancient societies were such that the leader's 'sources of preeminence [were] . . . apparent to every one'.[45] In stories linking monarchs to strongmen, physical strength symbolized earlier and presumably less mediated structures of social relation and hierarchy.

What is more important, Sandow used his celebrity and his conjunction with royal figures as a marketing tool. Over the course of his career, he endorsed everything from *Bovril*, a concentrated beef paste, to Spalding Brothers Sporting Goods. In this regard, he was a competitor not only with kings and queens but also with popular heroes like Henry Morton Stanley and politicians like Theodore Roosevelt, who were used as commercial icons. In Sandow's case, however, it was not a matter of achieving renown in a material sense and then having one's image appropriated by others, but – like later film stars – one of encouraging the use of his image and maintaining mastery over its appropriation.[46] A similar example of modern celebrity associated with monarchy was found in the career of an American, Washington Irving Bishop, who pursued his own version of a physique act with his use of 'muscle reading' to reveal what subjects were thinking. He was well known around the world as a magician and mind reader when he died in the same year as Sandow's purported visit to San Remo.[47] Bishop's unusual approach to muscles to read the mind indicated an enduring interest in the body and the anthropometric on the part of audiences. Moreover, his performances were marketed as having been seen by the monarchs of Romania, Greece, Sweden and Russia. For example, much was made in posters advertising his act of the acclaim he received from Czar Alexander III and his wife Maria Fedorovna. Bishop and Sandow both demonstrated how the realms of popular and elite culture were already regularly coinciding to a limited degree in the 1880s.

Although the celebrated figure of the bodybuilder was still typically grounded in traditional institutions such as the monarchy, the stage strongman's performance was often more 'real' than that produced by the spectacle of the rarefied royal court. The relatively new representation of the strongman was used frequently in political cartoons as a way of reifying the power of the political figure, for example the British Prime Minister Lord Salisbury's depiction as a Sandow-like figure in animal skin and holding a club, or a caricature of South African president Paul Kruger using a chest expander.[48] The link between the image of the elite aristocrat or gentleman and the bare-chested strongman remained a common theme. The contraposing images of Sandow clad in immaculate evening attire and then stripping to reveal his exceptional physique was one that he employed persistently. From his London début at the Aquarium challenge and on to his worldwide travels, he continued to refine his presentation as the muscular 'gentleman'.

Sandow's arrival in London in 1889 coincided with the ongoing expansion and upgrading of music hall venues such as the refurbishment of the Empire and Alhambra theatres in the West End into variety palaces.[49] Four years later, he was presented by impresario Florenz Ziegfeld in Chicago.[50] In a massive publicity campaign alerting the public to 'an unprecedented sensation', Sandow's image accompanied by the words 'the modern Hercules' or 'the perfect man' was spread throughout the city. The promotional assault paid off in a full house in spite of the muggy summer heat. Sandow 'held a man in the palm of his hand, bent a poker, opened a safe with his teeth, and balanced weights up to 300 pounds'.[51] His physique caused such a stir among the audience that Ziegfeld himself came out at the end of the act to proclaim that any woman willing to donate $300 to charity could come behind the curtain to feel the young man's biceps.[52] Socialites Mrs Potter Palmer and Mrs George Pullman did just that and a version of their backstage examination was to be found on the cover of the next issue of New York's *Police Gazette*.[53]

The *Police Gazette* image of Sandow examined by society women was reminiscent of the prizefighter's treatment as a kind of human 'racehorse'. The fact that women did the examining both under-scored and reversed the typical hierarchy of gender. Despite a reli-ance on new photographic technology, strength performance and postcard images of boxers and exotic women harkened back to a presumed natural state before industrialization.[54] Women weight-lifters were not unknown in the period, but like the armless and legless Matthew Buchinger they were considered odd or unusual. The strongwoman's categorization as strange or freakish valorized more normative notions of femininity.[55] Female performers usu-ally occupied traditional roles as wives or mothers alongside their unusual stage activities. Mademoiselle Arniotis, a 'slight wiry-looking' French strongwoman of the early 1890s, began her career through the traditional path of marriage.[56] The wife of a Greek horsebreaker and steeplechase rider, she first come into contact with the per-forming world through her sister's marriage to a member of the Hippodrome troupe in Paris.[57] Arniotis' strength was portrayed as an ironic counterweight to her conventional attractiveness as an object of desire for men. Her feats, such as lifting great weights with her teeth or holding up two men perched on a barrel, frequently invited male scepticism. A Dr Fourquier of Paris resisted the idea that she was not 'acting under magnetic influence' until he had witnessed her performances several times. The uniqueness of her talents was made more palatable by the insistence that she was 'born' and 'not made, a strong woman'.[58]

The music halls where Sandow and Mademoiselle Arniotis performed certainly had more female dancers than strong women. Shocking displays on stage of women in tights and shorter skirts became the subject of debate in newspaper letter columns in the mid-1890s. These were subsequently debated at the Licensing Com-mittee meetings of the London County Council.[59] Others were more horrified to hear about the female prostitutes trolling the five shil-ling public promenades of the theatres.[60] Indeed, there was more being revealed in the music halls than women's legs. When the question of renewing the alcohol license of the Palace Theatre of Varieties came up before the Licensing Committee in the winter of 1894, the propriety of an act entitled the 'Living Pictures' was raised. These were posed *tableaux vivants* similar to those enacted by Sullivan and others in the previous decade. These new *poses plastiques* used body make-up to give the impression of stone sculpture. Among other scenes representing the works of well-known artists, they were known for their use of semi-nude women who, except for the heavy white make-up (plaster of Paris and draped muslin), were some-times bare-breasted. One such depiction, entitled 'Ariadne', show-ing a seemingly nude woman on the back of a lion, was a particular focus of press attention. Tableaux like it were in fact not so new, and had been presented off and on since Lady Hamilton had posed as Hygeria in a quack doctor's 'Temple of Health' earlier in the century.[61] George Bernard Shaw, among others, commented that it was strange that women were not as equally debased by the sight of unclothed male athletes as men presumably were by undressed women.[62] One self-appointed critic of the licentious music halls, Mrs Ormiston Chant, claimed that 'men would refuse to exhibit their bodies nightly in this way'.[63] As Sandow demonstrated nightly, this was not true.

According to the theatrical and photographic codes of the day, strongmen typically appeared discreetly clothed in thick white tights and leopard skins that concealed most of their chests. This had been the case with Sullivan in the previous decade. Ziegfeld decided to break this convention and presented Sandow in a single spot-light, wearing only a pair of red silk shorts and a crown of gilded laurel leaves. His body was covered with bronze make-up and according to Zeigfeld's explicit stage directions he assumed a vari-ety of stationary classical poses. Neo-classical posing was not actually new, but in Sandow's act it was coupled with demonstrations of strength, the revelation of more skin and more well-defined muscles into the bargain.

In the introduction to English boxer Billy Edwards' *Pugilistic Portrait Gallery* (1894) it was noted that the arrival of a 'golden era of *muscular development* would soon lead to the establishment of a perfect manhood and womanhood'.[64] Of course, Edwards' collec-tion of photographs and brief sporting records of great fighters from the United States, Britain and Australia failed to include any examples of 'perfect womanhood'. He none the less claimed to answer a 'long-felt want' in the 'great sporting world' and beyond for images and information from the world of sport.[65] Whether such a need existed or not, the publishing of Edwards' book indicated the possibility of a market for fitness publications beyond that of the music-hall stage or single postcard image.

Like boxers and theatrical personalities of the day, photo-reproductions of Sandow were widely distributed in postal and other card forms.[66] By any standard, the postcard was a ubiquitous cultural form by 1900. Early in the century, Germany was said to use

'400 million post-cards per annum, on which it spends £10 000 in postage'.[67] Sandow was photographed by the highly successful Rotary Photographic company among many others. Rotary also published images of Sandow as well as an exercise series entitled 'Ideal Physical Culture' and a 'Health and Strength Series' featuring boxers like Tommy Burns, 'Champion of the World'. Sandow was also photographed by the famous Napoleon Sarony of New York. It was then customary for the photographer to pay a fee for the right to photograph and distribute postal card or cabinet photo images of famous subjects. But this had already begun to change. For example, Sarony photographed Oscar Wilde during his tour of the US with Gilbert and Sullivan's *Patience,* and the fee was waived in the hopes that the photographer would help make Wilde more familiar to American audiences. The fact that Sarony chose Sandow as a subject pointed to the strongman's possession of considerable fame already.

At the end of the century, fitness and exercise were just beginning to be popularly known by the catchphrase 'physical culture'.[68] Before the turn-of-the-century publishing wave initiated by *Sandow's Magazine,* the term was not unknown.[69] It was current enough in 1894 for Edwards to refer to it in his introduction. Sandow's choice of the term as a title served to greatly increase its use and symbolic value.[70] Only a handful of physical culture books were produced in Britain before the 1870s.[71] Along with Edwards, Sandow joined in a flurry of physical culture publishing in 1894 with his first book, 'compiled and edited under Mr. Sandow's direction' with G. Mercer Adam.[72] His entry at that point into non-stage activities was encouraged by his publisher Gale & Polden's growth as a military printer, a tertiary effect of an increase in the armed forces in the last decades of the century.[73]

In his early books, Sandow always overtly linked himself with the training of soldiers; in numerous publications, 'Sandow's System' was touted by himself and others as having been adopted by the British Army.[74] This was in fact never the case. Over the years, much was to be made of testimonials provided by the Inspector of Gymnasia at Aldershot, Col. G. M. Fox, and others. But the imprimatur of the Army Physical Training Corps, already then in existence for over forty years, was never given to the Sandow System.[75]

Sandow's second career in publishing was the culmination of his self-marketing as a 'professional gentleman' who also happened to be an entertainer and performer. In the frontispiece of his publication's initial number, he is shown dressed like any middle-class business-man, wearing coat and tie with a high white collar. This did not mean the discontinuation of Sandow the male pin-up: for many the simple inclusion of any muscular image of Sandow was enough to warrant purchase of the magazine. In most issues, there was always a sampling of both Sandow as the ideal body and gentleman publisher. As a burgeoning editorial writer, Sandow also appreciated the value of endorsements from recognized authors such as Arthur Conan Doyle and respected journalists such as W. T. Stead, whose testimonials on behalf of the strongman added lustre to the more credible opinions of the many medical doctors who pronounced Sandow the most perfect male specimen alive.

In the first volumes of *Sandow's* there was a pronounced effort to imitate more high-toned journals of the day. This mimicking of middle-class publications can be seen in the presentation of articles on athletics in antiquity and physical culture in childhood, as well as considerable space given over to reports on sports and activities such as cricket, cross-country running, curling, gymnastics, swimming, polo, golf, football, rugby, boxing and cycling. There were also articles dealing with the thorny issues of gender and class, such as matching pieces on 'Muscular Heroes' and the 'Muscular Heroine' in fiction, and in the realm of class politics, an article on the 'artizan and fitness', and another written by Mabel E. Cahill intriguingly entitled 'Lawn Tennis as a Social Reformer'.

Articles on physical fitness and the Jews, women and the rational dress movement and physical education for girls were also included. Legitimacy was also sought through references to prominent members of the social and political elite. Articles such as 'Strongmen of the Bench' highlighted leading jurists and MPs who were athletes or sportsmen.[76] The magazine also contained the three notes that Sandow successfully repeated in all his physical training publications: the perfection of the physique as a universal transhistorical technique, the need for fitness in schools, and the promotion of his own particular brand of training.[77] In *Sandow's System*, he outlined the rather simple training advice he sold over the next twenty years.

> The training I of course specifically commend is dumbbell and barbell exercise and of very lights, (for the generality of people . . . 4 or not more than 5 pounds) . . . nothing in my opinion is better than the use of the dumbbell for developing the *whole* system.[78]

Offering specific exercise advice and promoting individual and greater social change frequently led to questions concerning the term 'physical culture' itself. In the first issue of *Sandow's*, its publisher was quick to point out that, for most people, physical culture represented a common expression that few could define with any precision.[79] As Sandow noted later, it was surely a 'less severe and more euphonious and attractive name' than physical education.[80] Generally, he employed high-sounding, albeit vague, phraseology in his assertion that physical culture was to the 'body what culture in the accepted sense is to the mind'.[81] He stepped on to surer ground when discussing its more practical objectives and aims, for example the 'production of a perfectly sound body, that is Physical Culture!', or when speaking of undoing 'this evil' caused by a civilization that takes the body lightly.[82]

Following Triat's less ambitious publishing example, Sandow bridged the gap between the performance of bodily spectacle and the voice of textual authority in his transition from performer to publisher. In this sense, the general character of the turn-of-the-century health and fitness sector can be chiefly distinguished from the earlier Victorian era realm of patent medicines, therapeutic water cures and athletic revivals by virtue of the numbers it reached and its greater practical appeal across class lines. Performers such as Sandow as well as many popular boxers of the day were men from modest backgrounds at best. Some had escaped the misery of the slums by sole virtue of their bodily attributes and seemed to be living demonstrations that class divisions might be erased. Others, such as black and Jewish fighters from early in the nineteenth century, suggested that even ethnic and racial lines might be subsumed within the arena of physicality.[83] Which is not to say that physical culture regimens held any real promise of subsuming class distinctions. But class roles and relationships were changing and shifting, and the approach of physical culturists indicated their state of flux.

For late Victorians, the surface of the body provided a key basis for social categorization. More traditional means of assessment, such as the language of religious value, were less and less prevalent. The Salvationists and others found that an emphasis upon physicality was crucial to their success.[84] The possibility of acquiring an appearance of physical efficiency above and beyond a proper diet was presumably most attractive to a growing number of young men yet to marry, those between 14 (school-leaving age) and 27.[85] The urban clerk or labourer, still outside the defining bounds of marriage, may have sought and sometimes found a palpable sense of control in physical culture activities. Apart from complementing one's work-life with a quantity of personal autonomy, physical culture also provided an added sparkle to the capitalist myth through its regular linkage of exercise with material success.

To be sure, the proliferation of body images and promises of improvement relied upon more than simple vanity. Indeed, the fear of losing one's job for lack of fitness may have made some workers more vulnerable to early physique culture appeals. Economic down-turns and the threat of sudden unemployment were never far off in memory if not in reality. It was on the basis of such fears that one Edwardian worker regularly blackened his hair with butter and chimney soot so as to look younger and more fit.[86] To their credit perhaps, leaders within various labour movements understood that the acquisition of power was not simply vested in workers' literal muscle-power. An emphasis upon appearance as the marker of the self, and as the indicator of health (both mental and physical) was obviously not without its uses in medical and psychological diag-nostics. But the body, together with its related social identities or mental states, was not always so easily understood through a cur-sory study of the bodily surface alone. The idea of the body having any use-value at all was not the difficulty. Labour was not only a source of wealth but also an ostensible commodity. But the labour-ing of bodies in the gymnasium was not economically the same as working for wages. Physical culture sold the opportunity to 'work-out' beyond the space of the workplace. The play of sport was less a kind of work and perhaps a more effective way of taking one's mind off the exploitive nature of the system. It retained an aspect of freeplay even within the bounds of rules. But exercise, in and of itself, was more literally a kind of labour in its methods and the measure of its difficulty.[87] Like sport, however, such activities provided the satisfaction of exercising one's own body, of feeling engaged with others, of comparing and noting improvement.

Although crucially present as the locus of expanding male con-sumption, the actual body's articulation within health and fit-ness publications was primarily textual. As such, it was part of a larger range of discourse. Physical culture magazines were a small sub-genre within an overarching middle-class media that claimed to speak for entire nations and civilizations. From the beginnings of the mass British dailies in the 1880s, new media were understood as part of a single communicating voice with the power to set the limits of the respectable and the normal, even as they described the deviant in Victorian life. The correspondence columns of newspapers and magazines allowed for a kind of freeplay of opinion but these too were subject to publishers' and editors' prejudices and were expected to conform to the standard of an educated middle-class voice, or made to do so through editing.[88] Likewise, the use of pseudonyms, such as 'Praetorious' or 'Unknown Quantity', helped to maintain the impression of a dominant normative middle-class way of thinking and being. The frames of reference of the single speaking national subject thus represented were none the less many and diffuse. Because of its 'total' character, however, and the all-encompassing tendencies of its middle-class ethos, even expressions of diversity tended to operate within the bounds of a narrow normalizing discourse.[89]

Health and fitness magazine editors used similar means to substantiate the idea of diversity while at the same time perpetuating the idea of the ideal reader: an admixture of the middle-class and working-class self. The character of physical culture commerce, and its attempt to become an all-encompassing ideology, made for significant differences in the form and results of such practices. Because of its focus upon the body, the actual tone of health and fitness letters columns could be both more cryptic and open. For the same reason, they came to include men of more widely varied class and ethnic backgrounds. In letters and advice sections, publishers' replies were sometimes printed elliptically without the actual queries that had inspired them. In this way the body and its attributes, the presumed central object of discussion, were obviated. Thus, we have 'New Reader' being advised, '– Bathe in the open by all means', and 'H. Lewis' being told that '– A book on Artistic anatomy would suit you. We shall publish a series of anatomical photos next month'. Other intriguing responses include that to 'E.L.', '– you can see it privately if you make application', or to 'Depressed', '– My dear boy, letters like yours give me the heartache. Be a man, say to yourself "never again", and stick to it.'

More commonly the answers were more mundane, like that to 'Waverly', '– You will find hints for business men in the *Life Physical*, January number'.[90] In other letters sections, polite and carefully composed (or edited) testimonials to the efficacy of a physical culture course or book were published. Under the heading of 'Remarkable Recovery', correspondent A. George, a young worker in a foundry, told of his 'ailment'. Beginning work in 1904 at the age of 16, George found it impossible to 'do any manual labour, however slight'.[91] Following one of his 'usual attacks', he left work. Trying several kinds of patent nostrums to no avail, he was given a copy of Sandow's *Strength and How to Obtain It*. In the book he saw examples of other 'lads and men in the same predicament ... [who] had become not only healthy again, but strong'. He bought a 'set of developers' and soon began to feel the improvement. As he wrote in his letter,

> at the end of nine months steady exercise I felt as if I were a king. In the meantime I recommenced work, and everybody remarked upon my improvement ... now at the end of two and a half years I have become one of the strongest lads in the shop. I introduced your magazine in our Reading Club, and I am pleased to say they have taken it ever since, which I think has been the means of other lads going in for dumb-bells and developers. I have increased in height $1\frac{1}{2}$ ins., and weight 40 lbs.[92]

Whether George also benefited from an adolescent growth spurt is left in doubt. But his letter gives further indication of physical culture's potential appeal as a means to being more successful in work.

In 1894, Sandow was fictionalized in the first of several 'Dimenovels'.[93] Apart from personal testimonials and letters, characters from strictly imaginary works also had their functional value as physical culture 'role-models'. In Don Legat's 'The Influence of Fiction on Physical and Mental Culture', Sir Walter Scott and Robert Louis Stevenson were praised and the 'frivolous and unmoral if not immoral' quality of most contemporary fiction was condemned.[94] In 'Strong Men as Portrayed by Writers of Fiction', A. Weldon argued that censorship was needed to protect the young from 'cultivating morbid tastes and passions'.[95] It was asserted that the 'realistic and matter-of-fact readers' of the day required a useful depiction of fictional characters 'delineated with all the faithfulness of a photograph'.[96] The fitness culture press, in its attempt to be like other middle-class journals, flirted on occasion with the presentation of the ostensible fictional fitness tale. In Sandow's earliest registration issue, the magazine was primarily comprised of the beginnings of a serial adventure. Like the *Strand* or other mainstream middle-class publications, *Sandow's* thereafter published serialized fiction or single short stories typically depicting a male hero triumphing over criminals at home, and the occasional spy or recalcitrant colonial abroad.[97] Bernarr Macfadden, who also published a physical culture magazine in Britain, had his second brush with the courts as a result of the publication of *Wild Oats*, a serialized novel depicting the story of 'Reginard Barnes-Carter', a scoundrel with a congenital venereal disease who ends his life of debauchery as a lunatic who is burned alive.[98] Besides being influenced by Sandow and religious reformers like the British-born John Alexander Dowie, a medico-faith healer and founder of the town of Zion, Illinois, Macfadden was also an admirer of literary figures such as Upton Sinclair and George Bernard Shaw.[99] In each case, he was drawn to their social critiques, not to mention their potential marketing value as famous names.[100] Shaw and Macfadden shared a particular dislike for Anthony Comstock, Macfadden's nemesis and secretary of the New York Society for the Suppression of Vice.[101] Garish moral tales became the trademark of his later tabloid empire. However, in terms of the larger context in which Macfadden wrote his moral tales and in which physical culture developed, it is perhaps more revealing to look at better known writers.

The use of fiction within the fitness press indicated the increased power with which all fictional and journalistic discourse had been invested not only as an arbiter of taste but as a kind of political and social teacher. In both literature and physical culture discourse, what Holbrook Jackson called the desire for 'romance by Proxy' played no small part.[102] The decade that bred physical culture was a peculiarly self-conscious one. It was in the 1890s that the myths of the legendary lost generation began. The widespread awareness of the decade's distinct status was described by Yeats as no less than the 'crowning crisis of the world'.[103] More pointedly, *fin-de-siècle* self-consciousness was tied to important shifts in bodily awareness. The sense of a single decade and generation's self-consciousness and combined twilight and rebirth was fostered by the phenomenon of small magazines and an expansion in the markets for fiction. Part of a pervasive cultural desire for an answer to the chaotic temper of modern life's 'sick hurry', they paralleled the all-inclusive ideology of social relations manifested in physical culture and other popular movements.

In the pages of fitness magazines, the articulation of a techno-commercial order and new discursive aesthetic debates were intertwined. Physical culturists merged the aesthetic with the technical, and the imaginative with the scientific. In its technical novelties and gesturing towards efficiency, physical culture was in synch with the greater reading market. Indeed, desires to bridge fact and fiction, the useful and the beautiful, were not simply workable advertising ploys, but were also typical of many prominent writers in the period including Oscar Wilde, George Bernard Shaw, H. G. Wells and others. In the physical culture press and other genres such as boys' magazines, there was also a deceptively clear vision of the real: a focus upon imperial and national issues as framed within a neochivalric adventure narrative that validated simple class, gender and racial categories.[104] These larger issues were an abiding preoccupation of literate middle-class and lower-middle-class readers around the turn of the century.[105] Fears of decadence and campaigns for moral purity were thus important as subsidiary parts of what were thought to be quite pragmatic political concerns. Fiction as a form of information was portrayed at turns as dangerous, as in the presumed demoralizing effects of the penny dreadfuls, or as positive in the case of the works of G. A. Henty. The double-edged nature of the fictive device was thus seen as yet another bodily or virally conceived enemy, an agent of decadent forces, as well as a potential antibody defender against such social threats.

The great prophet of decadence and degeneracy, Max Nordau, ever alert to the dual nature of modern literature, singled out Britain's literary products as prime examples of escapism in response to the 'age and its disappointments'.[106]

> The light literature of England has long since ceased to be a faithful mirror of real life. When it is not describing with gusto, crimes and scandals of all kinds, murders, burglaries, seductions . . . it portrays a model society, in which members of the nobility are all handsome, dignified, cultivated and wealthy; while the lower classes are honest God-fearing people devoted to their superiors. . . . in short, a society which is in all respects an absurd idealization of that dilapidated, tottering structure of society as it exists in England at the present day.[107]

One of his least favourite authors was Oscar Wilde. The antithesis of any number of male icons of the age, such as the bumptious Theodore Roosevelt, there was no one less disturbed by the dangers of so-called decadent literature than Wilde. In eventually succumbing to scandal and a 'wasting disease', his demise was a fitting one according to the moral economy of his age. His own life story was a kind of physical culture moral tale, as 'obscene' in its details, if not more so than Macfadden's *Wild Oats*.[108] As the 'other' against which new normative terms such as heterosexual were being set and as a willing participant in a developing aestheticization of the masculine, Wilde played a key role in the construction of the sculpture machine's discourse on virilization. Like Sandow, he was a living example of the power of self-transformation. In his argument for a different idea of action in history, he argued that

> The one duty we owe to history is to rewrite it . . . not the least of the tasks in store for the critical spirit . . . we shall realize that the one person who has more illusions than the dreamer is the man of action. . . . Each little thing we do passes into the great machine of life, which may grind our virtues to powder and make them worthless, or transform our sins into elements of a new civilization.[109]

Wilde opposed the mundane 'doers', the banal poseurs like Macfadden, as well as 'real' men of action like Roosevelt. He allied himself instead with the poets, critics and chroniclers, for example those who 'did' something in a more sophisticated manner with language as opposed to the use or evocation of brute strength. This latter 'doing' he contrarily posed as doing nothing at all, while asserting the importance of actively 'doing' it just the same.

As physical culturists demonstrated, the combined brute force of the text alongside the muscular photographic pose was not necessarily inferior to the use of actual physical strength. In mocking the tenuous and theatrical performance of politics and culture as embodied by the military or physical culture hero, Wilde was an arch-realist. At the same time, his perhaps unserious attempt to turn even biology and the principle of heredity into subjects of aesthetic contemplation mirrored an omnipresent desire to reduce life to simple laws.[110] Beyond Wilde's own wish to demoralize social debates, there were those like Thomas Henry Huxley who actually wanted simpler answers. Or, there were those more to Wilde's taste, like the French historian Hippolyte Taine, who noted that vice and virtue were as much products of chemistry as were 'vitriol and sugar'.[111]

Wilde's specific literary attention to the body, its mortality and the growing ubiquity of technological representation as seen in *The Picture of Dorian Gray* (1891) can be interestingly contrasted with not only the crude narratives of Macfadden but also the didacticism of H. G. Wells.[112] As a progenitor of science fiction, Wells' treatments of the body and issues of contagion and decay are particularly relevant in examining the craze for reforming the physique. His initial fame as a novelist, as opposed to his later renown as a thinker, social critic and popular historian, closely paralleled the rise of physical culture. In his *The Time Machine* (1895), *The Island of Dr Moreau* (1896), *The Invisible Man* (1897) and *Tono-Bungay* (1909), Wells represented the prevailing 'biologisms' of his time and his own personal history of poor health. His shopkeeper father was known as a great working-class bowler in Kent. From time to time the elder Wells was even able to eke out the family income by playing cricket for pay.[113] As the younger Wells betrayed in a pamphlet of spiritual reflections about the afterlife, however, his youthful acquaintance with the life physical was largely one of illness.

> Tolerable health came only in my thirties. Muscular precision and hardiness I shall never know in my waking life . . . beyond the Happy Turning, I leap gulfs unerringly, scale precipices, skin up trees and am indefatigable. There are no infections there . . . to cough or sneeze would be to wake up and tumble back headlong into those unhygienic present-days realities where dirt-begotten epidemics have their way with us.[114]

Wells evinced an obsession with bodily health and fitness born of a disease-ridden and impoverished upbringing. His father was not successful as a shopkeeper and his mother was eventually forced to go back into service as a housekeeper. In turn, Wells was apprenticed as a draper's assistant at the age of 13 in 1879. An ambitious young man, he abandoned his apprenticeship in 1883 to become a pupil-teacher at a small country school. He subsequently won a scholarship to the Normal School of Science in London, where he studied under the biologist and Social Darwinist T. H. Huxley. During three years of study and afterwards as a badly paid teacher, the tubercular Wells' physique – he weighed less than 90 lb at one point – was the exact prototype of the ideal physical culture patron and reader. Like Sandow, he was impressed in his studies by the course having the most to do with the direct study of the body. According to Wells, 'The central fact of those three years' at the Normal School 'was Huxley's course in Comparative Anatomy'.[115]

In the late 1880s, Wells finished with a BSc degree with first-class honours in zoology and a second in geology. In this period his health reached a low point and he suffered the first of two protracted illnesses that left their mark on both his character and future literary efforts. Burst blood vessels in the lungs and loss of weight were indicative of tuberculosis. He was forced to turn to writing in order to make a living and soon found the success that provided the time and money for country air, walking exercise, and an improved diet. Because of his writing skills and good fortune, he left the ranks of those for whom a dose of physical culture might have seemed an attractive way of improving their lot in life. During a second physical breakdown in 1894–5, he reworked an old sketch into the serial which was eventually printed in book form as *The Time Machine: An Invention.* In the novel, Wells hypothesized a method for moving the physical body along a fourth dimensional path to a future world in which disease has been stamped out. But it is also a world cut through by an ineradicable class division based in bodily difference. Indeed, in spite of its triumph over disease, we are shown a dying planet whose rotation has slowed and whose sun has darkened.

Like the all-encompassing cult of the physique, Wells' system of the novel offered yet another totalizing framework for confronting the predominant social fears of the day. 'Brought up in a world of confusion and incompetence', he yearned for a single unifying explanation, a means of creating order in the face of increasing chaos.[116] In both the system of health culture and the Wellsian novel, the language of science, and a palpable sense of the frightful costs of failing to impose order on the body and society were key elements. For the would-be physical culturist, the patina of the scientific system provided a legitimacy, a reason for faith and a possibility that its hypotheses might be proven effectual. For Wells and his readers, the confrontation of the horrible possibilities of material progress left unchecked was counterpoised against a similar systematic cultivation of 'discipline, research and planning'.[117]

In Wells' *Tono-Bungay* the issues of degeneracy and the metaphors of bodily decay are also forcefully depicted:

> When I think of these inexplicable dissolvent centres that have come into being on our globe ... I am haunted by a grotesque fancy of the ultimate eating away and dry-rotting and dispersal of our world. So that while man still struggles and dreams his very substance will change and crumble beneath him.[118]

A substance he calls 'Quap' proves so powerfully dissolvent that it, alone, escapes commodization by that other great solvent power, industrial-capitalism. To ensure that his readers do not fail to recognize his metaphorical intent, Wells describes this 'radio-activity' as 'exactly what the decay of our old culture is in society, a loss of traditions and distinctions and assured reactions'.[119] For us today the metaphor of contagion has its own powerful resonances. In Wells' time, there had yet to be a generation of humanity unshadowed by the threat of epidemic disease. Alongside the persistent pall of syphilis, the global influenza epidemics which began in 1890 were still fresh in everyone's minds after the turn of the century.

In the chapter headed 'How we made Tono-Bungay hum?', Wells addresses the book's persistent theme, that of modern culture's transformation by commerce and industry.[120] In so doing he deals obliquely with physical culture as a commercial movement, and provides some insight on how it was also made to 'hum'. 'Tono-Bungay' itself, the other significant product in the novel besides the elusive Quap, is an everything for anything elixir typical of the golden age of patent medicines. The avowed first poster for the marvellous tonic uses the tag headline of 'Health, Beauty and Strength'.[121] Its sellers ask that 'penetrating trio of questions': 'Are you bored with your business? Are you bored with your dinner? Are you bored with your wife?'[122] Wells was clearly satirizing the discursive commercial realm within which physical culture had developed and still existed. As consumers, and patrons of the popular press, it was a field that his potential readers understood, the world of patent medicines, books and exercise products aimed at satisfying a whole host of amorphous and vague dissatisfactions with modern life. Through more directed and clever advertising, businesses promised more potent relief in various printed and liquid forms, including but not limited to a clean colon and the full restoration of sexual vitality. Wells links the rise of a nearly fraudulent patent medicine and the fortunes of its sellers to both the wild speculation of capitalism's pyramid scheme of stock trading and the fortuitous development and novel impact of 'smart' advertising. For example, he refers to 'That alluring, buttonholing, let-me-just-tell-you-quite-soberly-something-you-ought-to-know style of newspaper advertisement', as well as splashy posters and slogans, and 'the convulsive jump of some attractive phrase into capitals' that were omnipresent not only in physical culture advertisement but also throughout the media.[123]

Tono-Bungay was the product of a journalist familiar with the trends and workings of his trade's intimate concern with business, marketing and promotion. As such it provides an impressionistic, albeit satirical, view of the structural changes then taking place in the fast-changing marketplaces of things and ideas. The phenomenal success of the mythic tonic Tono-Bungay provides the hot air for the narrator's balloon's-eye view of an England shifting from a 'Bladesover system' of gentry-run villages into something vast and practically unnameable.[124] This was the world of the sculpture machine – in which the possibility of harnessing the present to the past and making the body more durable seemed both possible and necessary. The conditions that created these desires included the world market system, undergirded by capital and the monolithic modern state – hidden only partially behind the veil of a mouldering medieval ethos of national identity and honour. It was in this realm that Tono-Bungay did indeed hum. Though, not unlike a few physical culture enterprises, its fate was that of eventually humming down the road to bankruptcy and failure.

Physical culture and the new science fiction were both part of a more contemporary corporatist or consumerist ethic of sociability in which newly forged ideas of the unified self were constantly being asserted and eroded. The greater significance of Wells' fictional tonic lies in its existence as a cultural object that circulated in a universe that knew what physical culture meant. As a satirical reflection on the creation of a consumerist mass culture and the birth of an advertising-driven mass media, *Tono-Bungay* was produced within the context of the very commercial phenomena that its author describes. As a self-contained discourse on a changing social order and the seeming impossibility of fulfilling one's desire within 'traditional' economic and gender arrangements, Wells' book also provides a window into the assumptions underlying contemporary commercial appeals to individuals 'increasingly uncomfortable in ... [their] own skin'.[125]

Physical culturists and Wells began to find success in the period when the 'time machine' of motion picture technology was also being developed. As the more extravagant variety palace came to replace the older pub-based form of the music hall, the new apparatus of the phonograph (1892) and the presence of the bioscope as a recognized 'turn' at the end of the evening's events (the cinematograph was first shown at the Empire in 1896) brought together standard theatrical forms with startling new processes of mechanical replication and distribution. By 1898, London's famous Egyptian Hall, 'England's Home of Mystery', could boast of its presentation of Mr David Devant's 'inimitable electric shadows' and 'the Largest and grandest display of *Animated* Photographs ever exhibited ... with thrilling effects by Mr. Maskelyne's Electrical and automatic orchestra'.[126] In 1894, an advance was made upon the rigidity of the panorama and the earlier displays of Sullivan and Muldoon through the early cinematic commodification of Sandow's body. This was accomplished when his image was captured fleetingly with the new kinetograph machine by its designer William K. L. Dickson at the Edison Corporation's West Orange, New Jersey Studio.[127] Five years after jumping the stage at London's Westminster Royal Aquarium, Sandow's stock in trade was still his finely sculpted body, and it was upon this commodity that the steady unedited gaze of Dickson's kinetograph was focused. The resulting fifty-foot filmstrip was shown in over nine hundred peepshow viewers across the US and later adapted for viewing in more successful and widely attended projection theatres.[128] Showing him in brief shorts, the film revealed Sandow as he turned front to back and displayed his well-developed muscles.[129] Like typical postcards from the era, his 'flexing' in the 'Black Maria', and the staging of the short boxing film, *Corbett and Courtney Before the Kinetograph* (also filmed in that year), were unsophisticated renditions of standard sporting-theatrical events.[130] Despite its reliance upon a previous theatrical mode, and apart from the novelty of Dickson's invention, the filming of Sandow was important as a means of further familiarizing people with the changing codes of a dominant male subjectivity via the act of muscular posing. It also acquainted a larger audience with the phenomenon of strongman entrepreneurship which was already growing out of it.[131]

In the circulation of boxing and strongman postcards, Edison's film-strips, Billy Edwards' book and *Sandow's Magazine* we can see an attempt to refine and shape the market for bodily spectacle. What were often presented as seemingly transhistorical and common-sense ideas of the sexualized and gendered subject were in fact sometimes radical ideological products of intense cultural renego-tiation. The fitness postcard and the performances of Sandow cannot in this regard be considered apart from the cultural envel-ope of the time in which history, nature and varieties of the 'anthro-pomorphic cult' were being created, redefined and more strongly asserted. In fitness iconography, antique style and modern ideo-logy were combined with an aesthetic that was both more legiti-mate and to some extent more personally pleasurable or satisfying to larger numbers of the population. As a long-standing good within the realm of entertainment, the body of the strongman revealed on stage was more easily conceptualized as a commodity than a clas-sical sculpture derived from an unknown model. It was even more so when made literally statuesque on film and mass-produced in postal cards or peepshow filmstrips. The problem was one of how this procedure could be widened to include the bodies of individual consumers. The solution was to photographically make readers themselves statuesque and sell their bodies back to them as a kind of petrified commodity of the self made whole.

3

Sculpting the Heroic and the Homoerotic

Physical culture played an important role in the emergence of homosexual communities of desire. It was necessary, if the body was to produce the desired effect within advertising culture, to render it present in some ways, and invisible in others. This is especially relevant to the potential homoerotic reading of body images. In making the body into a more tangible commodity or circulating erotic good, photographs were crucial.[1] From its very beginnings, photography was used as a means of validating an ideologically and historically based social order which assumed an unchanging constitution of real space. If there was a literal sculpture machine, it was the technology of the camera. The realism of the photograph and other reproductions seemed at first a kind of antidote to the swirl of life's complexities as they were mirrored within the expanding print media of the *fin de siècle*.[2] Ideal sculptural images, both old and newly carved, or photographically reproduced, quickly assumed a new importance as evidence of the desired static self, representative of a stable history and a clearly concrete present. Photographically contrasting the heroic and the erotic was one of several oppositions that both inscribed and erased individual desires and experiences. Changing industrial technologies and nationalistic commercial imperatives made the mass dissemination of such oppositions not only possible but desirable. The use of the before and after photo had already been pioneered by Booth in promoting his conversion of drunks and vagrants.[3] The police mugshot was being used on a wider scale, and in medical and other reputed social-scientific analyses, photos of the diseased and degenerate were also being employed.[4] The means of reproducing photos had also improved and the means of having them taken were more readily available.

The colonization by health culture commerce of this relatively new space of identity formation was thus accomplished within the context of a developing mass economy in which men especially were more able to compare themselves, 'invidiously' as Veblen thought, to one another, and to ideal images. As a way of charting the self through life, the growing presence of photos had a marked influence on bodily conceptions generally. The objective stance of the pathologist could be adopted to some extent by any person in possession of a 'post-mortem portrait'.[5] This is an important insight in terms of the commercial selling of fitness. It implied a clearer notion of a standard of normalcy with regard to bodies and the creation of a seemingly concrete and absolute objective perspective quite outside of bodily experience. From such a seductive pathological standpoint the corporeal could be analysed and judged in new ways and in turn could presumably be reshaped.

The first of Sandow's 'Great Competitions' was introduced in the initial issues of his magazine. It was a contest that aimed to attract readers and students for mail order instruction, to provide the magazine with photos to publish, and create general publicity for Sandow's gymnasia and other enterprises. The contest response provides a look at the genesis of a modern male body image as a participatory process. Pictures were sent in from all over Britain. Some contributors posed formally in the ways that strongmen did on cheap postcards. A larger number of entrants simply faced the camera, while others stood with their backs to it, perhaps in order to hide their faces. Most men simply looked forward with their arms crossed across their chests. All photos were cropped so that the men appeared only from the waist up. Some wore moustaches, their haircuts were universally short, most were younger, a few middle-aged, some skinny, others brawny, or tattooed. A few wore singlets, though most were shirtless. Almost all of the photos were studio portraits with matt scenery backgrounds. Rather than revealing an obvious bodily ideal, the photos submitted presented a myriad of different body types. Although publications such as *Sandow's* constantly made reference to the symmetrical ideal of classicism, even the great strongman himself was shorter and stockier than typical examples of male perfection from antiquity. In this sense, the idea of normalcy was more complicated than it would at first appear to be.

Sandow selected the photos for publication 'haphazardly from a number', and kept a 'monster album' of all photographs sent to him at his headquarters ('Sandow Hall', Savoy Street, the Strand, London).[6] Gold, silver and bronze statuettes of Sandow were given as prizes at the first Albert Hall competition. The eventual group of 'splendidly proportioned men' (over 150 made it to the semi-finals) were judged not only by a classically trained sculptor, Sir Charles B. Lawes, but also by the medically trained Conan Doyle.[7] While the correspondent for *The Times* noted that the development of some of the men seemed 'abnormal',[8] the entire process of the competition still served to support the authority of a normalizing rhetoric by presenting concrete ideal models of maleness. It did so by combining specular aesthetics and the pleasure of looking with the comfortable validation of one's body being 'right' rather than degenerate or 'wrong'. Later, pictures of the winners were sold as a package. Other competitions followed and the practice of publishing photos continued in the form of 'Sandow's Portrait Gallery', which included pictures of men in the army or navy, colonial subjects such as a Mr Loo-nee (*sic*) from Rangoon, and even an occasional woman or baby. Presumably the continued publishing of these pictures, and the willingness of readers to submit them, was indicative of a marginally successful effort to construct physical culture and its bodily language of the pose as an act of mass self-definition.

In sponsoring such contests, physical culture media imitated the earlier subscription ploys of Lord Northcliffe and others in the mass dailies. More importantly, the addition of the self-revealing photograph created a space for male display and self-definition somewhat apart from actual gymnasia or swimming baths. This, alongside the confessional and 'parliamentary' forms of advice and letters columns, presaged a range of later publications that would cater to the vicarious tendencies of postwar mass circulation readerships. As the success of its photo-competitions indicates, physical culture offered men an attractive means of expressing their gendered identity. In physical culture participation and body building, the desire for fixing the self was fetishized or reduced to the level of prosaic action, to an exercise regimen from which all other goods, moral and intellectual, would presumably flow. The success of any physical culture programme or discipline was determined by an individual's access to information and instruction, that is to the expert knowledge of how to reform the self and the body. Ideal bodies like that of Sandow deemed more worthy of commercial display in printed form, and likewise the bodies of workers and the masses in general, increasingly became subjects of legitimate perusal and public concern. The freer enactment of bodily male power on the stage, which was even less regimented than the prizefight – although it too had its emerging codes – was complemented by the more static and flat expression of bodily order and normalcy articulated principally within the genre of the photographically illustrated periodical. Most often, its regimens were not presented as a mere indulgence of male vanity but as necessary tools for the preservation of family, nation and empire.

Sandow himself not only was filmed, which would be today's ideal form of apotheosis, but also was made truly statuesque through being rendered sculpturally in various forms.[9] However, it was not through the conventionally sculpted form that he provided the most significant testimonial of his impact on discourse and representation in this period, but by way of a special body cast made under scientific supervision at the British Museum.[10] In the October 1901 issue of *Strand Magazine*, along with the first instalment of Conan Doyle's 'The Hound of the Baskervilles', an article appeared concerning the display of the Sandow cast at the museum in South Kensington. Beginning in a satirical vein, the author describes a friend, 'the Superior Person', sputtering disapproval at the inclusion of the figure of 'Sandow the Strong Man' in the hallowed institution's halls. 'What will the museum be coming to next? A penny show with marionettes and performing dogs, I suppose ... music-hall people in the British Museum, faugh!'[11] The author disagreed and expressed no surprise that the authorities of the museum would choose to display such an item. As a cast taken from life, the statue was seriously presented as a scientifically valid anthropometric model. He argued that the museum would have been 'remiss in not seizing the opportunity of handing down to future generations a permanent record of the most perfect specimen of physical culture of our day – perhaps of any age'.[12]

In an interview with Professor Roy Lankester (curator of the natural history department), the point was made that Sandow's cast was of interest to the anthropologist not only as an example of the 'perfect type of European man' but also as a 'striking demonstration' of what can be done to perfect muscle by simple means.[13] Lankester also expressed his hope that he might eventually have such casts for all the races of humankind.[14] The article in the *Strand* was matched by another in *Sandow's* itself which included an entire series of photographs showing the process of making the cast with Sandow seated and classically draped like some latter-day Zeus. Much was made of the rigour and difficulty of making the cast.[15] Casts of Sandow's body were also eventually sold as fragments, usually a life-size arm.[16] The selling of competition photo sets and series, of Sandow live, or in cast form, revealed the importance of the pleasures of possession and the fetishization of body parts made possible by the dissemination of photographic images.[17] Similarly, cover composite photos of readers served to place readers in more direct correspondence with one another, within the inverted world of the multiple image.[18]

Towards the close of 1904, the physical culture press and no doubt Francis Galton's great admirer Sandow himself, were pleased by the University of London's endowment of a fellowship for a study of 'National Eugenics'.[19] Galton, in fact, reciprocated Sandow's admiration, and in his own studies complained of the difficulty of being able to compare his own countryman in the nude, and remarked on the shapelier bodies of people of subject races.[20] Galton's comments mirrored an enduring characteristic of the physical culture press in terms of its comparison-based consumerist dialogue and its own peculiar articulation of class and race as national and imperial properties in relation to bodily ideals. Although he was critical of the contestants in the latter's bodybuilding competitions, Galton was unstinting in his praise of Sandow's own physical attributes.[21] As to other competitors, Galton rather unscientifically compared them to Greek statuary, and found them to be quite unsuitable; they were not the

> best specimens of the British race to be ideally well made-men. They did not bear comparison to Greek statues of Hercules and other athletes, being somewhat ill-proportioned and too heavily built.[22]

Though disappointed with them from 'the aesthetic point of view', 'in respect to muscular power they seemed prodigies'. Sandow's 'statuesque posture' on the other hand was more to Galton's taste.[23]

A consistent thread in such competitions and other published photos, rather than a single ideal body type, was the language of the pose, fostered by the need to remain still for the camera. All of the entrants can be seen to have attempted to express a solidity of strength and potent force. To paraphrase a modern critic describing more recent male bodybuilding and posing, these photos evidence the attempt to embody the myth of phallic power through its association with the male erection. In this sense, the body is exhibited as totally taut; both literally statuesque and yet always capable of exercising force and power at the appropriate climactic moment.[24]

The language of the erect pose in which muscles were flexed to their best advantage was one with which men were conversant due to the distribution of Sandow's own image on postcards and in advertisements. In addition, editorial instructional articles were often accompanied by a series of photos cutting or fracturing the body into a range of poses according to the muscle groups being discussed, thus providing the readers with an important model of imitation; one in which bodily needs were configured as multiple, the body as series of separate bits, with particular commercial requirements. Here again, readers were also being familiarized with Sandow's variations upon the stances of classical figures. In these images the model's muscles were shown flexed and to their best advantage. In the process, the reader was given a photographic framework for seeing his own bodily self actualized through a similar set of poses. In turn, such images gave rise to a shared male community of understanding which could take part in the Great Competition.

Sandow's compact, stocky frame came to be synonymous for many with a turn-of-the-century ideal of masculine power. Unlike Sullivan, who often took on all challengers in his travels, Sandow's invitation to physicality was a less threatening and more inclusive one. By the end of the century, he had moved beyond the challenge of impressing music-hall audiences and cemented his position as the most imitated fitness entrepreneur and publisher in the period before the First World War. Sandow looked beyond the traditions of freakishness and fakery to other models in the display of the authoritative body as an object not only of awe but also of emulation. In the process, he linked the seemingly disparate realms of traditional aesthetics, practical exercise and social reform within a matrix of new consumer and media practices. In effect, he took Watt's idea a giant step forward by offering – for a price – to release 'beautiful Forms' more efficiently from living bodies rather than stone.

In other magazines, contests were also part of an attempt to increase readership, acquire material for publication and sell other products or membership in 'exclusive' readers clubs. In the early issues of Sandow's competitor, *Vim*, three different contests were advertised, including one for the best photo of an outdoor game, and a competition for the best description of a cure or benefit derived from the use of the 'Gem Bath Cabinet'.[25] In Macfadden's publications and the later pages of *Vim* and its successor, *Health and Vim*, competitions were also important. Along with its 'Readers Parliament', its clubs and societies with badges, oaths and special member privileges, there were frequent contests for the best developed male physique.[26]

In *Vim*'s 1902 inaugural issue, 'an illustrated monthly devoted to promoting health and vigour of the body and mind', its publishers (the makers of Gem paper clips) expressed their desire to help rectify the much talked about societal ills of 'exhaustion and degeneracy' then thought to be plaguing Britain.[27] *Vim* followed the lead set by Sandow and Macfadden and labelled their own efforts in this area as not only commercially inspired but a 'missionary endeavour' as well.[28] It was perhaps no accident that an evangelical tone was employed by the publishers of *Vim*. For preacher, reformer and business person alike, the successful example of the Salvation Army as a means for selling hydropathic equipment was an enticing one.[29] Sellers of health and fitness came to rely in varying degrees upon a format which successfully entwined the appeal of the pseudo-religious cult with the latest in scientific rationalism. In turn, the commercial evangelical approach helped to prepare the way for new appeals on the part of the twentieth-century state, both at peace and in war, a modern state even then growing cognizant of the new requirements imposed by a mass society.

In the new century, there were perhaps only a few who would have agreed with the Revd Hugh Price Hughes in his placement of the 'insane passion' for the 'idolatry of physical recreation' as one of the most 'menacing signs' of the times.[30] By the time of *Tono-Bungay*'s publication in 1909, the selling of 'muscular strength and beauty' had become an established service and media sector.[31] Its formulas were a proven method for any would-be fitness authority who might aggressively be employing their own or other people's bodies as marketing tools.[32] Like the sellers of Tono-Bungay tonic, physical culture publishers attempted to be all things to all comers. They tried to create a more immediate participatory medium for men of all classes to help develop what they frequently referred to as a new 'Physical Culture Society'. Constituted in one way as a commercial market of readers and potential buyers of exercise equipment, the participants in this phenomenon existed also as a market of individuals sharing some common, albeit vague, ideological ground with regard to the arrangement and reform of society. In the latter regard the physical culture press was part of a modern or twentieth-century trend by virtue of its mass marketing techniques and its desire to create the 'new man and woman'. Conversely, it was also a part of the Victorian sculpture machine in its desire to use new print technologies and methods of photographic reproduction to highlight classical ideas and imagery as popular ideals, to promote an historically based masculine ethos, rather than create an entirely new one.

Sandow's journalistic approach was always solidly middle-class, and when not posing in leopard skin and sandals or an oversized and well-placed fig-leaf, his frockcoat attire connected him to the masculine professions. For a time, at least, he was taken more seriously than he might be today.[33] Society took him in. Wilde's adversary, the Marquis of Queensberry, judged his physique competitions. Conan Doyle not only judged for Sandow but even went so far as to write a preface to a Sandow publication, something he claimed to have refused to do for other authors.[34] Many ideas similar to those of Sandow's concerning social and health reform were eventually enacted as part of the British welfare state and it was noted that he influenced most of the young men of the Edwardian generation. His schools were attended by persons of 'all sorts and conditions': 'city men', 'army officers' and 'athletes'.[35] To be sure, bodily images like those of Sandow and his readers were more accepted and commonplace in the new century, but the different ways of reading popular cigarette card pictures of languid female dancers as opposed to depictions of men remained significant.

As late as 1866 in Britain it was possible for a man to be prosecuted for 'indecency' because he had shown his legs while 'race-running'.[36] By the end of the century, legitimate representations of nearly nude male bodies were more common within a growing mass media. Indeed, physical culture pictures may have become more popular as sexual imagery after the 1870s and 1880s crackdown on the British trade in 'obscene' photographs.[37] The display of the unclothed male body within certain constraints was more common, but publishing photographs of partially clothed female bodies remained potentially illegal.[38] Whether posing in a neoclassical manner or simply reproduced from the legitimate realm of high art, women's images were more likely to be seen as titillating or appealing to prurient interests. This was the case in 1903, when Mr P. G. Huardel (a postcard publisher) appeared at the Bow Street Police Court after police had seized over 27 000 pieces of his stock.[39] The complaint filed by Mr H. Muskett concerned a picture of a woman in tights 'dressed precisely in the manner of a statue'.[40] The cards apparently came from France. Huardel promised not to import or sell others and was made to pay the four shillings' summons cost. He got off rather lightly, although 300 of his postcards were destroyed by the magistrates due to their 'grossly objectionable character'.[41] In Huardel's postcard trade publication, reference was made to a recent Glasgow case in which the chief constable judged a window display of prints showing works by well-known artists such as G. F. Watts and Lord Leighton, the president of the Royal Academy, as 'unfit for public consumption'.[42] Huardel enquired how it was that 'ballet dancers and seaside bathers [are] perfectly proper in the flesh, but horribly objectionable if deposited in a tiny photograph', noting that an image showing *Naissance de Nymphée* by Marold would be acceptable as a 40 × 22 inch print but possibly indecent as a postcard.[43] Our different way of receiving the opposing images of the woman in her inelegant bathing costume and the man clad in a single well-placed fig-leaf points to the importance of cultural norms and preconceptions on the part of the viewers of images. On the one hand, the seashore girl, once fraught with erotic potential, may now seem quite innocent, even frumpy, whereas the once avowedly heroic nakedness of the fitness poseur may today at least be seen to bear the possibility of an erotic reading. As exampled by the responses to the female body in the *poses plastiques*, notions of propriety were never so stringent as regards the nearly naked depiction of the bodies of children or adult males.

The depictions of women in the physical culture press and the reasons behind the media's persistent difficulty in attracting women readers raise the question of whether physical culture publishers really wanted women subscribers. In terms of hard numbers and revenue, they were surely interested in any potential buyer. But this leaves unanswered the question of their more precise tactical intentions in asking women readers to send in self-portraits. In this sense, the probability that images of physical culture women were sometimes used to attract male readers also pointedly suggests the homerotic potential of the magazines. Whatever their intent, the rationale of a liberating health regimen for female or male customers allowed for the display of bodies in ways that even then were seen as suspect.[44]

The body universal as a fashionable commodity contradicted many important social distinctions. For example, the industrial civilization frequently blamed for the effeminization of men could also be erected as a final bastion separating 'primitives' from the civilized neo-primitives who read the physical culture press. The love of elaborate and exacting codes of dress and finery have often been depicted in Western history as the weakness of the feminine sex or the fault of the prototypical dandy. But if we look at fitness commodification as the articulation of the body's surface as a kind of fashionable attire, we can see that the elemental differences in approaching masculine and 'other' bodies did not break along strictly genital lines of feminine versus masculine identity, or manliness versus unmanliness.[45] Strong and beautiful though she might have been, the female music hall weightlifter wore her body in the wrong way. In effect, she became a cross-dresser by wearing her body in a traditional male style. The strong beautiful male could also wear his body in the wrong manner. In this regard, the fluidity of the naked body as a common and concrete experience served to mask the specificity of pleasures and desires within in it.

For Sandow and most of his contemporaries, fine bodily appearance was the best indicator of a healthy brain and soul. In this regard, his first editorials reveal the lineaments of physical culture's pseudo-religious or cultic bases, and its reliance on antique imagery or at least his own particular fondness for it. Never part of the Purity Movement, Sandow consistently avoided explicit references to the dangers of immorality or masturbation. In his interpretation of the Greek 'golden mean', the moral strictures of religion and mortification of the flesh were to be replaced by the physical regimen of exercise and the body's liberation. In the substitution of secular discipline for spiritual, he argued for the interconnectedness of body, mind and soul. In this trinity, however, there was never any doubt as to which was more important. His belief in a kind of rationalist paganism was expressed in his hope for healthier and more perfect men and women who might 'beget children with constitutions that are free from hereditary taint. . . . the offspring of . . . the sons of gods with the daughters of men!'[46]

In physical culture, a gendered and moral status quo was both enabled and undercut by a history of thought and perception that both revealed and obscured the body. Based upon a Renaissance verisimilitude of 'real' social space within the timeless frame of antique sculptural and architectural orders, physical culture images and related products were made to reify past forms as they had already been articulated by historians, ethnographers, folklorists and others. Thus we have Edgcumbe Staley's *The 'Gentlemen' of Florence* (the first part in a series on the History of Florentine physical culture), or the repeated use of Reni's *Saint Sebastian* as romanticized evocations of an historically transcendent body.[47] Within an art historical or architectonic view, bodily needs and desires could be viewed as as being built into a necessitating framework of history. Men's desires were pliable as such, but typically only through direction from above, or by way of intercession on the part of the 'expert' physical culturist. The larger patrimonial practice of remodelling and reproducing the social order, which included the construction of a past, depended upon a similar articulation of an historicized subject body. In this sense, physical culture was the perfect expression of aspirations towards the sculpture machine.

Sandow's own adolescent conversion to health and fitness, as related to Ira Wood, a well-known physical culture expert in the United States, illustrated the value and use of antique imagery in the manufacture of consumer bodies.[48]

> So far as heredity is concerned I had nothing to be especially thankful for . . . still a mere lad my father's friends advised him to direct my studies toward the ministry. . . . 'Your son will hardly be fit for any more strenuous occupation.' Later our family physician in Koenigsberg, near the Russian frontier, told my father that if he did not take me to Italy for the winter I would never survive it such a weakling I was as a child. . . . Well, I went to Italy, and there my eyes were opened. The Greek and Roman statues I saw there inspired me with envy and admiration. I became morally and mentally awakened.[49]

In another version of the frequently told tale, he asked his father why there were no more such men. His father replied that in those days the rule of the survival of the strongest had not yet been mitigated by the cushioning effects of civilization. Then and there Sandow resolved to lift from himself 'the stigma of weakness'.[50] Even as he told this tale, the great health culturist emphasized that it was 'mental culture first, physical afterwards'.[51] The real commodity he was selling was not technique, nor training, nor mental culture, but rather a more amorphous satisfaction of desire, an answer to the 'envy and admiration' he himself professed to have experienced on that first visit to Italy.[52] Certainly, many of his contemporaries would have understood the similar 'stormy emotion' also experienced by the young Viscount Esher upon visiting the sculpture gallery of the Louvre.[53]

The reliance on a sculptural body in the age of photography was due to an abundance of statuary and monuments and the invention of industrial processes for making cheaper metal cast images. In this context, Sandow and other physical culturists really had something to sell: the opportunity for men beyond the elite sphere to take possession of their bodies in a new way, by social comparison, initially through a pleasurable identification with the comforting and timeless beauty of statuary.

In this regard, Oscar Wilde was certainly not alone in his attraction to a combined modern/ancient aesthetic of bodily freedom. The interest in antiquity was also enjoyed by many who did not share his passion for Oxford undergraduates and working-class youth. As we have already seen, its forms were frequently employed in the pictorial selling of health by the physical culture press. None the less, Wilde's prosecution in 1895 illustrated that the late Victorian body remained constrained by tightening moral codes even though it was an ever more present focal point of consumerism.[54] The Bradlaugh case, the Parnell divorce and the Sir Hector MacDonald and Wilde scandals were all examples of institutional, legislative and judicial responses to changing perceptions of the sexual body as a social danger.[55] By the end of the century, hard labour in Reading Gaol had become a presumably more humane punishment for the sexually deviant than the Regency hangman's rope. But the definition of sexual misconduct among males had widened to include more than mere genital contact. Of course, the precise sins of the 'degenerate' could not be discussed or protrayed in any detail. Indeed, they could be prosecuted only within a framework of body politics that revolved around veiled readings of the body that distinguished the heroic from the erotic and the complex realm of homosocial Victorian friendship from its dreaded antithesis. Wilde's own thoughts on the tractability of language, style and the bodily pose were proven correct even as they were employed against him. He was depicted in court and the press as the embodiment of 'gross indecency', in opposition to the implied innocence of the 'boys', 'lads' and 'youths' he was accused of corrupting.[56] He was convicted as much for his impudence in the face of authority and his ideas as he was for his 'immoral' practices. As with the Marquis de Sade, the inextricable bonds linking bodily behaviour and ideas were made more pronounced through the persecution of a philosopher who dared to practise what he preached.

The Wilde trials were a contest between two opposing ideas of the gendered and sexualized self.[57] In the end, the 'rule-bound violence' of aggressive British masculinity triumphed. Wilde's loss to Queensberry on his own turf – the highly conventional arena of British justice – was a win for a progressively masculinized and repressed society that was embracing institutionalized sport wholeheartedly.[58] And yet, the same society that gave rise to mass sport and physical culture continued to harbour spaces in which male–male love could be legitimized if not always easily indulged.[59]

Physical culture was part of a larger media that helped reconstruct dominant and subversive images of sexual practice. The music halls where Sandow performed were frequently peopled by male (as well as female) prostitutes.[60] From early in his career he travelled not only at the shadowy fringes of the music hall and circus, but also in the dubious realm of the artist and the model. Often working-class or foreign, artists' models played an important role in constructing heroic and erotic imagery. In a rare physical culture article written by a women, Mrs Frank Elliot illustrated a common objectification of the foreign male body.

> With regard to male models the regular studio type of young man is often Italian. Italians are as a rule more picturesque and plastic than the average English model. Although the latter may be found seriously cultivating his muscular system at the halleturnberein [*sic*].[61]

Sandow began his career as just such a plastic foreign body. Indeed, before his first trip to the United States, he was 'picked-up' in Italy by an English painter.[62] His often-told formative experience in the realm of body representation also took place in Italy, a traditionally well-known site of homoerotic imagery and transgressive sexual practice.[63] In yet another version of the visit to Rome he asked his father 'why our modern race had nothing to show in physical development like those lusty men of olden time? Had the race deteriorated, or were the figures before him only . . . ideal creations of god-like men?' His father replied that the race had suffered from 'sordid habits' and 'fashionable indulgences'. In this telling, the historicized body was presented as a nexus of individual autonomy and national health. Again, Sandow carefully situated himself as chaste in his identification with antique images of male power and his appreciation of their bodily beauty and perfection. But the stories of his visit to Italy can still be read as tales of his 'coming out' as an admirer of the male physique if not an actual *aficionado* of male eroticism. Pointedly, his admiration of the masculine body was presented as distinct from the increasingly taboo physical act of men loving men, just as racial and national bodies were desexualized and shorn of erotic potential while retaining their power as symbols of white male dominance.[64] The public denial of the erotic was proof of the extent to which elite discourse held authority over the definition of the body. The question was then not so much one of how same-sex relations between men became criminalized in the period but rather how other male pleasures like those encouraged in physical culture were at the same time asserted as legitimate.

In this context, the supposedly non-erotic images of the male body found in the physical culture press need to be carefully assessed. In 1905 F. W. Haslam, a professor of classics, spoke before a physical culture society in Canterbury, New Zealand. Haslam argued against the failure to link citizenship with military duty and bodily fitness, scornfully noting that its lamentable results included the tendency for public gymnasia to be taken over by time-wasters, 'professional athletes, pretty boys and their friends, who made their exercises a cloak for immoral practices'.[65] His allusion to this aspect of gym life reads as a common example of homosexual panic from the period.[66] As a classicist, Haslam was no doubt aware of the 'unspeakable' sexual practices of the Greeks, and was at pains to remind his listeners that the rise and fall of such ancient civilizations provided an important lesson for contemporary physical culturists. The problem again was one of how any degree of male affection, or admiration of the body, as evidenced by physical culture posing, was possible at all in a repressive atmosphere characterized by the sentiments of Haslam and others.

The open-ended possibilities of the naked body's interpretation meant that Haslam had a point. To argue that the admiration of the body had to remain pure demonstrated some knowledge or belief in its potentially impure reception. The centrality of dynamics of repression and liberation to Victorian processes of desire meant, of course, that the unspeakable would at the very least continue to be whispered. Despite the institutionalization of the delineation between the homosexual and the heterosexual, the spectral processes of the sculpture machine foreground the inherent difficulty of socially constructed categories of sexuality being mutually exclusive and strictly binary.[67] The assumptions by Haslam and others, considered alongside the outcome of the Wilde scandal, meant that physical culture media were that much more important for men who desired simple comradeship or sexual pleasures focused upon other men. Legal repression worked on one level. But an upper- and middle-class-dominated demi-monde of homosexual practices did not disappear in the wake of Wilde's conviction. Consciously or not, physical culture media catered to the overarching 'pornographic' gaze of consumerism as well as an elite penchant for sexually cross- ing the class divide. Classifieds, letters columns, photo-contests and the homosocial character of such publications provided a space for a variety of men to enjoy and imagine the male body, to commun- icate, and even meet one another. Indeed, by the middle of the twentieth century, its successor publications were being avidly cross- read by men who had begun to identify themselves primarily accord- ing to their sexual activities. In this sense, fitness magazines were a major step in the creation of a homosexual subculture based on something more than overt prostitution or chance encounters in public places.[68]

Haslam's interpretation of the Grecian example had in any case been preceded by opposing views in addition to those of Wilde. As Charles Kains-Jackson, Lord Alfred Douglas's friend and fellow homosexual activist, argued in the 1890s, England no longer needed to concern herself with 'population' now that she was 'militarily stable'. In an article in the spring 1894 edition of *The Artist and Journal of Home Culture*, Kains-Jackson reasoned that a real civiliza- tion might thus flower, producing a 'new chivalry' founded upon a spiritual and intellectual foundation of male love.[69] Like Haslam, he made a linkage between romanticized martial life and bodily fitness.[70] In arguing for his new version of knightly camaraderie, he was alert to the predispositions of his special audience and that of late-nineteenth-century British society in general, which was easily seduced by romanticized chivalric as well as classical analogies. Within the readership of *The Artist*, he was preaching to the con- verted in so far as his arguments concerned erotic male associ- ation or the possibilities for a latter-day Theban band. Certainly, his very use of the chivalric metaphor emphasized the continuing power of martial imagery in the construction of both an imperial mythos and his own particular eroticism. In this regard, Haslam and Kains-Jackson illustrate how physique photos of strongmen posing as Greek statues, and a variety of other illustrations of male bodies in the physical culture press, could be read as both erotic fodder and inspiring imperial imagery.[71]

As Wilde's trial and Haslam's lecture illustrated, any new chivalric or martial model, in so far as it allowed men to take any pleasure in their own bodies or in homosocial activities in general, was destined to develop along rather circumscribed and conventional lines. None the less, the emphasis on embodied maleness within a romanticized framework of martial skill served to support and to varying degrees undercut the contradictory rationales that lay behind racist, ethnocentric and gender paradigms. Although less visible, the same was true of sexuality.[72] The male body was beautiful, good and heroic. Each of these were qualities that could also be eroticized. More importantly, the fact that they could be de-eroticized provided a rationale for the nurturance and concealment of individual desires that were socially inappropriate, if not illegal.

In suggesting some of the conditions that allowed for the admiration of the male body while the actual sexual act between men was being actively persecuted, Oscar Wilde's tour of the United States – which took place a decade earlier than Sandow's own travels there – and the career of the founder of Scouting, Robert Baden-Powell (BP), are relevant.[73] Wilde's presentation in the pose of the aesthete in association with a tour of Gilbert and Sullivan's *Patience* had the commercial purpose of attracting audiences for the operetta. On Sandow's tour, he too entered the marketplace as a posing product, and as a result of Florenz Ziegfeld's management became a more saleable one at that. Side by side, photographic depictions of a nearly nude Eugen Sandow and a clothed Oscar Wilde as both photographed by Sarony of New York revealed two very different creatures indeed. Anxieties over the line dividing the sexes or the normal from the perverse were thus subsumed in such new forms of representation that supported various interpretative visions of the natural past, for example the weakness of the effeminate dandy versus the apparent power and historical weight of the neo-classical sculpture as imitated by the music hall strongman.

Both were engaged in the same commercial activity of selling a photographically manufactured self. But Wilde's body was hidden beneath clothes and Sandow's was undressed for all to see. In further comparing the two, however, a reversal takes place in which the nearly nude Sandow stands as the more opaque figure while the pallid and lank young Wilde fully dressed and in lace cuffs appears as the more transparent. Sandow asserted himself as the epitome of modern embodied manliness. Wilde resolutely refused to conform to any normal idea of embodied masculinity.[74] Sandow simply posed and rather than subverting or violating middle-class sensibilities, represented an aesthetic philosophy more firmly grounded in an ideology of male power expressed through physical beauty, muscular strength and proportion.[75]

The case of Baden-Powell, on the other hand, provides a mediating figure between the two and some clues regarding the different ways that physical culture as sexual imagery may have fitted into the lives of some of its readers.[76] As a complement to Sandow and Wilde, he provides an impressionistic example of not only the mindset behind the physical culture publisher and promoter but also that of their readers and spectators who were comfortable in a predominantly homosocial culture.[77]

The inordinate amount of time that Baden-Powell spent with the men under him can be attributed as much to his enjoyment of male camaraderie as to any Christian Socialist desire to 'improve' them. Indeed, his love of the empire's far-flung places was not only about the 'flannel shirt life', but also about the greater opportunities to take part in a male culture that prized and displayed the body regularly. He held an 'emotional and aesthetic affinity' for the 'well-muscled males who were taming nature in these remote places'.[78] His concern with typical 'manly' activities was belied by his enjoyment of many 'feminine pastimes' such as interior furnishing and the design of embroidery patterns for the wives of the regiment.[79] However, his enjoyment of so-called feminine activities was not matched by a liking for women's company or an appreciation for representations of their nude bodies.

Baden-Powell's attitude toward the body in general was keyed toward the typical pattern of physical culture gender differentiation. Emphasizing 'clean manliness' in an unpublished draft article titled 'A Dirty Age', he condemned the depiction of female anatomy.[80] He considered the tenth Scout law to be the most important – 'A Scout is clean in thought and word and deed' – and was especially concerned with 'keeping the racial member clean'.[81] His concern with male purity and female contagion can be linked to his position as an invisible spectator of male erotica. Baden-Powell made special trips to see A. H. Tod's collection of photos of nude boys at Charterhouse and his appreciation for nude imagery extended to the spectacle of actual nude young men as well.[82] In 1934, he railed against the police banning of boys swimming naked in the Serpentine.[83] Watching bathers had long been a London pastime. In the nineteenth century, Francis Galton had 'often watched crowds bathe, as in the Serpentine' and, as noted earlier, complained of the relative lack of such opportunities to 'scientifically' compare his countryman in the nude.[84] In Baden-Powell's lifetime, such public opportunities diminished as the body became a greater focal point of movements like Scouting and physical culture.

In the trauma of Baden-Powell's own jump from childhood to adulthood and its financial burdens, we can see how the pictorial depiction of clean youths and the 'boys' own' associational appeal of the physical culture club or league might have been attractive to him and others. To be young and male was to be exempt, in Baden-Powell's canon, from the usual tyranny of social distinctions. His love for the ambiguity or 'betweenness' of boyhood was linked to his own experience of adulthood as a dangerous phase of life, a kind of death of youth's idyll wherein work and the need to make an income took precedence over frolic and play.[85] Like Sandow and Wilde he had to make his way in the world. As Benjamin Disraeli quipped, success required either blood, a million or genius. Much like Sandow and Wilde, Baden-Powell demonstrated some modicum of genius in his ability to market himself as a successful author, publicist and entrepreneur of the imperialist ethos.

Sandow's career in Britain began with his presentation as both Wilde and Baden-Powell's preferred object of desire, the 'ephebe', positioned in the state bordering youth and full adulthood. Acquiring a moustache, he soon proceeded to occupy the role of the 'mature athlete', a relatively new image of male eroticism by comparison with the dominant Victorian objectification of the youthful adolescent as epitomized in photographs by Baron Von Gloeden.[86] The mature athlete was different from the boy-Ganymede but similar in the poseur's willingness to become vulnerable to the camera's eye. The heroism of youth was that of vulnerability associated with innocence. The heroic stance of the mature strongman was characterized by control – the exertion of power and the promise of mastery. By way of muscular posing's conflation of power with simple physical strength, there was a push against the prevailing experience of a machine age in which the body was in some ways less exalted as a productive resource. Likewise, in the assertion of a neo-classically inspired muscular aesthetic, particular notions of beauty and sexual positioning were sublimely and causally linked with an abstracted and still palpable exercise of male power. But these were never hard and fast ideas and relations. Individuals who fantasized physical encounters with such images could make them into objects of possession as well as icons of potential domination. A given subject might desire, in fact, to possess the mature strongman master or be dominated by the adolescent youth. Another might find equivalent pleasure in imitation, assuming either or both bodily costumes in fantasies or actual enactments of same gender and opposite gender sexual encounters.

In opposition to Wilde, the seemingly unconcealed figure of Sandow, like the uniformed hero of Mafeking, provided real refuge in its assertion of the big lie, that of an overarching and bodily indexed manliness within which specific desires, including homoerotic ones, might be kept secret. In this regard Sandow's body was a kind of uniform, as well as its own mask and mediator, acting as a greater metaphorical body that could be mistaken by thousands of others for their own, one in which specific individual desires might be diffused within an experience of the physique somehow anterior to its socially determined existence and being.

It was expected that technologies like the photograph revealed the true nature of bodily difference. Although the body was the cipher or sign of the self, the essence of the individual remained intertwined with ideas of moral good and rational optimality. The apparent control of the body as well as who did the looking, and why, were all critical questions. There was perhaps nothing more obvious than the weakness of the woman in her 'underthings' or the limpness of poet-aesthete versus the strength of the well-muscled and naked male. But such distinctions between men, women and effeminate men were fundamentally reliant on the assumption that different poses by men, 'inverts' and women reflected their inner desires and fundamental constitutions. The strategic juxtaposition of certain types of men – those with exemplary muscles – versus representations of the self-conscious powerlessness of the effeminate underscored such assumptions. Images of strong or degenerate men and exotic women were read within a world that believed in the premise of male superiority. In fact, neither the belief in male primacy nor the ideals in male or female representation conformed very closely to people's actual lives.[87] The weedy degenerate clerk, unfit for military service, who was the presumed client of the physical culture huckster, made for an interesting contrast to the growing numbers of women who energetically played sports at school, avidly rode bicycles and, in short, were making a hash of traditional representational distinctions.[88] As did the guardsmen and others who conformed publicly to archetypes of masculinity, even as they sold themselves as prostitutes or had sexual relations with their male comrades.[89]

For men who desired other men, playing the double game was enabled and encouraged by dominant presumptions about the readability of the body's surface. A large part of the success of physical culture was its assertion of the male body as heroic rather than erotic, in the body's depiction as under control rather than out of control. In pictorial practice, magazines like *Sandow's* clearly provided space for a readership of men at least desiring to look at or compare themselves with other men. In every case, the reader brought individual experiences and desires to bear in consuming physical culture products and images. Underneath the controlled body there was always the threat or promise of its opposite. In some cases the presence of the erotic was more obvious. Eugenicist Francis Hutchinson, for example, in one of several physical culture articles he contributed, described his 16-year pursuit of measuring and photographing a large number of young men in the nude. In his arguments for nude male physical culture he proposed the mass production of live body casts to be displayed in gyms and museums, and the circulation of books of honour containing photographs of the very best bodies.[90] Like Baden-Powell and Francis Galton, his standard of perfection, though based on the gathering of numerous young men's measurements, was taken from antiquity. Despite Hutchinson's supposed objective of maintaining the quality of the racial stock, it is difficult to picture youths posing awkwardly in the latter's New Zealand garden with any real objectivity.[91] The slightly awkward innocence of naked youth can be viewed now as then in distinctly erotic terms. In Hutchinson's case he obviously liked to look and certainly desired to see more. Arguing that such exemplary male images were only useful as a means of improving the race, his rationale left open the question of the aesthetic and erotic standards that underlay his ideas of racial improvement.

Sandow's Magazine – especially the Great Competitions – encouraged the growth of a male community that could both enjoy viewing male bodies and improve their own physiques. In some ways it is all too easy for us today to read such physical culture magazines as both crassly commercial and implicitly gay-coded. This is not to say that any body was always naturally erotic underneath the scrim of cultural disavowal, but rather that erotic readings of the body were as legitimate as heroic ones for either gender. Eugen

Sandow's ostensible aim was always that of improving the health of the nation. In his editorials he often employed a kind of religious rhetoric in identifying the neglect of the body as the worst of all sins, a sin 'against nature'.[92] Indeed we might view the body as a much more precious commodity in the *fin-de-siècle* period when the ravages of viral threats were an historical constant with little precedent for their eradication. However, Sandow's conclusions regarding the sin of bodily neglect were certainly atypical in their rationalization of pleasure. Indeed it was a peculiar kind of bodily temperance for which he argued. It was, he wrote

> Not the temperance which consists of rigidly abstaining from all the 'pleasant vices' but the real temperance which teaches a man when to say 'NO' . . . to indulge in all that is conducive to happiness without being in danger of . . . overstepping . . . the boundary line, which leads to misery.[93]

Here Sandow left a large space for interpretation concerning the placement of that boundary line. His rhetorical style and ethical tolerance were decidedly unlike the exacting moralism and hectoring tone of competitors such as *Health and Vim*, which argued, in a rather salacious way, for sex as a sterile and pseudo-religious experience intended only for procreation. Sandow put forward an ethic unbounded by traditional Christian morals, dependent upon circumstances and consequences rather than rigid taboos. Baden-Powell, Wilde, Galton, Hutchinson and Sandow participated in different ways in the promotion of an admiration of the male form that went somewhat beyond their professed intellectual or reformist motivations. Whether physical culturists intended them to or not, men like Edmund Gosse, Viscount Esher, J. A. Symonds and significant numbers of others were likely to have read the illustrations and photographs in their press as homoerotic. We can only wonder about the extent of the space it provided for other such individuals who not only enjoyed Sandow's display of his own and other male bodies but also desired the experience of their touch and feel as well.

The rhetoric of the media heroicized 'thinking' man of action, later expressed by T. E. Lawrence, emphasized the cultural eclipse of Wilde's own version of the living thinking-posing man of literary action. The record of outright denial and distortion of Lawrence's sexual predilections demonstrates the dropping of a new kind of curtain between the male subject and his audience in a media-engulfed world. Indeed, in this regard, media-made individuals such as General Gordon, Lawrence and even Sandow had more in common with Wilde than with any less practical ideal of the heroic. As enactments of the spectacle of gender, the modern male hero exists within a medium that encourages a focus on appearance and consumption as markers of self in spite of all accompanying action to the contrary. The physical culturist was especially engaged in this outright fetishization of the male as statuesque poseur, as an opaque surface representation of natural strength. In relation to certain traditional ideas of the gender dynamic, this was fundamentally subversive, as the body was in effect being constructed as yet another product that could be easily changed, and that concealed as much as it revealed.

In the realm of the physical culture photograph's production and reception, actual desires and wants were enmeshed within seemingly common-sense oppositions of the pure and heroic set against the deviant and abnormal. Postcard or magazine images of nude or partially clothed boxers and strongmen poseurs ostensibly linked the athletic pose with physical power and ideal manhood. In the process historicized ideas of masculine beauty and bodily autonomy were placed above other abstractions or experiences of the self. But the emphasis on the unclothed body was regularly complicated by issues of gender and sexuality, as well as race and class.[94] A morally infused rhetoric of a male/female, heroic/erotic hierarchy served to cut through the tangle of contradictions epitomized by physical culture's articulation of a universally reformable body. The issue of manliness or rather the problem of the 'unman' increased in this context, as fitness industries and the greater political and cultural emphasis upon the body developed. Because it was incumbent upon the physical culture client to protect and improve his own bodily honour, and because his physique was something that might be lost and perhaps never restored, male readers were in effect being 'feminized' by the very consumer ethos that promised them a restoration of their masculinity.

The heroic was a handy way of erasing and concealing the possibility of the great majority of men's actual lack of self-control or indeed, their lack of political power. To be sure, the concern with bodily control through the assertion of the heroic pointed to the body's crucial elusiveness as an ideological construct in both its gendered definition and in the conflation of social identity with sexual practice. In the flesh and in the physical culture photograph, the body and desire were re-read, constrained and controlled. They remained, and remain today, elusive experiences. Practices that aimed to discipline them were avowedly repressive in many cases, and unexpectedly liberating in others. In their variety and complexity they constitute traces of a dimly imagined future that includes the contradictions of present-day body consumerism and a commercial aesthetic that continues to separate and fuse the heroic and the erotic pose.

4

Imperial Mirrors

As the late-nineteenth-century imperial land grab accelerated, Britain's pre-eminent position began to be threatened by US and German economic competition.[1] Fitness entrepreneurs relied upon the fears of British decline and expanded their ambitions to an imperial scope. Both imperialism and consumerism were in fact intimately connected within physical culture's romanticized, aggressive and redemptive conception of empire which reasserted the value and worth of the individual male body.

The fact that subaltern peoples could be seen as both warlike and effeminate pointed to the variability of the body. Baden-Powell's belief that other races could excel physically and remain degenerate demonstrated how the body could be read as a kind of clothing that covered more profound failings.[2] Warlike Rajputs, Jats, and Gurkhas of India could be seen as superior to the supposedly more 'effeminate' Bengali Hindus, and could, at the same time, be viewed as inferior to Europeans in terms of political and technological achievement. As the use of the feminine term indicated, the strategic employment of the hierarchy of gender was important.[3] Oftentimes, in fact, gender categories were seen as more natural and deeply embedded than those of race and nationality. Crucially, they could be easily conflated with other social categories including emerging ones concerning sexual practice. The 'jellyfish' or 'waster' versus the real man relied on the notion that those who were not self-reliant and hardy were not 'men'. Simple bodily ability required linkage with other ideological conceptions of manliness. Correct behaviour or how one wore the clothing of the body was thus significant above and beyond strength, speed or skill.[4]

The conflict with the Boers in South Africa was the first test of the British empire's might pitted against fellow Europeans since the Crimean war. In the 'Black Week' of 10–16 December 1899, three of Britain's generals were defeated in quick succession. This did nothing to quell the huge volunteer response to the war. The reasons behind this rush to enlist cannot entirely be attributed to 'patriotism' pure and simple. Concern over the nation or empire's

81

welfare was clearly evinced by sharp increases in enlistment in the volunteers forces during the Eastern crises of the later 1870s and early 1880s, the 1884 invasion scare, as well as the botched attempt to rescue Gordon Pasha in 1885, and the first Boer war.[5] Such rises in numbers may be more meaningfully linked to interests that shaped physical culture: desires for adventure, comradeship and gainful employment.[6] The enthusiastic volunteering has been called 'something approaching a rehearsal' of the rush to sign up in 1914.[7] 'Impelled by the lust for glory', nearly 11 000 volunteers alone were raised in late December 1899 and in the early months of 1900 and many more could have been raised.[8] Most of these were clerks and the like, who also comprised the larger part of the then emerging physical culture press's audience.[9]

By the outbreak of the Russo-Japanese was in 1904, physical culture had become a widespread and popular phenomenon, with its fitness and strength publications, instructional schemes, devices and organizations present throughout the West, and many parts of the colonial world.[10] The quick spread and popularity of physical culture among different classes and ethnic groups points to some significant contradictions within fitness discourse. The apparent democracy of the commercial body flew in the face of many prevailing racialist and class presumptions of the day. Physical culturists were not immune, however, to influences that undercut or negated the egalitarian appeal of their advertisements. In practice, most fitness media tacked a course between the two: veering back and forth from a hysterical rhetoric of biological degeneration to the more euphoric positivism of their own methods that aimed to socially reconstruct the body.[11]

The genetic elitism of eugenics was never reconciled with physical culture's persistent utopian promises of bodily empowerment for all. Despite Sandow's admiration for eugenicist goals, Francis Galton's views on ideal typologies were in conflict with some key assumptions and practices of those in the fitness media and related industries. Physical archetypes and ideals were vitally important to Sandow and others. But the physical culturist's aim of inducing individuals to imitate such ideals and actually change their bodies was less scientific and more 'democratic' in its implicit promise that a majority of bodies might attain some movement towards the ideal. Eugenicists focused on the possession of good genes and the ability to pass them on. In terms of greater government policy, they were in alignment with typical middle-class views of social hierarchy and heredity. But eugenics was not to be the vehicle for answering fears of national decline. The more programmatic and less controversial exercise methods of the physical culturist were to become more important within educational reform.

Fitness media were not only important within the widening gambit of health and exercise didacticism, but also significant in the formation of national or racially based ideas of self-definition.[12] Ideal bodies were used as tools of domination in both class interactions and in imperial contexts. At the same time, the very plasticity of any bodily ideal created ruptures for workers and subaltern peoples. By 1905, the generation that was to be decimated in the First World War was already experiencing the globe as cultural and economic totality. Anyone who had the income to purchase physical culture products or the leisure time to put its principles into practice was a potential physical culture participant. In this sense, physical culture's ambitions were theoretically coextensive with the borders of the massive global economy itself. Careful to observe the representational conventions of the day, *Sandow's* physical culture message was by virtue of its circulation in magazine form, never reserved for the socially elect or withheld from the marginalized. However, the democratic, even revolutionary, implications of it were only dimly grasped as women, colonial subjects and the working class began to apply his formulas of corporeal empowerment for themselves.

As Sandow disembarked at the English port of Dover on 18 September 1905, a military band struck up his personal signature tune, Handel's eulogistic 'See, the Conquering Hero Comes!'[13] His stately attire of black frockcoat, grey trousers, and silk waistcoat was counterbalanced by press descriptions of 'his fair hair curling under the broad brims of a trilby hat'.[14] His return to Britain followed a lengthy tour to British India, Dutch Java and Japan. By the time of Sandow's journey to India, cinema's impact – at either the so-called core or periphery – had yet to be felt. However, in those parts of India he visited in 1905, a not dissimilar pre-cinematic relationship between audience and performer was enacted as his image and celebrity drew audiences that may have cared little for, or known nothing of, his specific message. Traditionally, the model hero was either a purely fictional character or that of a person who had demonstrated actual moral or physical bravery. Sandow's 1905 visit abroad illustrated not only the possible cross-cultural appeal of his particular message but also a new level of interest in a largely popular culture personage whose accomplishments were purely performative in nature.[15]

The means of distributing the images of theatrical and sporting celebrities had accelerated rapidly during the last two decades
of the century. The earlier intellectual celebrity exemplified by Mark
Twain, Charles Dickens or Oscar Wilde had developed within a
nineteenth-century lecture circuit which reached a relatively small
number of people.[16] That the German-born Sandow published in
Britain and the US and travelled around the world preaching his
gospel of health and strength, illustrated the extent of capitalist
consumerism's global scope. The content of his message, and his
practised performer's sense of marketing, attracted thousands into
his travelling tent in India with equal numbers turned away.[17] In
Britain and the US, his celebrity status – part entertainer, part athlete – captured just as many. The distribution of Sandow's ideas
and image outside of Europe illustrated how physical culture reproduced typical power relations and provided possibilities for resisting them.

At the turn of the century, Sandow's image could be found in
the drawing-rooms of mansions in Newport, Rhode Island,[18] as well
as among the debris of battle in far-away South Africa. In 1901, an
'interesting Boer Relic' was sent to *Sandow's* by a Lance-Sergeant of
the 2nd Coldstream Guards then stationed at Graaff Reinet, South
Africa. The relic was a photograph of Sandow found on the veldt,
'evidently dropped by a Boer admirer'.[19] The photo was republished on the occasion of his later visit to South Africa in 1904.[20] In
both cases, the picture was used as an example of the strongman's
presumed appeal beyond the shores of Britain and even among her
enemies. Similarly, in 1902, the magazine presented photos of fit
British troops and Boer prisoners at the Diyatalawa prison camp in
Ceylon; these appeared with the assertion that both 'our "Tommies"
and "our friends the enemy"' inside the wire enclosure were equally
interested in Sandow's system of physical training.[21] With the use
of other such letters and photos from around the world, physical culture became a window on the nation and empire.[22] Later, Sandow's
life-sized plaster cast became one of the most popular exhibits in
the 'gloriously eclectic museum' of the Gaekwar of Baroda, Sayaji
Rao III (1875–1939), along with items like a stuffed buffalo calf with
two heads.

Even before his trip to the Far East, the new name of Sandow's contest scheme – the 'Empire and Muscle Competition' – demonstrated
the currency of imperial rhetoric and imagery.[23] The fitness media's
depiction of the exoticism of empire was one of several themes that

were intended to produce a dependency on the part of the reader for a monthly or weekly peek at empire through the looking-glass of the physical culture press. One underlying idea was that 'reality' was being experienced somewhere else, and that the medium of the magazine gave one reliable, albeit secondary, access through the medium of self-comparison.[24]

Sandow's trip to the Far East also indicated the politically subversive potential of physical culture as well as its inherent malleability.[25] Well before his visit, the currency of bodily empowerment in India had already been specifically tied to nationalist activity by the writings of Sarala Debi in the 1890s.[26] The world-renowned Hindu revivalist and reformer Swami Vivekanada argued that the key to success for independence lay in the 'three Bs: beef, biceps and Bhagdvad-Gítá'.[27] Physical exercise was also later incorporated into the nationalist terrorism movement by groups such as the Simla Byayam Samiti, a physical fitness club founded in 1926 by a follower of the Yungantar terrorist group.[28] Such examples were expressions of the recognition that physical discipline and strength could be useful in the struggle of resistance, if assiduously cultivated by politically committed Bengalis, Punjabis and others. Such bodily fitness became identified with an exacting exercise regimen, a constant and organized life routine, and sometimes even included a meat-based diet. Like other implements of colonial rule such as military equipment and transportation technology, it was not considered inherently or uniquely Western, but as separate from its user, and capable of serving any master. The cultivation of physical strength thus offered the attractive promise that the British might be beaten at their own game.

Sandow's visit to Britain's Indian empire coincided with a period of political turmoil. This unrest was indirectly connected to the increased expectations of nationalists in the aftermath of Japan's stunning defeat of Russia – a demonstration of Asia's capacity to thwart European ambition. Sandow's visit occurred near the time of the conclusion of the war between Japan and Russia and also the signing of the second version of the Anglo-Japanese alliance, which included within its scope the protection of Britain's Indian interests. Nationalism in India under B. G. Tilak, L. Lajpat Rai and others grew stronger from that point on. More immediately, Indian politics were ignited by the actions of the Viceroy, Lord Curzon, particularly his disastrous partitioning of Bengal in 1905. From that moment, an escalating dialectic of repression and resistance, concession and unflagging pressure commenced, thus defining the basic dynamic of imperial rule up to its demise in 1947.[29] The travelling strongman entered this charged environment equipped with a message that delighted Indians without threatening the British. Because he was not 'political', the celebrated colossus was viewed by all with pleasure and amazement, but his import was dramatically different as seen from opposing cultural perspectives. The London *Standard* wrote that Sandow's winter sojourn to India had dramatically

> incited the emulation of native athletes, he has been hailed as 'Sandow-Pahlwan' and challenged to single combat by a champion who styled himself Gamun Baliwala Pahlwan pupil of the late Mohammed Buta famous as the Rustam of Hindustan.[30]

The great Gamun was 'ready to wrestle with Sandow-Pahlwan before the public so that all classes of the people might see and appreciate our good points'.[31] That Sandow had been taken into the hearts of Indians was evidenced by the use of the name 'Pahlwan', a name applied generally to indigenous athletes and more especially to popular wrestlers.[32] The *Standard* speculated

> Whether the Indian government will hasten to avail itself now of Mr. Sandow's services is not known but as we frequently hear of a lack of strong men in the administration there might be room for one of his unquestioned vigour. Personal strength has before this enabled English officials in India to maintain the prestige of the empire even more than the alleged superiority of western intellect.[33]

For the British, Sandow could be viewed as an exemplary specimen of a determined will applied to a naturally gifted Anglo-Saxon physique. For an Indian prince such as the Gaekwar of Baroda, he might have been seen as a marvel plain and simple, his plaster cast yet another item of conspicuously luxurious consumption.[34] For other more politicized Indians or those of less exalted classes, he could be viewed as a prototype for a legion of warriors campaigning for a greater cause than worldwide physical culture. In Bengal, as Gamun Baliwala Pahlwan demonstrated, Sandow epitomized an indigenous art, once thriving but now dormant, which might be rekindled to serve largely political ends.[35] Sandow himself was clear in his belief that his methods were for everyone, as he was quoted from a series of articles in the *Indian Sporting Times*,

The native Indians have a fine foundation for her [*sic*] building of large Physical Men. It is only because of their lack of proper food and systematic exercise that they are thin and haggard.[36]

Sandow denied that exercise was limited by climate, a frequent basis for evolutionary-based racist rationales, and observed that 'seldom have I found a country where I want to exercise as much and as often as I do here'.[37] Attempts to write off such peoples as Macaulay did with his description of the Hindu 'race' as 'weak even to effeminacy', were countered by citations of Indians 'quite as brawny as any English public school boy'. For example, 20-year-old Chaudra Perkh of Calcutta, son of a rich merchant, opened a well-attended physical culture class, and had been practising the Sandow system since the age of 15. Another improved 'native specimen' was Ram Narayan Acharryya, who at the age of 11 had been thin, weak and almost without muscle. Yet another Indian, Surest Chandra Das Gapta of Bengal, sent in to *Sandow's* a table of measurements (taken from age 15–16 between 1904 and 1905) which showed an increase in chest size from 27 to 31 inches. In all, Sandow assured his readers that

The interest displayed in the . . . movement augurs well for the future of this great peninsula and will lead to an amelioration of the condition of its teeming millions of inhabitants.[38]

In Sandow's day, if not also in our own, it was exceedingly hard for a crafted male physique to escape its destiny as the representation of a fighting machine. Brute strength was not without its uses in colonial affairs, and as some contemporaries acknowledged. It might also be harnessed to efforts that could foment the undoing of imperialism. In Sandow's tour there was some proof of J. A. Hobson's notion of extra-economic factors in the maintenance of empire. Sandow's intent was surely selfishly pecuniary but at the same time he was the quintessential salesman for the 'savage survivals of combativeness' which Hobson argued lay at the root of modern imperialism.[39] By the time of his return from the Far East in 1905, the political value of his methods had become a kind of commonplace back in England. As the *Morning Leader* noted on the occasion of his return, Sandow's bodybuilding blueprint had been introduced into the British Army, no doubt to the relief of officers and the successors of Wolseley who had been troubled by the undersized dimensions of many of its soldiers' bodies.[40]

After 1905, the example of Japan's *Bushido* model of rationally marshalling its small island resources in pursuit of conquest was a salient one.[41] The fascination with Japanese success, apart from its racial implications, was further evidence of a harkening back to a romanticized idea of feudal man-to-man combat. Even before the Russo-Japanese conflict, the interest in Japan as a physical culture exemplar was apparent.[42] Articles such as 'An Exhibition of Japanese Sword Fencing',[43] and G. S. Surrey's 'Wrestling in Japan', appeared in the first years of the twentieth century.[44] More typical were pieces focusing on individuals such as the wrestler Higashi. In 'Sharkey and the Japanese Wrestler', the latter was described as 'no larger than a good sized American boy of 15 years'. Like Japan herself, size was of little importance, as Higashi triumphed handily over the 240 lb wrestler.[45] Following upon Japan's victory over Russia, the numbers of advertisements for ju-jitsu and Asian martial arts schools increased markedly.[46] Along with the usual ads for the healthy benefits of Fry's Cocoa, banner tag lines such as 'Victorious Japan' heralded the services of the Ashikaga School of Ju-Jitsu in Liverpool.[47] Athletic notes sections now included the ju-jitsu category as a sport.[48] In addition, typical observational assessments asserted the better quality of Japanese health.

> In the whole of Tokio [*sic*] . . . I have not seen a single soldier who is flatfooted, narrow chested, or slouching. The army is the cream of the nation. It is a thousand pities that the same thing cannot be said of the modern Tommy Atkins. I have seen many soldiers in London with all three of these drawbacks.[49]

In both *Vim* and Sully's *Physical Education*, similar preoccupations with physical training in Japan and the potential dangers of too much sports spectatorship as opposed to participation were also evident.[50] Like Brabazon or Esher's cursory comparisons, the emphasis was upon the body as it seemed to appear within shifting hierarchies of physical typology. Of course, the Japanese example was a complicating factor in terms of other ideas about race. Because of the clear bodily differences between the white European and the Japanese, the elevation of the latter to the status of an ideal type was in decided conflict with typical views of white superiority. Further articles and more ju-jitsu ads were also regularly found in *Sandow's* and other physical culture magazines.[51] In terms of the physical culturists' egalitarian conception of the body, it made perfect sense. In this respect, what Sandow taught about and revealed in his tent was indeed something that persons of 'all sorts and conditions' could understand and profit from.[52]

The synthesis of individual concerns with larger ones was crucial. In spite of the popularity of the pseudo-science of the eugenicists, Lord Esher was not far wrong in his assessment that scientific thought was 'uncongenial to the British temperament in commerce or statecraft' and that other more evocative ideas were necessary. In his own arguments for national military planning in 1904, Esher placed a typical emphasis upon the individual body, noting that 'Imperial rule can have no other ultimate basis than adequate and organized physical force'.[53] The fact of Britain's military forces increasing reliance upon new destructive technologies rather than the valiant body of the soldier was not lost upon others such as Brabazon and Wolseley. And yet, there was a need and desire to retain the ideological flavour of past military glory.

In one sense, there was a relatively easy absorption of differing race examples of health and strength within physical culture rhetoric. There had long been an abiding interest in digging up examples of physical culture in differing cultural and historical settings.[54] One frequent example of this was the interest in the 'virility' of the Jewish population.[55] The assimilationist possibilities for the middle-class Jew in the latter half of the nineteenth and early twentieth century in Britain were not insignificant. Of course, for those of a different skin colour, circumstances were much more complicated. To those considered to be of different races (which might include the Irish, Indians and Sub-Saharan Africans), the world of sport and fitness seemed to offer an easier means of social acceptance than would have been possible in other areas. In the case of Arthur Wharton, a 'young gentleman of colour', who in 1886 became the first athlete to run 100 yards in 10 seconds, 'the old association of black athletes with boxing' was transcended, and he became one of the first of Britain's modern black sporting figures.[56] As a presumed example of the 'salvation of the fittest' or 'success of British imperialist ideology in action', Wharton was a problematic case.[57] However, like the boxer Peter Jackson, or Jesse Owens or Joe Louis, 50 years later, Wharton's sporting success did not and could not alone demolish embedded structures and habits of racism or ethnocentrism.[58]

The taint of degeneracy believed to be the result of miscegenation or race-mixing relied upon clear notions of racial superiority. Notions of sporting ability and physical vigour as being more natural or primitive in character could none the less be used as a convenient rationale for explaining the black man's superiority over whites in the discrete realm of sports. This was demonstrated by the appearance of an African male on the cover of *Health and Vim* in 1909. The use of a member of a 'savage race' as a 'presentment of typical "health and vim"' was carefully explained inside. The Zulu tribesman on the cover, although admitted to be the 'South African black at his best' and 'the finest type of all the black races', was regrettably, none the less, a member of a 'degenerate nation'.[59] His lean frame was clearly at another extreme from the Greek-inspired ideal seen in most physical culture representations of white European men. A similar example was seen in Felix Martinas' article on the 'The Champion Wrestler of the East', Mabul Khan, a Baluchi of the Mier Shadeensai caste, who is described as being of those 'turbulent races' possessing 'warlike tendencies'.[60] Other similar articles lauded the abilities of Pacific islanders while at the same time referring to the 'Savage Athletics' of Tonga and Samoa.[61]

As participants within the empire, those of a different colour were to some extent offered a promise of equality at the level of the body if not in terms of culture and technological achievement. Thus, in the November 1902 *Sandow's*, we have the example of 'A Sketch of the History, Customs, and Life of the Africa East Coast Natives', by Mkvazi Lo Twitshi.[62] In 1903, a similar colonial perspective, 'On the Hills with a Rifle' by Gurkir-Pal Singh Mann of the Punjab appeared, and in 1904, *Sandow's* printed 'A Young Ceylon Athlete' by Francis De Zoysa.[63] But such contributions by actual colonial individuals, like similar articles by actual working men, were the exception rather than the rule. Letters from individuals such as P. M. Deva Varma of Bengal on the value of physical culture in healing weak lungs were more common.[64]

As with the poor, middle-class white males took a proprietoral interest in the fitness of subject peoples. In a 'Notes of the Month' from 1902, for instance, there are two photos of a Gurkha Hill scout in loincloth, sent in by Captain Watt of the 2nd Gurkhas, Abbottbad (Punjab) India, and another photo of a C. G. Bruce, who had once attended a Sandow school, with another Gurkha, Harkbir. All were hill scouts in Bruce's regiment, and rather than attesting to the empowerment of their subordinates, Watt's and Bruce's presentation of physical culture results had more of the cast of one horse trainer talking to another.[65] In another issue, the dark-skinned body of Norbert Malcolm Whiter of Lahore is shown as evidence of the results obtained from Sandow's *Strength and How to Obtain It* following two years of training. Included with this pre-mortem photograph is a medical certificate from a Dr P. Womey attesting to Whiter's health. Situated nearby in the same issue is a photo of a $14\frac{1}{2}$-year-old boy, H. D. Pratt of the London Orphan Asylum.[66] In both cases, the powerlessness of the two subjects in class and racial terms stood in direct contrast to any assumption of autonomy on their part as practitioners of physical culture.

The effort to show physical culture to be pan-racial continued with the printing of letters such as that of F. Horace Gonzales from St Joseph Trinidad, British West Indies,[67] who sent his photo as proof of his transformation after four months of using the Sandow grip dumbbells. But what imperial rhetoric might join together was offset by other articles pointing out racial and national differences, such as John Macdonald's essay on France and 'The Strong Strenuous Purposeful Teuton'.[68] The article argued that Germany's young men were taught how to take care of their bodies and protect their nation, which resulted in 'a virility of thought and action' that was a 'menace to the rest of the world'.[69] As time went on, testimonials became less common than the growing use of examples from the world of wrestling or entertainment proper, such as Higashi, Mabul Khan, or Smaun Sing Hpoo who performed at the Lyceum as the 'miniature hercules'.[70]

The limitations of appeals framed in these ways were perhaps made most apparent by *Sandow's* ceasing the publication in 1907. Increased competition from a growing number of fitness periodicals, waning interest in the physical culture craze and a desire to diversify into other product areas such as prepared foods led Sandow to suspend publication of his magazine. Upon his return from the Far East, Sandow was said to be preparing the inauguration of a national institute of physical culture at a new centre in London.[71] Despite the imminent closure of the magazine, his visit to the Far East underlined the contradiction of developing international linkages and mounting breakaway nationalisms, both rhetorically and in practice, that characterized the growing capitalist global economy.

After disembarking at Dover in 1905, Sandow embraced his 'pretty little nine year old girl who enquired whether her father had brought any nigger boys for her to play with'.[72] The reporting of the comment indicated that the actual roles of colonial subject peoples, as well as that of the city clerk or working person, within the great physical culture movement, was typically more that of marketing pawn than active participant in a great movement. In fact, Sandow reportedly 'collected a native inhabitant from every country he visited'.[73] The 'nigger boy' or 'collected' primitive was thus not only a crucial symbol in the ideological articulation of the white man's burden, but also a veritable plaything in the endless selling strategies of fitness sellers. That some colonials on the empire's periphery and many persons within its core might have eked out a sense of self-autonomy was perhaps not a bad thing. That such personal satisfactions were actually possible was certainly a tertiary concern of physical education professionals, fitness businessmen and even social reformers. However, as a 'working man and trade unionist' wrote in response to an article on the weeding out of the unfit, the emphasis upon the precious resource of the body served to avoid a central issue within the commodification process: that of money.[74] As the correspondent wrote, the best definition of 'fitness for the present day battle of life' was not good genetic material alone but rather 'the possession of money' that might assist one in making the best of their physical endowment.[75]

Physical culture was part of a consumerist economy whose products and services were emphatically supra-class oriented and at times intent upon transcending even the boundaries of race. As with the rationale behind degeneracy, physical culture's implicit critique of the effeminizing effects of civilization and its rampant technological advances could, in fact, be turned back upon its white middle-class progenitors. In its focus on the controlled and, thus, honourable body universal, certain hegemonies were supported more than others, mainly that of a male-dominated protomilitaristic culture. However, if maleness and 'primitive' strength were the signs of effective power and dominance, other more palpable markers of white European superiority were in some sense obscured. As physical culturists often implied or argued directly, bodies were bodies, and the ways to strength and beauty were in many senses truly democratic. This created a problem of how to distinguish between bodies. Here, moral questions, and that much denigrated quality of civilization, came back into play. One answer to the problem was the strategy of transformatively tainting what were otherwise positive 'white' heroic physical traits whenever they were found elsewhere. A seemingly liberal racial view of colonial peoples could then compass the denigration of the physically robust and militarily indispensable Irish as both 'savage' and weak by virtue of a lack of self-control.[76] Or as Baden-Powell proved, fine bodily qualities could be separated from character and moral bearing whenever questions of racial superiority arose.

In day-to-day practice, the attempt to articulate the rhetorical frame of a worldwide physical culture movement was not all that easy. Indeed, the maintenance of the idea of empire itself was a project fraught with considerable difficulty. And yet, the imperial ethos remained all the more important in spite of the practical failings of physical culture as a sub-imperial movement. The earlier nineteenth-century struggle for rational recreation reflected a longstanding concern with the maintenance of categories of social differentiation of manners and morals which seemed to predate the new mode of capitalist production and democratic institutions. The possibility of a return to a pre-industrial past was encouraged by a resurgence of imperial rhetoric and its numerous examples of 'traditional' social organization which seemed to necessitate the cultivation of an old-fashioned paternalism. Martial and Meiji Japan was seen as a special exemplar of this. As Kenneth Ballhatchet and others have suggested, ideologies of the 'ruling race', based in martial strength, contributed to the renewal of gentlemanly ideals with new mass cultural appeal, as presumed aristocratic class attitudes were transformed in an imperial setting into racial ones supporting an expanded 'class' hierarchy of nations and cultures.[77] In this sense, the promise of personal autonomy offered by fitness proponents and sellers was given a crucial functional link: the role of the white male citizen, regardless of class position, as a defender of the realm, a person valued as a member of a larger metaphorical body, of an elite nation among nations.

It was the avowed goal of Sandow and his fellow physical culturists to make people happier and healthier. Such goals were never completely disconnected from more traditional models like the military. Following in the footsteps of social reformers, it was always expected that some more elevated purpose above and beyond mere money-making or the pursuit of personal pleasure was necessary to rationalize the selling of fitness. In this sense, militarized imperial objectives could be tailored to fit the ends of many social aims in addition to individual consumers' very personal desires.

It is my ambition to revitalize the youth of this generation and make them physically fit for the highest duties. I have been at work in London for some years to this end, preparing soldiers for the frontier and firemen for the crowded city, with schools for physical culture everywhere and an enrollment of twenty thousand pupils.[78]

Sandow worked at this project for nearly a decade as a magazine publisher and continued to promote the cause through his institute of physical culture afterwards. Its result in terms of profits for himself were not inconsiderable. Significant changes in general health and exercise habits, however, cannot be so easily assumed.

The overall effect of fears for the health of the nation and empire, fed in part by the horrendous Boer war recruitment statistics, included substantial policy changes such as the 1906 subsidization of school meals and the enactment of compulsory school medical inspections in 1908.[79] Sandow's own emphasis on exercise for children fitted in with the interests and concerns of many others during 1906–11, including Lord Rosebery and Winston Churchill. Churchill specifically linked education and proper diet to military recruitment in his analysis of the 'seeds of imperial ruin and national decay', while Rosebery grandly argued that 'Health of mind and body exalt a nation in the competition of the universe'.[80] The specific effect of physical culturists' efforts upon the greater male populace's health and habits is harder to gauge and cannot in any case be easily separated from the efforts of many other proponents of fitness in the period including eugenicists, moral purists and national efficiency proponents.

As part of a much larger expansion in a host of activities that can be loosely called leisured, exercise media like physical culture played a role for many in their individual attempts to quiet the disturbing emanations of the *fin de siècle* and the new century.[81] As indicated by a photograph published in *Health and Vim* of a newsagent's stand covered with fitness magazine promotions, physical culture periodicals had attained some measure of drawing power by 1909.[82] By that time, commercial health clubs and such were more common. New names in the business such as Thomas Inch (who started by sending in his photo to *Sandow's*) began to achieve prominence.[83] In 1911, Inch was listed along with Sandow and others as yet another fine embodiment of physical culture, as a poseur, author and teacher.[84] Older fitness sellers were still active, such as Atilla, who was busy with his 'Elysium of Exercise' at the Crystal Palace Health Institute.[85] Along with more traditional physical culture approaches, some different trends were apparent. For example, the publication of journals such as *Physical Perfection* and the *Journal of Scientific*

Physical Training more closely linked physical culture with new professionalizing health and fitness educators.[86]

Many such publications illustrated an increased interest in purity that surfaced in the years before the First World War.[87] Fears of unproductivity and the 'solitary Vice' were omnipresent throughout the century of the sculpture machine. 'Dullness of eye' and 'thickness of skin' were not the indicators of being worn down by responsibility and work but were instead the physical 'MARKS OF SIN'.[88] The objective of using exercise as an answer to the presumed problem of young men's sinful sexual practices was commonplace.[89] Although different from the 'Uranians' of the 1890s, groups of physical culturists continued to link body culture to the cultivation of chaste male friendship. In this period, *Health and Vim* started their 'association of honour', which was yet another participatory scheme with badges and other paraphernalia aimed at building circulation figures.[90] Later, a grand prize competition to boost membership in the association was offered. The first prize was a course from the international correspondence schools, and, perhaps more appealingly, the second and third prizes were a graph-o-phone with 12 records, and a rollifilm camera.[91]

Of course, young men were not the only ones subject to the evils of sin. Ladies' pages also alerted women to the dangers of idleness.[92] Typists and 'girls in service' were warned of the dangers of immoral reading, especially those writers who approached purity matters in the 'wrong way'.[93] Likewise, the ominous threat of the so-called white slave trade was mentioned frequently.[94] More generally, the reliance on classical models continued with articles such as F. A. Wright's 'Some Lessons from Greek Statuary' in which statues from antiquity were argued to be of special importance in producing feminine beauty and strength.[95]

At the same moment, as part of the growing debate over national health and efficiency, new preventive approachs to moral problems were put forth in opposition to earlier repressive criminalizing efforts such as the Contagious Diseases (CD) Acts.[96] In 1911, the National Council of Public Morals (NCPM) announced its support of positive prevention as an answer to the usual threats to empire and the nation's economy posed by other nations and falling birth rates.[97]

For over a decade physical culture publishers and advertisers successfully cultivated the public's interest not only in watching bodily competitions but also in the training and improving of their own bodies through 'rational movement'. By 1911, the author Arnold Bennett could rely on a sizeable readership of people who were presumably either consumers of physical culture or had some knowledge of the growth of body 'culture' during the prior decade. Bennett's own transatlantically published book, *Mental Efficiency*, trafficked in an 'appeal' derived from physical culture as a means of advocating an analogous methodical improvement of the mind.

> If there is any virtue in advertisements – and a journalist should be the last person to say there is not – the American nation is rapidly reaching a state of physical efficiency of which the world has probably not seen the like since Sparta. In all the American newspapers and . . . monthlies are innumerable illustrated announcements of 'physical-culture specialists', who guarantee to make all the organs of the body perform their duties with the mighty precision of a 60 h.p. motor-car that never breaks down.[98]

Bennett noted that such advertisements were multiplying in his own country as well, observing that 'Our muscles are growing also', although in a 'more modest British fashion'.[99] The author, in fact, admitted that he too once 'went in' for muscle building, contorting himself daily according to the fifteen diagrams exhibited in the physical culturists' *'magna charta'*, the wall chart.[100] Indeed, the mass craze or fad for improving the body, which began just before the second Boer war and the Spanish–American war, showed few signs of abating as the century entered its second decade. Conceding that the many advertisements for body culture were not cheap, Bennett expected that they must generate substantial profit, and whether they were a sign or a precipitant of a particular firm's wealth, they were intimately linked to demand which, for Bennett, meant that 'vast numbers of people must be worried about the non-efficiency of their bodies'.[101]

The unstated premise was that people may not have always felt so, and that they were being made newly conscious of their bodies' deplorable condition by physical culturists' articulation of a purpose for the products and services they supplied. The atavistic provenance and modern applicability of a still resilient physical culture was demonstrated at the time of the coronation of the King-Emperor George V. *Health and Vim* featured an item praising the monarch as the 'sailor king', a term that had been used to describe Victoria's uncle, William IV.[102] Using the symbol of royalty to demonstrate the

explicit patriotic zeal of commercial endeavours such as fitness publications was scarcely unusual, especially during a coronation or
jubilee. Periodicals of the day frequently used national figures to
sell products and enhance their circulation numbers, and no national
symbol was as effective as that of royalty. The commodification of
royalty that tentatively began with the Hanovers was a standard
practice by the early twentieth century, and, as living links with the
past, the appeal of royal figures in a modernizing culture might
even be enhanced through their association with more up-to-date
commercial ventures.

Moreover, given that much of Europe had already moved towards
a society characterized by the metaphors and practices of commodity
circulation and scientific calculation, it seemed suitable to modernize
monarchs by referencing them to a dynamic economy. The emerging
mass order – at least as reflected in a realm of public discourse that
recognized its rise – required that the hybrid corporate-ancestral
body represented by royalty should be couched in contemporary
terms.[103] In pursuit of this, *Health and Vim* related the monarch to a
society of calculation and circulation by conferring on George V
not only the sobriquet of the 'sailor monarch' but also that of the
'business king'. With both titles he was explicitly and personally
linked to the naval might and industrial and commercial interests
of the British empire. The two names welded together hinted at
systematic changes which had already occurred in the interaction
between leisure and commerce on an international scale. As exemplified in the fitness magazine's depiction of George V, a multifaceted
concern with both the individual and the national imperial body
was exhibited and exploited by the health and strength industry.

The new King-Emperor, like the former US President Theodore
Roosevelt, was frequently depicted as a vigorous and athletic exemplar of bodily cultivation.[104] The British throne could also be refash-
ioned as a 'bully pulpit', if more subtly so, with occupants like the
robust King George or his photogenically active heir the Prince of
Wales (later Edward VIII). The point that needs to be stressed here
is that British royalty and American statesmen were increasingly
being rendered as vigorous well beyond the bounds of the physical
culture press. The healthy dynamic body exhibited in energetic
service to nation and people was a pervasive emblem of the times.
And, in its commercialized form, it played a key role as a model for
the early-twentieth-century consumer-citizen.

On the eve of the First World War, the King-Emperor appointed Sandow as his official physical culture trainer.[105] A growing concern with strong bodies, and an underlying obsession with weak ones, thus coincided with the intersection of former traditional rituals and institutions like the crown and military with newer commercial forms and popular entertainments. The pervasiveness of its popularity as a social topic was also evidenced by the 1911 reference to the 'King as a Physical Culturist' and the latter's taking up a course of physical exercise so as to better 'withstand the great strain . . . during the coronation season'.[106] The editors asked whether the nation could 'possess a more representative head?'[107] Probably not. The king was heralded as both a symbol of commercial efficiency and as 'a great patron of manly games'. As such he was an important legitimizing image in the selling of gendered and class ideals within fitness, as well as being a symbolic linchpin in the greater fad for efficiency.[108]

As evidenced by the King's appointment, Sandow did not entirely disappear from the public spotlight after 1907. Doubtless, the xenophobia that accompanied the First World War influenced the German-born health culturist with his Kaiser-like moustaches and German accent to adopt a lower public profile between 1914 and 1918. As early as 1903, there had been some concern expressed in *Sandow's* that its publisher's foreign birth might be a problem. An item from another publication praising the contribution of 'aliens' like Sir Ernest Cassel, Baron Reuter and others was printed in October of that year.

> Germans are supposed to be the bitterest enemies of this country, but Britain owes big debts to many individual Germans – and to none, perhaps greater than to Sandow, who has instituted the revival of scientific physical culture.[109]

By the time of George V's coronation Durbar in India as King-Emperor, important changes had already occurred within the physical culture market. At that point, the term physical culture itself was beginning to be displaced by the catchword of 'efficiency' which, as Bennett's book demonstrated, could more easily encompass the commodification of both mind and body. The efficiency movement was different from physical culture with its accent upon a qualitatively enhanced industrial product or result. The objective of the former in Britain was the renewal of manufacturing and agricultural economies for 'Bismarckian rather than humanitarian reasons'.[110]

Physical culture's stock in trade, the more amorphously individual pursuit of 'thy self' spoke to rather more premodern notions of cultivating the personal and husbanding local resources. As such, its concerns were regarded as organic in nature, and, while many times scientifically sound, they had to be harmonized with a putatively immemorial moral order.

The examination of how physical culture's more organic and process-oriented prescriptions came to be eclipsed by the mechanical, end-results orientation of the efficiency movement exposes some of the obstacles as well as a few of the opportunities that confronted the former in the prewar years. Because physical culture assumed many guises as a media genre and cultural practice, its impact became diffused and diluted thus enabling other institutionalized forms of media and leisure, at once less general and less explicit, to overtake it. At the same time, it is important to recognize that the elusivity of physical culture was also its chief asset. It could be and was frequently used interchangeably with the terms fitness and recreation, or as a synonym for physical training or education. It was thereby capable of attaching itself to other ideals and practices that were attractive to the millions. However, its malleability made it a difficult property to control in terms of profit-making.

As 'National Efficiency' demonstrated, business entrepreneurs, military men bent on better national preparedness, empire-builders and numerous proponents of the political status quo all found the rationalization of the body and its control as a cultural sign to be an attractive proposition. As Bennett wryly observed, the possibilities for rationalizing the body according to some standard or ideal had a fundamental personal appeal for many middling or petit-bourgeois male consumers.

> We compare our arms to the arms of the gentleman illustrated in the ... advertisement, and we murmur to ourselves the classic phrase: 'This will never do'. And we set about developing the muscles of our arms until we can show them off (through a frock coat) to women at afternoon tea.[111]

Physical culture both reflected and capitalized upon the changing value and broadening scope of the image and spectacle in modern life, changes which helped to facilitate the development of a larger mass media and the early cinema. The use of the exemplary body as a focal point of comparison was a key to the physical culturists' successful marketing of their services and products before its eclipse by efficiency and the coming exigencies of the First World War. The movement responded to different requirements in varying social climates and resonated in divergent ways within different populations. Its magazines and ephemera, like all representation, were and are elusive historical artefacts that cannot be easily tethered to any particular nation-state, racial or ethnic grouping. Its magazines and postcards circulated widely and freely throughout the world. In this sense, physical culture was a peculiarly interactive international phenomenon. Thus, even an exemplary body such as Eugen Sandow's was also crucially that of yet another consumer-citizen of the world. More importantly, his was a physical form that might be enjoyed vicariously as well as imitated outside printing and photographic processes, by any 'body' regardless of race or class position if one was only willing and able to pay the price in money, time and discipline.

5

Slaughter Machines

Significantly, physical culture emerged during the era of the Spanish–American and Boer wars. Such colonial conflicts took place as concerns about manliness as a nationalized physical property grew ever more palpable and as methods of selling and marketing products and services became more sophisticated. By the turn of the century, however, Britain's citizens were perhaps more united as a nation of sporting spectators than they were by the dual ideologies of monarchy and empire. Despite rapidly changing naval and firepower technologies, massed ground forces remained the rule of the day, and discussions of the male population's fitness for outmoded forms of warfare continued apace. In 1899, following the English football final, *The Times* trumpeted the truism that sport was of inestimable value in the 'battles of life'.[1] As physical culturists illustrated, whether lazy or obstreperous, sickly or menacingly robust, it was widely thought that the bodies of workers and soldiers needed to be controlled, trained and rationalized. In this sense, the early First World War recruiting poster 'Rally Round the Flag – Every Fit Man Wanted' neatly built upon earlier fitness marketing in its synthesis of the nation with the healthy male citizen's body. In a similar vein, Prime Minister Herbert Asquith's comment on Field Marshal Kitchener, 'He is not a great man. He is a great poster', summed up a central message of the age of the sculpture machine.[2]

The generations that participated in both physical culture and the First World War were influenced by several events and social changes including fears of degeneracy and the effects of mounting international competition. It has been argued that the move towards the First World War was characterized by the persistent struggle of the landed aristocracy to maintain its place at the top of society. In key ways, the era encompassing the reign of Kaiser Wilhelm II and the spectacle of George V's imperial Durbar in New Dehli reveals an *ancien régime* 'fighting to prolong its life' and a rising 'industrial capitalism bent on imposing its primacy'.[3] The publicity-attuned Kaiser and the British 'business king' each demonstrated that the so-called atavistic elements of monarchy and aristocracy did not always oppose the modernizing ethos of capitalist consumerism.

In this sense, physical culture discourses complicate notions that the First World War took advantage of a natural or necessary desire to act out masculinity or vent supposedly more primitive forms of aggression in an over-industrialized society. Indeed, we can glimpse in physical culture the beginnings of consumer dynamics based upon pleasure rather than ideals of patriotic duty or military heroicism, processes that began to allow for the 'movement, colour, adventure and drama' presumed inherent in battle, to be partaken of in more domesticated ways.[4] In the years immediately preceding the war, the consumer was already being constructed as needing ever new experiences and products, as continually liable to the presumed boredom of commercial civilization. In this context, physical culture sought to stabilize and perpetuate itself in an emerging consumer culture that thrived on incessant change. But the war as yet another 'consumable' experience adding colour and verve to an otherwise dull existence, turned out to be much more like the drudgery of the factory than it was like a Boy Scout outing.

It has often been implied that an increasing emphasis on athleticism was unproblematically 'in the air' at the turn of the century, its climacteric being the First World War.[5] But neither the seepage of an atavistic and intensely masculine military or public school ethos into broader society nor the hypothesis of an aristocracy experiencing its last agonizing death throes suffices as an explanation on its own. Each eschews a more multivariant analysis of events which in each case seem to proceed inevitably towards war. In this regard, the primarily male arena of physical culture offers a prism not for establishing the causes of hostilities but for reassessing the reasons behind the early enthusiasm for the war, and how those on the lines and at home coped with its horrors after the first flush of glory had passed. In addition, the ways in which physical culture weathered the war years reveals much about the workings of the century of the sculpture machine. In this respect, health and fitness commerce and ideology also offers a more popularly accessible discourse on the nexus between the individual and the nation in the period.

As evidenced in physical culture and earlier fitness discourse, Britain's comparatively anti-military civil culture was nonetheless prone to connect athleticism with national defence. The same athleticism fundamental to public school life was eventually superimposed on the conduct of war by leaders such as Field Marshal Haig, who emphasized the playing-field spirit, 'pluck' and backbone rather than intellect, even at the staff officer level.[6] Such ideas were as useful in marshalling a common language of duty and respectability in rationalizing mass conscription and home front support as they were in the processes of healing over the experience of war. In this sense, however, the 'fourth Balkan War' is too easily constructed as a movement of mass forces: whole populations collectively sick of civilization's empty materialism, national 'bodies' that welcomed war as an antidote to boredom if not something grander and more purposeful.[7] The galvanizing of conscripts took more than the simple act of presenting a nation with the *fait accompli* of actual hostilities.[8] Whether 'civilization' was indeed collapsing or not, the machinery of international conflict founded upon growing reserves of armaments, colonial rivalries and heightening jingoism had long been in place. In this sense, the myth of any truly collective and sustained response to the war revolved more around hyperconscious visual and textual images: media depictions of partly staged crowd scenes; sometimes apocryphal descriptions of orgies of celebration greeting the outbreak of war; and the self-rationalizing memoirs of middle-class and elite individuals.[9] As more recent scholarship seems to indicate, the many fears and desires of Western Europeans in the last quarter of the nineteenth century cannot be so easily understood through the muddied retrospective gunsights of the war.

In Paul Fussell's *The Great War and Modern Memory*, he presents the image of a 'former athlete, both legs and one arm gone, [who] sits in his wheelchair in a convalescent park listening to the shouts of boys playing at sunset'.[10] Fussell's description of Wilfred Owen's poem 'Disabled' is particularly poignant with regard to the first generation of physical culturists and exercise faddists, many of whom eventually experienced the horrific life of the trenches in the First World War.[11]

> There was an artist silly for his face,
> for it was younger than his youth, last year,
> Now, he is old, his back will never brace;
> He's lost his colour very far from here,
> Poured it down shell-holes till the veins ran dry,
> And half his lifetime lapsed in the hot race,
> And leap of purple spurted from his thigh.[12]

The aestheticized and politically conscious 'body culture' of the prewar period – despite its military antecedents – stood in stark opposition to the experience of Owen and many others in the First World War. One of the many macabre paradoxes embedded in the crushing carnage of 1914–18 was that prewar physical culture was as much about building up a healthy and athletic soldier citizenry as it was about taking pleasure in the individual physique. In a comparison of Owen's poem to A. E. Housman's 'To An Athlete Dying Young', Fussell answers his query of why the young athlete enlisted with two words: 'Physical vanity'. The line from Owen read 'Someone had said he'd look a god in kilts'.[13] Doubtless for many men who rushed to join up in 1914, vanity played its part. As the example of physical culture demonstrated, such narcissism was part of crucial changes in modes of bodily self-definition characterizing the years before the war.

In comparing warfare in the past to the banality of the already technologically overdetermined battle of the late nineteenth century, there was always an implication that previous ages revealed the better side of military glory. The massacres of the Somme and Passchendaele were in some ways comparable to the ritualized and regulated contests of outdoor games. The war was most like actual mass sporting events in that much of it was spent waiting and watching. Soldiers were as much spectators as participants. Some in the trenches, in fact, never experienced battle; even those who did spent most of their time miserably waiting for the push that never quite became a breakthrough. Ultimately, the masses who went in enthusiastic droves to see athletes compete and marched off in similar fashion to war in 1914, found the latter to be a dull if not decidedly unchivalric affair; its battles were so horrific and unprecedented in scope that no scrimmage on or off the playing fields of Eton could have provided anything like an adequate preparation. Nonetheless before and during the war there was a frequent recourse to chivalric terminology.[14] For example, substantial chivalric vocabulary was employed in much of the poetry commemorating the First World War.[15] In their own pursuit of regaining the harmony of the lost pre-industrial world, physical culturists' textual discussions of improving the body also tended to emphasize a combination of atavistic and modernist imagery. In this sense, physical culture was an inheritor of a predominant Western martial ethos in its linking of functional activity – health or character improving – with a decorative or aesthetic ideal. The cult of the beautiful athlete merged the stability of biological necessity with bodily pleasures in the same way that the ancient Greek knight unified the 'beautiful and good'.[16]

The spread of an individualizing commercial body culture was similar to medieval chivalric discourse in its prescriptive character and its definitional elusivity: in its being 'tonal rather than precise in its implications'.[17] In the fashion of the chivalric 'self-help' books of the sixteenth century, for example Thomas Elyot's *The Gouernour* (1531), or Baldassare Castiglione's *The Courtier* (1528), the late-nineteenth-century interest in the upward training of bodies was likewise focused on the link between militarized bodily discipline and individual self-creation.[18]

Like the commodious shell of traditional chivalry, forms of consumer sport and leisure as appropriated within physical culture were thus ideologically flexible and inherently bound up with an ever-growing capitalist market culture. Physical culturists built upon the media-articulated desire to demonstrate manliness apart from work or the role of father. The latter roles were not so much diminished in importance, indeed physical prowess was often touted as a means to being better at them. But, in a print-driven society where virility suddenly seemed to matter more, physical culturists claimed to provide effective techniques and nostrums capable of curing not only the waning manliness of the person but the ills of a masculinized body politic as well.

For military theoretician J. F. C. Fuller, the socialization of the mass of young men presumably starved for community and a sense of purpose was best accomplished through the comradeship of military organization, which he saw as a mainstay of promoting a sense of national identification. The increasing popular awareness of the psychological ought not to be underestimated as a factor contributing to the success of the physical culture media or in responses to the war. In the works of individuals like Col. Fuller, a need was expressed for a moral sense which would mitigate baser instincts and sentiments when reason and intellect failed in battle. Echoing the sentiments of the physical culture press, Fuller opined that honour, duty, patriotism and self-control were all functions of a sublimation of the individual to the requirements of the group, a necessary social discipline upon which all armed force, the nation and the empire relied.[19] British politicians of the period, among them Arthur Balfour, also recognized the unifying power of comradeship that seemed to arise from playing and watching games.[20] It was frequently argued that a combined protomilitary and public school ethos could be spread beyond the barrack square and playing fields and into larger society. Indeed, in many ways it had spread through the increased numbers of Old Boys, the army's adoption of promotion by merit, the thriving genre of juvenile public school fiction, and the articulation of public school values in the political and literary discourse of the day.[21]

Stephen Graham's memoir, *A Private in the Guards*, emphasized the obedience springing out of the comradeship and hero-worship that were fundamental to physical culture's success before the war.[22] Older non-professional soldiers, like Irish MP William Redmond and Sir Maurice Baring, lauded a similar neo-chivalric heroicism in their writings about the war. In his *Trench Pictures from France*, Redmond sentimentally describes the grave of a French infantry-man, 'red poppies and blue cornflowers nestle around the little cross, and with every breath of wind nod and point to the words, "Dead on the Field of Honour!"'[23] Baring attended mass on the anniversary of Agincourt at the cathedral of St Omer and could not help but think of Henry V participating in the same ritual before going into battle in 1415.[24] Such a shared cultural experience made it more likely that many men would reach back to a romanticized heritage in confronting and interpreting their experience of war. Physical culturists responded to and helped shape this shared ethos of romanticized Anglo-Saxon heroism. The story of its success helps us to see how individual readings of shared culture provided resist-ance to the reduction of the body to 'a "political" force . . . maximized as a useful force' at the least cost.[25]

Alongside physical culture clubs and associations of honour, protomilitary cadet corps operating independently and in the pub-lic schools during this period provide further evidence of the iden-tification of masculinity with physical attributes best developed through pseudo-war activities.[26] In practice, of course, the presumed excitement and adventure associated with traditional warfare never quite panned out. More importantly, the realities of battle even when knighthood was in flower were arguably as brutal as those found in any form of organized and rule-bound killing as seen in the First World War, and were far worse in some cases than the relatively 'painless' imperial expeditions upon which its generals were weaned. In the end, even those who were comforted by the ethos of fair play or had been seduced by the 'foul literature of "glory"' were doubtless equally worn down by the lengthy and often inconclusive annihilation of modern warfare.[27]

By the beginning of the First World War, there were larger num-bers of single males, the prime focus of fitness sellers.[28] A great deal of the movement's steam came from its presumption that these customers needed help and could benefit from physical culturists' claims that they could make right what urban living had put wrong. In particular, they argued for the renewal and development of the empire as an answer to the prototypical male clerk's plight. Again, the success of physical culture demonstrated, in part, a desire for association and community that was unsatisfied in an increasingly secularized urban industrial society. As the war drew near, there were continued and frequent attempts to link physical culture with the success of institutionally successful groups like the YMCA, or more often the Boy Scouts through the creation of special boys' sections and the highlighting of Scout activities.[29]

Urban clerks were still presumed to be the press's staple readers, but in the wake of Scouting's success, boys became a new focus. A representative example, just before the war, was an issue of *Health and Vim* which included a typical photo of 'Bank Clerks as Gymnasts' from the London Central YMCA, in addition to one of the many attempts to connect Scouting to physical culture.[30] As in the final issues of *Sandow's*, *Health and Vim* continued the usual pleas for photos from readers in the final months before the First World War.[31] Generally, posing competitions remained popular schemes.[32] A larger physical culture community seemed to have come into existence, although it had to compete with a growing number of other sporting activities and leisure pursuits. In one ad for the *Health and Vim* 'Developer', a kind of double-wall pulley device, testimonials from presumably well-known figures appeared: they ranged from a black athlete, 'Kid' Harris, to gymnast Sergeant F. Mills, and P. C. Humphreys, captain of the London Police Force tug-of-war team. In marketing appeals at least, such disparate individuals fit comfortably enough within a prewar physical culture rubric.[33]

Overall, there was a sense of open free-market competition with numerous ads for items and services not associated with *Health and Vim* appearing in its pages. Besides an advertisement for J. Nicholson's British Health Institute,[34] there were ads for Edward Aston,[35] Professor Danks and Victor Spartan,[36] Lionel Strongfort and T. E. Black, and Thomas Standwell's Curative Physical Culture Institute, whose fee 'was within reach of every working man'.[37]

Just before the war in June 1914, an article praising Germany's support of the Olympic Games and gymnastics appeared in *Health and Vim*.[38] The piece highlighted the value of physical preparation in times of national emergency. By August of that summer, physical culture was itself argued as being 'a form of national service'.[39] By September, the dominant war cry, and accompanying platitudes echoed throughout the physical culture press. Germany's traditions of fitness and encouragement of physical preparedness were now couched in quite different terms. The war was not an attempt to 'annex territory, but to fight and kill the last shreds of military despotism in the civilized world'.[40] Whether Sandow indeed suffered at the hands of xenophobic prejudice, the commercial possibilities for making money from physical culture were clearly on the wane during the war. The expanding number of competitors and supply problems resulting from the war were important factors. In 1909 Sandow Ltd ventured into the corset business. His company also started selling a special Sandow cocoa in 1911. A new cocoa factory was begun in 1913. Bigger companies quickly cut their prices in response. After the war began, the company suffered from bad publicity because of its use of German cocoa waste. By 1916, the company had lost over £20 000, its failure principally attributed to the war and the 'non-supply of corsets ordered'.[41]

In a world where making corsets, cocoa and war production were inextricably linked, there were those few who recognized that as daily economic and social life had changed, so had the character of battle. Some were even so perspicacious as to note that perhaps it had never been so glorious as some made it out to be. In this sense, abstractions like dying for 'King and Country' or a belief in the 'cult of the offensive' are less helpful than those referenced to the maintenance of individual respectability. As one anonymous veteran later wrote, 'There wasn't one in a hundred of us who, if he could have crawled home with a shred of honour, wouldn't have taken the opportunity'.[42]

The fitness press joined in this sort of discourse with vigour, always alert to ways of using it to appeal to more customers. As sales declined during the war, physical culture publications freely employed guilt as a selling point. With the arrival of the war the dreams of the physical culturist came true in part: the nation was put on a war footing and the necessity for the fit and 'capable man' became seemingly obvious. The war put physical training at the forefront and injected an actual element of heroic risk into the practice of body culture. Many fitness sellers and not a few publications played upon the self-hatred of those failing to pass the exam on the first try with offers of physical culture tuition that would make them fit for war. After the war Sandow sold his 'success' in helping

1. A 'representative' body from mid-century popular culture. 'Portrait of Mr. Van Amburgh as He Appeared with his Animals at the London Theatres', by Landseer, 1847.

2. Hippolyte Triat, French strength performer and reformist, antecedent of later physical culturists. Undated.

3. Publicity-conscious Lord Wolseley, the 'very model of a modern major-general' and one of the founders of Gladstone's NPRS. Undated cigarette-card.

4. (*left*) Oscar Wilde by Sarony, 1882.

5. (*right*) Eugen Sandow, *c.* 1889.

6. Eugen Sandow taken in Italy, *c.* 1887.

7.   Anthropometric exhibit, World's Columbian Exposition, 1893. Peabody
     Museum, Harvard University.

8.   'The Ladies Idolize Sandow' *Police*
     Gazette, 1894.

9.   Physical culture reader, Mr. B. C.
     Gazdar, *Sandow's*, 1899.

JOHN McNEIL HUNTER (Glasgow), 71
Silver Medal.

G. JONES (Denbigh), 26
Silver Medal.

E. LAMB (Staffordshire), 122
Silver Medal.

J. M. ROBERTS (Leicester), 86
Silver Medal.

DOUGLAS SHEPHERD (Forfar), 49
Silver Medal.

HARRY CALOW (Lincoln), 8
Silver Medal.

G. RILEY (Bedford), 10
Silver Medal.

A. B. ALLAN (Renfrew), 119
Silver Medal.

H. WESTER (Hants), 3?
Silver Medal.

H. S. HOYLE (Yorkshire), 14
Silver Medal.

G. HAYES (Worcester), 142
Silver Medal.

F. C. T. WORTH (Gloucester), 54
Silver Medal.

E. J. HORNE (Derby), 28
Silver Medal.

J. W. TALL (Warwick), 134
Silver Medal.

R. E. GOLD (Glamorgan), 51
Silver Medal.

ALFRED E. FRANCIS (Antrim), 4
Silver Medal.

W. J. MORGAN (Monmouth), 103
Silver Medal.

G. A. HICKLING (Nottingham), 114
Silver Medal.

11. Sandow and Judges review contestants at Royal Albert Hall, *Sandow's*, 1901.

12. Anthropometric chart showing Eugen Sandow as a masculine standard and the Venus de Milo as the feminine ideal, *Sandow's*, 1901.

SANDOW'S ANTHROPOMETRICAL CHART,

Giving the Ideal Measurements of the Human Body according to Age, Height, and Weight.

AVERAGE MEASUREMENTS OF MR. SANDOW'S PUPILS AFTER THREE MONTHS' TRAINING.

13. 'Gurkha Hill Scout', *Sandow's*, 1902.

to taking cold. Sometimes they cover their bodies over with clay. In all kinds of weather they go about barefooted and bareheaded—in fact, the whole body bare. They are not very fond of bathing, but, being unclothed and exposed to the air at all times makes bathing less necessary for them than for civilised folk.

Whenever one of these natives

that their health begins noticeably to fail. It seems that these children of Nature cannot well bear the ways of civilisation.

Their principal food is corn. When it is young and tender they eat the green corn. After it is a little older they cook it, simply putting it in an iron pot with a little

14. A 'Zulu Tribesman', *Sandow's*, 1907.

15. 'Four Native soldiers', *Sandow's*, 1907.

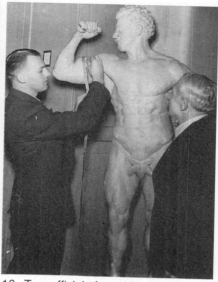

16. Two officials from *Health & Strength* magazine measure the Sandow Cast in the British Museum *c.* 1930s.

17. The remains of a First World War British soldier, Chemin des Dames, France.

18. The Sandow Cast today alongside miscellaneous bones from the Royal College of Surgeons.

men pass their First World War enlistment exams in *The Power of Evidence*.[43]

Health and Vim readers who were less than healthy were hectored: 'Every Unfit Man wanted to join health and vim army'.[44] Assertions that the 'Nation with the quickest and greatest recuperative energy . . . will win' employed the usual body equals nation analogy.[45] One editor displayed the typical physical culture 'concern' for the rejected: 'Some of my readers are possibly disappointed recruits, young men who with a little training might easily become efficient and so pass the army test, and thus help to swell the tide of swift victory.'[46]

Emblazoned on the back cover of that same issue was 'Have you joined the Health and Vim Army . . . special war offer of 10/6 cash'. It was parenthetically followed by the hopeful reminder, '(while war lasts)'.[47] The war was also used as a way to advertise the International Correspondence School. One advertisement referred to its importance in the great 'War on German Trade', asserting 'We cannot all be soldiers but we must be men.'[48] Common ads for varicose vein treatments now used war as a hook. Since the condition was a bar to service, a cure was promised from which enlistment would presumably follow.[49] As a morale-builder, such appeals may have had some positive effect. All in all, they evidenced a shameless promotionalism masked as patriotic participation.

Throughout the war, military covers were used routinely and the press became more interested in issues of exercise directly related to martial health and efficiency and consequently were much less interested in sports.[50] By August 1918, *Health and Vim* had become *Health and Efficiency*, and its price had been raised from two to three pence.[51] As the war came to a close, business as usual continued.[52] Advertisers sent out the cry: 'Wanted – Unfit Men',[53] and physical culturists Danks and Inch were appointed physical education instructors for the army.[54] *Health and Vim*'s October 1918 cover showed a physical culture man in uniform with equipment and a gym behind him. The caption read 'Here I am!'[55]

A more positive result of the war was that purity campaigns were derailed. The presence of regulated military brothels tacitly acknowledged the wiser course in preventing venereal disease among the troops. Purity efforts at home began to be criticized for even broaching the subject of sexuality. Two years into the war, there was a brief notice in *Health and Vim*, 'Objections have been raised to the manner in which we have endeavoured to promote

our purity campaign. We have decided to withdraw all books dealing with this subject.'[56] In the next month's issue it was explained
that legal restrictions on the discussion of purity had been the cause
for the withdrawal.[57] In 1917, the social purist and eugenicist the
Revd James Marchant argued for a renewed link between religion
and science in the pursuit of all 'moral reforms for the regeneration
of mankind'.[58] Within the often 'amoral' pragmatism of running the
war, however, the currency and usefulness of purity appeals lessened. The practical need for healthy troops and presence of palpable foreign enemies seem to have had more traction with the public
than the purists' war against premarital sex and masturbation.

The desire to escape the 'sordid' commercialized world, of which
physical culture was a part, continued during the war, with its
publications continuing to be infused with images of healthful sport
and cleanliness. Lieutenant Henry P. Mainwaring Jones, killed 31
July 1917, in a letter to his brother four days earlier depicted war as
clean by comparison to life back home: 'ordinary life runs on a commercial and selfish basis; if you want to "get on" . . . you can't
keep your hands clean'; he ended by referring to the feeling before
a big battle, 'The only thing that compares to it are the few minutes
before the start of a big school match. Well, cheer-oh!'[59] The day-to-
day experience of actual war was not so easily disconnected from
more abrasive modern imagery. As one soldier described the echoes
of battle as 'a sound like a motor-cycle race – thousands of motor-
cycles tearing round and round a track with cut outs . . . it is really
a pair of machine guns firing'.[60] Images of machine-made blood
and mud were as directly contradictory to prewar physical culture
rhetoric as they were to Rupert Brooke's prewar anticipation of
young men 'into cleanness leaping'. Brooke, a public school Old
Boy, found the camaraderie of preparation for mobilization exhilar-
ating. Likewise, in the letters of F. H. Keeling we get a glimpse of
the enthusiasm for the 'fine life' of preparation for war, which he
describes as the 'greatest game and finest school for men in the
world'.[61] As Captain Theodore P. C. Wilson wrote to his aunt in
April 1916 with reference to Brooke's 'cleanness':

> War is about the most unclean thing on earth. There are certain
> big clean virtues about it – comradeship and the whittling away
> of non-essentials . . . but it's calculated death, the deliberate tearing
> of fine young bodies – if you've once seen a bright-eyed fellow
> suddenly turned to a goggling idiot, with his own brains trick-

ling down into his eyes ... as I've done, you're either a peace-maker or a degenerate.[62]

Similarly in Owen's 'Anthem for Doomed Youth', the image of young soldiers as 'those who die like cattle' created 'an imaginative join between industrial meat processing and human killing'.[63]

Many like Charles Carrington recognized the futility of the war, but saw no other course for 'a plain, honest man' but to join up.[64] Though disenchanted by the war, Carrington epitomized the individual who equated prowess in war with a heroicized concept of masculinity. Castigating those who 'squeal' when faced with hardship, he emphasized the value of risk and comradeship. Quoting Lawrence, Carrington described the uniform's capacity for making a crowd appear solid, giving the slackness of the masses 'the singleness and tautness of an upstanding man'.[65] In such responses we see the coming endpoint of physical culture's exaltation of the body. The years 1914–18 betrayed the overarching importance of the one body, and the need to blur hundreds of thousands of possible physical culture patrons into the normal and the average needed in war. For many, the sculpture machine would thereafter be eclipsed by their experience of the war's slaughter machine. In the process, the twin generations of physical culture and the First World War were connected to a more appropriate postwar bodily exemplar: that which lay beneath the monuments that commemorated unknown soldiers.

In the First World War there are no stories similar to the one of Sandow's picture left on the battlefield in the Boer war. Instead, we have images like that found in reminiscences of a Canadian clergyman, F. G. Scott, who upon seeing the dead body of a young man covered in yellow mud, thought of a bronze statue, the youth's 'beautiful face, with finely shaped head covered with close, curling hair ... looked more like some work of art than a human being'.[66] A similar story of dead bodies covered by the masonry dust of a bombed-out house, posed 'like a terra-cotta group', was described by Lance-Corporal Harold Chapin, an American citizen killed in France in 1915 at the age of 29.[67] Tellingly, actual photographs of dead bodies, whether statuesque or not, were not published during the war.

Forcing the harshness of war into the framework of classicism was matched by a recourse to mechanical and other worldly metaphors that articulated the democratic inclusiveness of death. Describing the effects of the severe shortage of water at Gallipoli, Joseph Murray wrote of those on the front line as 'savage ghosts' living in a world where 'Rich or poor, the chances of survival are equal. . . . Those that are alive at this moment are not fully conscious of the fact. They are mechanical ghosts; all the fighting men are ghosts – officers and men alike.'[68] Although at the beginning of the war Vera Brittain found it difficult to conceive of so many 'poor disfigured bodies heaped together', her own loss of her brother and future husband was followed by her experience as a nurse at the front. There she confronted the actual horror of 'gruesome human remnants heaped on the floor', the laboured breathing of 'poor things burnt and blistered' by mustard gas and the 'wax doll' faces of the dead.[69]

The incomprehensible losses of the war were underscored by the painstaking efforts made to find, identify and bury individual bodies. This rejection of traditional collective graves and the 'Victorian aesthetic of death' created two different strategies of remembrance: that of the generic body of the 'unknown soldier' and the commemoration of names that acknowledged the democracy of mortality.[70] Ultimately, the representational fragmentation of bodies in physical culture was horribly replicated in life as countless 'clean' young men were blown to bits; their bodies become ghosts of remembrance. If not sent home with missing limbs like Owen's former athlete in the poem 'Disabled', the survivors were often at the very least severely traumatized by the numbing routine of modern war's brutality, if not shell-shocked. For some of the disabled who survived, the artificial reformation of the body became a mechanical reality with the design of prosthetic limbs that could be directly connected to industrial machinery.[71]

In the end, the well-sculpted physique of the physical culture patron was of little use in combating the power of the artillery shell. In the case of Rupert Brooke, physical beauty and a self-styled higher sense of duty counted for nothing in the face of an infection that knew neither glory nor moral purpose. And yet, all these same qualities were ironically made more precious in the face of the death and destruction. In John Dos Passos' postwar novel *Three Soldiers* (1921), there is an exchange between two enlisted men swimming naked after undergoing a tough inspection. They are interrupted by a 'YMCA man' who points out the close proximity of two French women, and suggests that they show some modesty. One soldier asserts that they might as well look, since there may not be 'many people who get a chance'. The YMCA man fails to understand the soldier's point. The latter responds, 'Have you ever seen what a little splinter of a shell does to a feller's body?'[72]

Along with the public school graduates, the Uranian poets and other writers, and painters like Henry Scott Tuke, Frederick Walker and William Scott, physical culture publishers and sellers of fitness products provided a textual and visual ground which helped men to initially frame the war as heroic and, in turn, cope with its unheroic realities.[73] Ultimately, they also may have helped many of its survivors and the mourners of its dead heal their emotional wounds if not obliterate the facts of its grim experience. In this sense, physical culture was as important a part of the world that fomented and experienced the First World War as the boys' books of G. A. Henty or 'male-romances' of Rider Haggard.[74] Like the neo-chivalric model that could then encompass the very differing public and perhaps similar personal desires of a Kains-Jackson and a Lord Esher, or a Baden-Powell, physical culture offered and, at the same time, masked other kinds of consumer enjoyment besides those explicitly tied to disciplining the body as a national resource. In this regard, the war was not simply a victory of the heroic over the erotic, nor of the machinery of war triumphing over the physical culture body.[75]

The First World War was the site of a whole range of pleasurable male relationships some of which might have otherwise been proscribed. Physical culture, in advance of the war, similarly provided a space in which the pose of heroic action or national duty did not necessarily preclude pleasures of personal vanity, male friendship or even those based in sexual enjoyment.[76] The tenderness of Wilfred Owen's poetic descriptions of his fallen and injured comrades illustrated the sharp antagonism between the intensity of fellow feeling created by the war and its unutterable hideousness. The connection of the war experience to the articulation of new communities of desire was illustrated by a shortlived increase in interest in sexuality that followed 1918 – for example, A. E. Housman's pamphlet 'The Relation of Fellow-Feeling to Sex', written in the charged sexual atmosphere of the 1920s.[77]

The power of nostalgia for lost youth and the preciousness of aestheticized bodily perfection found in response to the First World War was presaged in Baden-Powell's poignant reference to the commonness of death in the Matabele campaign. In a blunt and yet touching comment, he foreshadowed the style of many memoirs of the First World War. He had been speaking to a trooper. Later the same day, he recognized the young man, his body slung across a horse's back with some of his 'brains bulging from his short-cropped hair'.[78] This was perhaps the most painful reality of military life for Baden-Powell as well as many others in the war who felt most at home in its male-only environment – the confrontation of the actual death of youth, the heroic-innocence of life unlived.[79]

Linkages between watching or participating in recreative activities and the evocation of the romanticized past within the rhetoric of national defence were commonplace not only in the discourse of the *fin-de-siècle* period but well beyond 1918.[80] In the outcome of the First World War, what were presumed to be dominant or elite values, and indeed typical masculine martial ones, came into conflict with a vast technological system of industrialized warfare. Here the noble ideals of character and bodybuilding were of less importance than the more practical affective qualities of any male group.

The British elite's martial ethos generally opposed the so-called 'entrepreneurial qualities' of creative imagination and openness to innovation characteristic of businesses that included physical culture.[81] The attitudes which made a man suitable for participating in parliamentary politics or civil administration at home or overseas, in which loyalty, group deference, cautious leadership and other unwritten codes of behaviour were of paramount importance, made him perfectly unsuitable for preparing for or directing the first modern war. For millions of Victorian men, whatever the variables were in their struggles to reconcile public ideology to their own desires, the First World War marked the stop point of their carefully negotiated strategies of masculinity.

The homosocial basis of physical culture, along with that of the military and the public school, allowed for a continuation of an adolescent athleticism that relied on the opposing image and reality of a 'home' or family life that was constructed as feminine.[82] George Mosse has described the First World War as an 'invitation to manliness', an opportunity to regain a sense of masculine identity that was based not only upon the 'honourable' sacrifices of war but also upon social relationships exclusive of women.[83] As Baden-Powell's, Field Marshal Haig's, Lord Kitchener's and T. E. Lawrence's misogyny testifies, the exclusive maleness of the military, as in the empire, was an incentive for more than a few. Indeed, as Sandra Gilbert has also argued, the desire for male comradeship was often augmented by a fierce rejection of femininity. But the feminized antithesis of 'home' was intimately part of the ideology of the playing field and ethos of the gymnasium. The experience of the gym and physical culture 'home course' were perhaps no more or less helpful than a public school education in confronting the war. The more important end result was that the social background of most officers – which remained largely homogenous up until 1939 and continued to include a classical public school education – did not enable them to bring the war to a close without unparalleled destruction.[84]

At the end of the First World War there was a need to distinguish physical culture from its old bedfellow military training. The wrestler Bernard Bernard argued against the linkage with military training as war robbed physical culture of 'its noblest mission, i.e., to honour, beautify, and prolong healthy human life'.[85] Bernard addressed the sober echoes of wartime 'efficiency' that continued to dominate physical culture rhetoric and – in a larger sense – the forms of military comradeship, among public school Old Boys or working-class mates, that persisted beyond the Armistice. Such comradeship, however, proved evanescent, and efforts to link physical culture with military preparedness dwindled in a postwar climate unconducive to scaremongering.

In November 1919, the pictorial cover of *Health and Vim* returned, and the focus on sports, especially wrestling, was revived.[86] Remaining physical culture periodicals adopted larger formats and became far more interested in selling copies than preaching a particular gospel of health and strength. In June 1920, *Health and Vim* changed its name to the *National Magazine of Health, Physical Culture and Sociology* and the cost per issue rose to six pence. In September 1919, Sandow returned to publishing with a title that referenced the destruction of the war, *Life as Movement: The Physical Reconstruction and Regeneration of the People*.[87] Indeed, the bodily legacy of physical culture's numerous interests, the experience of war and the face of the future were perhaps best represented over a decade later by the publication of Dr Jacques W. Maliniak's *Sculpture in the Living: Rebuilding the Face and Form by Plastic Surgery*.[88] Maliniak did not argue for a particular physical ideal, stating that 'there is no universal standard of physical perfection'.[89] But the title and the flyleaf illustration of his book were revealing. The illustration did not depict the 'shattered countenance' of a soldier made whole nor the 'legitimate reconstructive' transformation of the 'new woman'.[90] Instead, it was a photo-reproduction of a statue from the Museum of Naples, the Venus of Capua, a statue that the young Sandow may well have been familiar with from his first visit to Italy.[91]

The physical culture search for statuesque bodily harmony was made possible by the mundane desire for profits and the grandiloquent discourses incited by the rivalries between nations. In its development, we can seen some of what Veblen called the displacement of a pre-industrial body by that of a machined figure, a body like Sandow's that could be admired, imitated and industrially reproduced.[92] These were the uniformed masses, the countless individual sculpture machines that played their role as industrial inputs and as mass-produced heroes. A decade later, even the new technologies of the surgeon who might reshape the body devastated by war continued to be romanticized as a kind of aesthetic physical culture, the pursuit of the 'Perfect harmony of form and proportion' that was the primary aspiration of the age of the sculpture machine.

6

Conclusion

Eugen Sandow, Oscar Wilde and many of their Victorian contemporaries admired the strong and the beautiful body. Prized as they were, beauty and strength had to be considered in the context of ideologies of race, gender, sexual behaviour and class. In the 'play' of the music hall, enactments of gender were predicated on the idea of the heroic and pointedly de-eroticized warrior male versus the eroticized and controlled woman. But such distinctions were almost always superficial. Even the surface of apparent simplicity seen in nineteenth-century bourgeois male dress was no less complicated than that indulged in by women, and no more or less restrictive and enjoyable. Men were also the focus of rational dress rhetoric, since they too often wore confining garments like corsets in order to conform to an ideal figure.[1] But, no matter what women or men did, where they did it and how it was interpreted by a male-dominated culture were of tremendous significance.

In physical culture and in Wilde's aesthetic philosophy, flesh and intellect were joined in a realm of the sublime that both relied upon and questioned Victorian bodily hierarchies and categorizations. In his reference to history as the 'great machine of life', Wilde acknowledged the growth of a practically indifferent market culture, one without a precise ideological, gendered or moral trajectory, which could just as well transpose our present-day sins into virtues over time as it could make them into the reverse.

As the cultic master of a seductive new biophilosophy, Sandow was the 'charismatic warrior hero'.[2] In the realm of the market there were ample opportunities for the similarly 'self-ordained' to work their magic upon nascent buying populations. In opposition to modern complexity and bureaucratic domination, he and other physical culturists employed scientific and rational appeals, while adopting anti-rational heroic stances. In their pursuit of 'booty and, above all gold', fitness entrepreneurs always implicitly rejected notions of rational economic conduct.[3] Indeed, it was this inherent contradiction between the obvious pecuniary interests of fitness sellers and their mystical and anti-economic mission which accounts

117

for much of their success. Never deriving his recognition as a 'master' from any manner of election, the physical culture hero relied upon the constant demonstration of personal strength. As a prophet of fitness, Sandow had to perform the 'heroic deeds' appropriate to or expected by his constituency. In turn, his followers had to be seen to 'fare well' in their surrender to his domination.[4]

Physical culture was emblematic of the age of the sculpture machine because it was a complex commercial medium that welded together elements of nationalist and imperial ideology, aesthetic-dandyism, gothic and classical models, Social Darwinism and nineteenth-century racism, and many other elements in a cohesive format that sold products and magazines.

The overriding aspiration of health and strength proponents was to contain competing leisure interests within a single moral and political ethos and sell products at the same time. In its reaction against the crowded urban industrial environment with its insalubrious environment, the fitness media were influenced by late Victorian reformism's predominant assumption that work and beneficial exercise might be brought into greater alignment. In a growing age of image and symbol, the heavy burden of maintaining such a cross-class and even internationally mediating ethos proved to be too much. It was highly conceptual, not quite a potent and recognizable cultural sign that required little or no explanation, such as 'health' or 'fitness' has practically become today. As a result it required constant redefinition and aggressive marketing. At the same time it was a self-starting commercial enterprise always tainted by its associations with more vulgar entertainments like the circus and lesser sports such as wrestling and weightlifting.[5]

The old-style fitness media adopted a framework of opinion formation and exchange whose parameters were set by a middle-class ethos that sought to orchestrate a single national voice. In addition, physical culture's appeal to all classes and, implicitly, to a range of differing sexual, gendered and racial or ethnic subject positions, was founded upon a more elastic definition or representation of the normative body. In this the universal language of the body's pose was marginally more important than the (middle) class-specific language of the advertisement text or of the magazine's correspondence columns.

Defining the normative body in the face of so many unique bodily experiences and for so many different identity groups was a process that was both easier and more problematic than the reproduction of the single middle-class voice. The 'building' of a normative neo-classical body in relation to the correlates of health and fitness could be gestured towards in ways that might practically obscure racial difference, or deny and even erase sexuality and gender at the specific point of its appeal to the individual within the mass. At the same time, in reverse fashion, physical culturists might seek to reinforce difference at those identical points of appeal if they thought it would augment sales. In this regard, the privileging of the individual body and its optimality, pleasure or satisfaction offered a space in which physical culture's collective national aims might be contravened in the pursuit of actual personal satisfaction and enjoyment, or anti-discipline if you will.

In the main, photographs of actual bodies and reproductions of contemporary and traditional sculpture and painting were used as a means of articulating the body as a stable transhistorical entity. The body was useful in this respect but its seeming solidity was also chimerical. In one sense, physical culture's principal commodity was the very physique of the consumer. In another way, its product was always and forever present in the form of an endless supply of other people's bodies to be looked at and imitated, and of course, both desirable and obtainable in the form of purchasable images. Victorian panopticism's avowed purpose was to amplify power and its exercise within the seamless functioning of a new social whole. Ancestry was to be replaced by normalcy, and ascribed status by new measurable criteria.[6] The army, prison and asylum were its original models. In the 1880s Bentham's presumptions about the centralization of surveillance and reform were complicated by the emerging mass press and the soon to follow golden age of the periodical publication and twentieth-century consumerism. Within these developments, the masses' supervision of their own surveillance and their ability to challenge the regime of the panopticon were expanded within the imbalanced give and take of a consumer oriented mass society.

Popular body phenomena as seen in the music hall and physical culture were creatures, in part, of a highly politicized range of nineteenth-century bodily discourses on social degeneracy and national preparedness. Different kinds of bodily displays helped shape twentieth-century public perceptions and policy debates concerning body-related issues such as the spread of venereal disease, conscription and compulsory physical education for children. Whether it was on the parade ground, in the music hall, in the physical culture magazine or even in front of the consumer's bed-room mirror, displaying the body had numerous political implica-tions in a bodily obsessed society. In this regard, 'real' political activity was never simply relegated to the workplace or union hall.

Throughout its heyday, physical culture remained a vague and often contradictory health regimen that was never as programmatic and organized as either Scouting or the YMCA. Its fundamental objective was oriented towards its sellers rather than its buyers; it allowed anybody and everybody who might adopt a professorial or athletic pose to sell services and training methods as well as a multitude of related products. Depending on the often unpredict-able desires of its readers and buyers, it thus remained a necessarily protean concept, its precise meaning functionally obscured within the vagaries of the commercial market.

In the age of the sculpture machine, biological sex, race and indi-vidual desires intersected in an intricate fabric of social definitions and hierarchies focused on the body. More obvious in their effects were those methods and systems that sought to define and con-trol the body. Other less obvious and complicating factors included the desire to make a profit or simply enjoy one's own body. In the case of physical culture readers, individual experiences and desires were key factors in prompting the consumption of body products and images. Like the double-edged discourse on degeneracy, which stressed simultaneously the fears of growing working-class power and mass society's accelerating decay, discussions of indecency and sexual and gender identity created further fear and uncertainty.

Physical culture media were thus illustrative of an overall crisis in the definition of gender ideals and attempts to control and con-cretize sexual practices in relation to pictorially centred ideas of self-identity. Because of all these processes' relevance to the intim-ate lives of individuals and their ideas of duty to their gender, race and nation, physical culture media were also a noteworthy part of a social landscape that helped determine responses to the catastrophe of the First World War. Within physical culture, tradi-tional heroic models of masculinity were asserted within the com-plex arena of a new media form. In the process they were transformed by the very commercial purposes to which they were tied, and as well by the personal requirements of their readers. Thus, by their very attention to issues of self-identity and gender, such maga-zines underscored the presumption that such systems and structures needed to be constantly reinscribed within people's lives. On the one hand, the media asserted what were presumed to be 'natural' visually apparent categories; on the other, they were very much in the business of alerting their readers to how tenuous and protean those same categories could be.

Physical culture's broad range of publications, instructional schemes and exercise products existed in the context of other contemporary movements that were reactionary or nostalgic (for example, the Olympic movement and early fascism). They were also part of the age of High Imperialism. The physical body's commodification as an object of social reform was significantly linked to the depiction of the globe as an understandable totality. In this period, both Europe and the United States turned to the seas and entered a new age of imperialism that was enabled by new technologies of transport, communication and warfare. Indeed, if the world could be conquered and understood, why not the body? More elaborate international communication linkages allowed nations to be defined and compared as if they were physical bodies. And, just as bodily analogies were used to describe geographic units and national phenomena, these were in turn used to describe the experiences of individual bodies. In a sense, bodily metaphors helped make the unification of the globe possible at an ideological and conceptual level if not always so in actual practice.

The presence of new figures of bodily power like Triat, Atilla, Macfadden and Sandow, along with the new means of representation within popular and commercial culture, offer an additional framework for examining the flexible nature of what Joseph Schumpeter called the 'steel frame' of the *ancien régime* as it adapted to the 'new direction of governing power'.[7] In its approach to its varied readers, physical culture demonstrated the complex responses of the age to the desire to fix social differences from above and to employ them from below as a means of self-empowerment. Its periodicals helped to 'solidify' new markets, though, ironically, the hooks first employed in creating new consumers for magazines and fitness products harkened back to ideas and images that were in many cases never a part of the experience of the majority of their buyers.

In physical fitness commerce the body was focused upon as a design space wherein the principles of surveillance, discipline and efficiency might be employed by anyone who could afford a postcard or magazine.[8] In the process, elite values and traditional depictions of the ideal male body were applied and in some cases transformed. As the example of the British monarchy attested, even the signs of the eagle and the sun, or rather, the unlikely imperial personage of the 'widow of Windsor', could be profitably commodified.[9] The spectacle of the music hall strongman was thus even more easily packaged and sold.[10] In this, the advent of successful fitness media and its associated industries corresponded to a shift from an earlier 'macro-politics of monarchy and Empire' to a postwar 'micro-politics of the body and gender' that persists today.[11]

Beginning as medium-sized journals, physical culture periodicals were largely tabloid in form with more illustrations and increasingly provocative covers by the start of the First World War. They continued to be characterized by their use of images that emphasized the physical form as evidence of mental clarity and moral purity. Unique to the age, such media expressed aspects of four trends: a growing popular awareness of scientific methods and therapeutic ideas; a seemingly more liberal attitude towards discussing and revealing the body; an increasing concern over national efficiency; and the changing configuration of work and leisure. Trends like these would continue to shape society over the following decades, but neither physical culture nor any of its competing bodily discourses was destined to become the unifying commercial or political ideology their various creators had hoped for. In their British context, moral purity and national efficiency would each fade, along with old-style physical culture, in the interwar period.

In the context of our own ever-changing medical and imaging technologies, physical culture has become quaint, its visual remnants yet another anchor for mass cultural nostalgia. Within our own mechanisms of picturing and understanding the body, the penchant for the better body remains. Although its ideal figures seem ever more technologically determined, they continue in many ways to mimic the same heroic postures of antiquity. In this regard, the metaphor of the sculpture machine remains an apt one today as countless new versions of the heroic in art and advertising are manufactured as a means of glossing over the ruptures and complexities of the impending *fin de millénaire*.

Language and the visualization of the past are intimately connected to our current understanding of bodies. History and the body have become more significant within the 'hyper-reality' of new communication technologies, along with the ever-expanding accumulation of pictorial and other cultural representations. The first generations of physical culture patrons were only just becoming familiar with the defining visual technologies of our age: photography and the cinema. They had never seen a twentieth-century superhero comic book or a Charles Atlas advertisement. Indeed, before the articulation of a fitness media most individuals lacked both the forum and perhaps even the visual and ideological language for 'policing' their own bodies or comparing themselves to their peers in any rigorous or standardized fashion.

The nineteenth-century practice of forging parallels between a long-lost heroic past and a quasi-menacing present began in some sense with the Renaissance retrieval of Greek and Roman architectural and sculptural forms. Looking at physical culture within this historical frame helps to make it understandable as part of a continuing reconstruction of spatial and societal order. Comparing Sandow to the Farnese Hercules did not erase the differences separating physical culture images from the represented body in Antiquity and the High Renaissance. The ideal physical culture body had a new relation to the mass of individuals that such images had never possessed before. As a societal standard of 'truth and conduct', the appearance of bodily force retained a place as a metaphoric property within a more cohesive worldview based upon technology and the machine process. The circulation of the image of a genuine body achieved through effort, rather than one whose status was ascribed at birth or referenced symbolically to that of a distant ancestor, was thus part of a process in which the photograph was ever more seen by society as a validation of truth and reality. Here physical culture offered a new possibility, the chance to 'produce' your own body through the myriad technologies and discourses of the sculpture machine. In such a self-production, external discipline and individual empowerment were intertwined.

The architectural redesign of bodies in the media and in the gymnasium helped to create the citizen as an agent of bodily change: both as a viewer of other body-specimens and as a self-oriented consumer. In this sense, physical culture bridged a gap between an era in which the photographically based mass press was relatively new and one in which society quickly became saturated by both photographic and cinematic images that feigned experience and produced a contradictory and active-passive form of consumer participation. Photographs and images were crucial to the fitness media, but for the most part their use within an old-style physical culture that was more ideologically specific proved no match for the increasingly garish tabloid press, the expanding cinema and live spectatorship.

For a time, however, physical culturists adeptly captured and combined in one genre varying readers' topical interests, from the nobility of sport and political bombast to cheap thrills and cure-alls in various forms. But their success was shortlived, partly because the 'everyman' or 'everywoman' to whom the first physical culturists wanted to appeal never existed in quite the way they thought. Middle-class trappings of the gothic or elements of classicism and political posturing probably satisfied the vanity of the magazine's editors and publishers more than their readers. And much of this was easily jettisoned when simpler formats proved successful during and after the First World War. None the less, the amateur gentleman posture donned by the successful 'strength performer' or entrepreneur was a remarkably effective one to the beginnings of the First World War.

Sports figures from football and wrestling, from the cinema and its satellite publications, quickly took centre stage in the late 1910s and 1920s, creating different and more diverse models of self-actualization.[12] Many other fitness sellers and poseurs followed in the footsteps of Sandow and Macfadden, including the Englishman Thomas Inch, who was 'discovered' by Sandow; George Hackenschmidt, a Russian émigré promoted by Hopton Hadley who was the founder of *Health and Strength*; and the American Angelo Siciliano, later Charles Atlas, who found his first fame as a winner of a Macfadden competition in 1921.[13] Bernarr Macfadden's first major success came then with his publication of the archetypal confession magazine *True Story*. That the character of the international field had changed was also apparent from the postwar shift in editorial emphasis of the German magazine *Sport im Bild*. By the time Erich Maria Remarque was working for the publication in the 1920s, it had adopted the slick mien of high society and abandoned its more sports-oriented prewar approach.[14] In Britain as well, the exigencies of war and the changed consumer market that followed in its wake demanded that the ubiquitous moustached image of Sandow, the civilian harbinger of a new physical culture order, be replaced by new images, initially by that of the imperial Field Marshal, Lord Kitchener, and subsequently by the more overtly sensual and erotic representation of film idol Rudolph Valentino.[15]

The immediate postwar period was one of unprecedented flux for physical culture. After 1918, a new structure for comparing bodies by way of the cinema and a wider range of magazines was firmly in place. The appeals of body culture were challenged in novel ways by other consumerist-oriented media. Its audience shrank as men became markedly outnumbered by women consumers (physical culture was unable to adapt itself to this demographic change).[16] Attempts to stem further losses rarely went further than changing names. Thus, in the 1930s, the company that had published *Health and Vim* (Health and Vim Publishing Co.) became known as Health Promotions. In a similar fashion, the objectives of many fitness sellers became less grandiose. But the earlier predominant ideology and atavistic ethos that their commercial practices had once matched so well were by no means gone.

In Italy, Macfadden's great admirer, Mussolini, spoke in 1932 of the young men of the First World War that had gone 'joyfully' to their deaths and argued for the necessity of motherhood for women, heroic action for men, and military preparedness for all.[17] In the mean time, the body in Britain began to be concealed again; by the 1920s, the locus of an aestheticized body culture had returned to its earlier home in Germany. There were significant changes in sexual norms throughout North America and Europe, but bodily modesty and repression were perhaps even more characteristic of the interwar period in Britain and the US.[18] For the next quarter of a century, the tight control of the mail and the press exemplified in the First World War would be used to push against attempts to match or outdo the pictorial traditions established by the first physical culture magazines. In response, pseudo-art magazines began in Britain and the US and persisted for the next two decades. The age of Charles Atlas and Joe Bonomo that arrived with the 1920s saw the separate pictorial and health philosophy strands of the old physical culture diverge almost completely. By the 1950s physical culture existed in name only as an evocative rationale and instructional decoration for male physique magazines consciously catering to professional bodybuilders and a readership of men who simply liked to look at other men.[19]

In *Road to Wigan Pier* (1937), George Orwell criticized several assumptions concerning progress, including the bleak, though no less utopian, Wellsian idea of a future race of robust 'godlike men'.[20] Reminding his readers of the common wisdom, and perhaps his own belief that all progress is somehow a swindle, Orwell notes that the very material conditions which produce such figures we might recognize as 'godlike' would certainly be the unlikely results of a cybernetic society ruled by a machine ethic of efficiency.[21] Orwell demonstrates his own orientation in the thinking that created the nineteenth-century sculpture machine. But he also helps us locate Wells by asserting that 'In the last analysis the champion of progress is also the champion of anachronisms'.[22] In his own argument for an Orwellian 'plainspeak' of common sense, there are similar contradictions that deserve addressing. Within Orwell's text and the works of Wells he criticizes (specifically *Men Like Gods* and *The Dream*) there floats a common though unreified image of the body. It is, of course, a masculine figure, specifically a worker, alternatively freed from labour or malevolently alienated from the 'good' of production. It is a body, like most subjects of political economy in the broad sense, 'built' up from personal impression and gestured towards by means of sweeping generalization.

In *Wigan Pier*, this implied body is tightly contained conceptually on the one hand by material conditions in opposition to disaster, pain and difficulty. On the other hand, it is a will-o'-the-wisp figure of embodiment lacking actual historical or practical specificity. Orwell is right, in pointing to the desire to square a circular idea of forward progress feeding back on a purer past. But his assumption of a single or monolithic ethic of the machine tending towards optimal efficiency obscures the possibility of human agency interacting with, making, relying upon and even resisting mechanization and its material effects.[23] He presumes that in a future Utopia men would 'do dumbbell exercises to harden muscles which they would never be obliged to use'.[24] But by the 1930s men, and even some women, had been doing exactly that for over half a century, and it was for a complexity of reasons other than the arrival of Utopia.

In their heyday, physical culture publications demonstrated a different phenomenon from that found earlier in Germany, a desire to make the body respectable rather than simply freeing it from constraint.[25] The later health worship movement played its part in sharpening the tools for attracting and perpetuating a mass consumerist culture and in turn its audience was enticed to move on. That they had moved on was evidenced by the passing of Eugen Sandow from fame's spotlight in the postwar era. During his career, Sandow maintained the social clout of a professional gentleman without substantially sacrificing his appeal to workers and other non-elite members of society. More accurately, he transcended class and other distinctions by aiming at the 'body universal'. Despite his 1911 appointment as His Majesty's Professor of Scientific Physical Culture, the German-born 'lion of London's' image was noticeably absent from newspapers and advertisements during the First World War. Ironically, he had given generously to both the territorial army and Lord Esher's 1909 appeal.

After the war Sandow officially retired and lived with his wife in a cottage outside London. In the summer of 1925, his old impresario Ziegfeld came to visit him there. It had been over thirty years since their American tour. As legend would have it, the great Sandow suffered a stroke a few months later, after driving his car into a ditch during a rainstorm. Unaided, the 'modern Hercules' attempted to lift the car up out of the mud. He died shortly thereafter in October 1925 at the age of 55. Not unlike 'Sir Dan' Donnelly, it is perhaps more probable that he suffered an aortic aneurism as a result of tertiary syphillis.[26] What remains of 'the most perfect body in the world' now lies in Putney Vale cemetery. There is no monument. The exemplary plaster cast of Ernst Sandov Müller taken from life remains in the possession of the Natural History Museum at Kensington. The image of the erstwhile father of physical culture is kept deep in the bomb shelter that serves as extra storage space for the museum. Infrequently displayed, the partially dismantled armless cast of the most perfect human specimen rests in a cupboard among several burlap bags of unmarked bones from the old Royal College of Surgeons. The greater trend he helped to begin and the sculpture machine's focus on making and possessing an ideal bodily-self to live in persists in our own search for representative and timeless bodies.

The tenuous sense of progress we feel today in terms of faster transportation, better hygiene and increased political rights does not certify an absolute march forward in terms of bodily liberation. In fact, the appearance of new disease strains and continuing debates about race and civil rights indicate quite the reverse. As the record of war and genocide in this century attests, the attenuated advances made in our understanding of body politics and the appreciation of their importance should alert us to what can be and sometimes has been lost. More importantly, it might also help us transform some of the gratitude we feel for the bodily health and pleasures we enjoy in the present into a respect for what others endured in the past.

Documents, objects and images of whatever provenance can be given more or less plausible meanings, but the boundaries of interpretation are never necessarily limited by the fences of logic nor are they sharply delineated by the borderlands of the absurd. The seeming solidity of the world and our need for at least the pretence of sense always send us back to some lode-star of stability. The body figures prominently in our search for the real and the stable. But even the palpable physical reality of self-existence and the mass of bodies that surrounds us defy easy definition and simple speculation. Language and thought are perhaps more imprecise than the body is malleable. But we are as trapped within language and thought as we are within our bodies. Even the exemplary life of health is a process of increasing loss of control and bodily failure. But this does not mean that we cannot increase our knowledge of the body in both its ideological and experiential forms.

In the preceding study of the sculpture machine and physical culture I have attempted to draw together several important currents. In investigating how self-improvement information and practices from athletics to simple exercise became quasi-religious substitutes, physical culture provides an alternative point of view, variously giving primacy to changes in material production, the awareness and experience of the body and larger contextual events relating to the desire to socially control it. As the following quotation from a marketing letter for a recent health and strength magazine indicates, the importance of information as a fetish in the successful triumph of the modern individual is no less consequential today: 'it's not the good who die young – it's the uninformed'.[27] Further on in the same letter it is asserted that men have 'come to realize that taking care of the physical machine is not only for wimps, women and doctors'.[28] A similar, albeit crude, approach was neatly summed up at the turn of the century in the physical culture marketing dictum, 'weakness is crime, don't be a criminal'.[29]

As the more recent letter illustrates, health promotions continue to play upon the fear of the loss of self, of the possibility that gender roles might become confused or abandoned altogether. In foregrounding the healthy idealized heterosexual body's seductive potential the importance of a gendered and historicized ideal of pure existence is underscored. Such a heroic ideal is a figure that retains its power; a power that is unproblematic (and masculine), a physique that is erect and never flaccid, a physical form that promises to miraculously escape time and even death. The central and most inescapable fact of life is that it does not last.

And yet, at the heart of this book is the idea that individual agency is important and that our ideas about bodies can alter what might seem to be the natural and concrete limits of physical experience.

As the reach of our own biotechnical grasp and the frontiers of commercial desire seem to ever advance, we reflect upon who we are with the aid of inexpensive images that record our ongoing physical changes from the moment of birth, and even before with sonogram technology. Indeed, Watt's dream of an actual sculpture machine seems newly possible as recent designers have begun to perfect a process called stereolithography that fabricates sculptural models directly from computer-aided designs.[30] The more important issue, however, is not the existence or possible development of such mechanisms but our continuing aspiration towards making life and bodies timeless in a variety of ways: through science and technology, as part of the ideological life-cycle of the historical nation, and in the endless pursuit of physical pleasure and sensation. What we want for and from our physical selves contributes to the way we define and shape our lives. Indeed, our own era continues to be defined by its body technologies, politics and therapeutics. In this sense we need to continue to investigate how we build our own bodies and identities as well as the global consumer culture that relies on them.

Notes

1. For an analysis of machine metaphors and the impact of technology in imperial settings see Michael P. Adas, *Machines as the Measure of Man* (Ithaca, NY, 1990). See also Anson Rabinbach, *The Human Motor* (New York, 1990).
2. *Les Jeux Olympiques, 776 av. J.C.–1896* (Paris, 1896) 108.
3. *Ideal Health and How to Obtain It by Physical Culture*, by 'M.D.' (London, 1909) 1.
4. The problems with studying the body in the context of private life in this period have already been cogently laid out by Michelle Perrot (ed.), *A History of Private Life: From the Fires of Revolution to the Great War* (Cambridge, MA, 1990) 1–5. Even most sociologists, who are typically less tradition bound than historians, would admit that there is as yet no sociology of the body, only a diffuse and cautious effort to begin collecting bodily related data. As Anthony Synnott argues in *The Body Social: Symbolism, Self and Society* (New York, 1993), psychologists and philosophers as well as historians have tended to ignore the body. Groundbreaking work by historians of gender and sexuality such as Judith Walkowitz, Peter Brown and Thomas Laqueur are notable exceptions in this regard.
5. See David Landes, *Prometheus Unbound: Technological Change and Industrial Development in Western Europe from 1750 to the Present* (Cambridge, 1969) 357.
6. Ibid.
7. Like the geographical nation, biological categories such as gender often implicitly finesse questions about their specificity and substance. These are taken for granted as the visible which denotes the underlying truth of differences.
8. Despite Britain's position as the centre of English language health and fitness publishing, the US has received greater attention in terms of the refashioning of Victorian manliness into a more consumer-oriented gender ideology. This is due in part to an understandable tendency to view the US as a dominant political and cultural force. Accordingly its successes are related to a gendered paradigm associating all power with maleness. As a working category, masculinity begins to escape our analytical grasp once it becomes overly 'nationalized', or too much identified with a specific state/cultural hegemony. On American exceptionality, see Myra Jehlen, *American Incarnation: The Individual, the Nation, and the Continent* (Cambridge, 1987).
9. Other significant events in 1829 included the founding of the centralized London Metropolitan Police by Sir Robert Peel. Moving bodies about became easier too. Franz Ressel invented the screw propeller

for steamships in 1829. Besides the opening of the first Liverpool–Manchester railway, 26 steam cars were operating in London by 1830. In anticipation of later mass health crazes, American clergyman Sylvester W. Graham linked fat, meat and white bread to poor health and the stimulation of carnal appetites in 1829. In the same year, his fellow Massachusettsan, physician Jacob Bigelow, coined the word 'technology'.

10. For an explanation of the graphic revolution and another view of this era that includes the present, see Daniel Boorstin, *The Image: A Guide to Pseudo-Events in America* (New York: Vintage, 1992).

11. Synnott, 262–3.

12. For more on this concept and a somewhat dated but interesting take on sociopathology and technocracy see Lewis Yablonsky, *Robopaths: People as Machines* (Baltimore, MD, 1972). See also Shoshana Zuboff, *In the Age of the Smart Machine: The Future of Work and Power* (New York, 1988).

INTRODUCTION

1. From a letter concerning Watt's new invention for copying sculpture, 11 May 1811. See also the 'Machine for Copying Sculpture' (1811) in H. W. Dickinson, *The Garret Workshop of James Watt* (London, 1929), and reference to a 'sculpture-machine' in Samuel Smiles, *Lives of Boulton and Watt* (London, 1865), as quoted in Humphrey Jennings, *Pandemonium: The Coming of the Machine as Seen by Contemporary Observers, 1660–1886* (London, 1985) 130 and 303–5.

2. See Mollie Sands, *The Eighteenth-Century Pleasure Gardens of Marylebone, 1737–1777* (London: Society for Theatre Research, 1987) 15. Novelty acts or simple displays like that of a 'giant and a dwarf' could be seen at Marylebone as well. Ibid., 65.

3. The German-born Zoffany's combination of neo-classical poses with contemporary subject matter was seen in his portrayal of William Hunter giving an anatomy lesson at the Royal Academy (*c.* 1772) and in the classically modelled *Death of Captain Cook* (*c.* 1789–97). Benjamin West, the first American painter to study in Italy, shocked London's Royal Academy with his similar neo-classical depiction, *Death of Wolfe* (1770). The shock was not a response to the fact that West had used classical postures and gestures but that he had painted Wolfe, a commoner, and that the figures were depicted in contemporary dress.

4. Apart from *The Gladiator*, his other works included such images of eighteenth-century science as *Experiment with an Air Pump* (1768) and *The Orrery* (1766).

5. See the discussion of the simile of the sculptor in Havelock Ellis, *The Dance of Life* (London, 1929) 264–8.

6. See Veronica Kelley and Dorothera E. Von Mucke, *Body and Text in the Eighteenth Century* (Stanford, CA, 1994).

7. Johann Huizinga, *Homo Ludens*.

8. At the end of the eighteenth century the personal caricature was in its infancy as a media tool and images of public figures seldom looked like the people they were meant to depict. See Kenneth O. Morgan (ed.), *The Oxford Illustrated History of Britain* (Oxford, 1984) 367–9.

9. Harold Perkin, *The Origins of Modern English Society, 1780–1880* (London, 1969) 96. Watt to Robert Milne, engineer of the New River Water company in the 1790s, Boulton and Watt Papers.

10. Apart from the concern with prettifying his own body, George IV showed a Rabelaisian interest in bodily matters of size as well. He was said to have measured a Mrs Vaneck's behind with a handkerchief and showed the measurement to 'most of the company', from G. W. E. Russell, *Collections and Recollections* (1898). In a quote from a contemporary 'unpublished diary' he was also said to have relished telling a story about the very large penis of one of his brother's, from *A Persian at the Court of King George 1809–1810*, trans. and ed. Margaret Clarke (1988). He was not so happy when others alluded to his own growing girth, as in the apocryphal story of Brummell referring to him as another's 'fat friend' or when the poet Leigh Hunt was jailed for two years for calling the recently appointed Prince Regent 'a fat Adonis at fifty'. All anecdotes from Elizabeth Longford (ed.), *The Oxford Royal Book of Anecdotes* (Oxford, 1991).

11. See Perrot, *A History of Private Life*, 47–50, 87–9. Middle-class criticism of upper-class 'indolence, their corruption, their immorality was at its height in the 1820s and 1830s; it subsided as the aristocracy and gentry became more attached to domestic values'. Ibid., 89.

12. The fighter's arm is now on display at a pub in County Kildare. In his 1887 tour, John L. Sullivan made a point of visiting the site in Kildare where Donnelly beat Cooper. See Patrick Myler, *Dan Donnelly, his Life and Legends* (London, 1976); Allen Abel, 'Dan Donnelly', *Sports Illustrated*, 82 (7) (1995): 164–73; and Michael Isenberg, *John L. Sullivan and his America* (Urbana, IL, 1988) 245.

13. Prizefighting can be viewed as the most immediate non-military cross-class antecedent of late-nineteenth-century male body culture. Needless to say, the various roles of fighters, touts, trainers, patrons and gamblers continued to be allotted by virtue of one's economic class. It is important to note that it was largely a spectator phenomena rather than a participatory one. Elliott J. Gorn, *The Manly Art* (Cornell, NY, 1986) 30.

14. Carlyle was none the less a great one for employing the metaphor of the hand-to-hand fight, see Walter E. Houghton, *The Victorian Frame of Mind, 1830–1870* (New Haven, CT, 1957) 206.

15. Bruce Haley, *The Healthy Body and Victorian Culture* (Cambridge, MA, 1978) 3–4.

16. Suffering through years of blindness and debilitating prophyria, the King's illness required Parliament's official enactment of a regency (1811–20).

17. J. P. M. Pannell, *Man the Builder: An Illustrated History of Engineering* (New York, 1964) 100–1. Alongside Huskisson, the trains carried over 700 other dignitaries including the Duke of Wellington.

18. Huskisson was a former MP and recent President of the Board of Trade. From the *Mechanics Magazine*, 25 September 1830, as quoted in Jennings, *Pandemonium*, 177–8. Apparently, Huskisson had been crossing the tracks in order to take the extended hand of the Duke. Other guests such as Prince Esterhazy were only narrowly pulled to safety at the last second. Ibid., 178.
19. From Fanny Kemble, *The Records of a Girlhood* (1878). Ibid., 179.
20. Ibid.
21. Ibid.
22. Richard Aldington, *Four English Portraits, 1801–1851* (London, 1948) 50.
23. Roger Boutet de Monvel, *Beau Brummell and his Times* (London, 1908) 196.
24. Longford, *Anecdotes*. Journal of Mrs Arbuthnot, II. During the King's lying-in-state on 6 July 1830.
25. His work on 'clothes' is found in *Sartor Resartus*, which was begun in 1829. The chapter entitled the 'Dandiacal Body' has been described as serving as 'the Victorian epitaph for Regency Dandyism'. It was published in book form in the US in 1836 and in England in 1838. See Ellen Moers, *The Dandy, from Brummell to Beerbohm* (Nebraska, 1960) 178.
26. Balzac was perhaps the first writer to take clothes seriously as a modern sociological study, as noted in Anne Hollander, *Seeing through Clothes* (New York, 1980) 433.
27. *Frankenstein*, 12. Like Goethe's *Faust*, Shelley's work confronted the double-edged problem of the inventor's desire to step beyond the confines of conventional wisdom and moral rules. Ibid., 11.
28. The forced labour of the slave trade provided much of the impetus for the capitalization of industry, from the seed money for Barclay's Bank to the financing of Watt's steam engine. See Walter Rodney, *How Europe Underdeveloped Africa* (Washington, DC, 1985) 85. See also Eric Williams, *Capitalism and Slavery* (Chapel Hill, NC, 1944).
29. On the regimentation of soldiers bodies see Robert L. O'Connell, *Of Arms and Men: A History of War, Weapons and Aggression* (Oxford, 1989) 154; and with regard to workers see Marx and Dickens.

1   BRIDGING REFORM AND CONSUMERISM

1. C. M. Smart, Jr, *Muscular Churches: Ecclesiastical Architecture of the High Victorian Period* (Fayetteville, AR, and London, 1989) 4, 15. Even the light and airy Crystal Palace attested to the strength of industry.
2. 8 October 1851; from the *Journal of Gideon Mantell*, ed. E. Cecil Curwen (London, 1940).
3. Ibid.
4. There were prominent exceptions, such as Marianne as a national symbol in France. See Susan Rubin Suleiman (ed.), *The Female Body in Western Culture: Contemporary Perspectives* (Cambridge, MA, 1985).

5. In critiquing trends frequently associated with his father, Matthew Arnold argued that relying on the unexamined English idea of freedom or even the religiously inspired ideal of the muscular Christian was to demonstrate an uncultivated and 'unfruitful' reliance on the mechanistic; to put faith in population, railways, coal and wealth and a 'mere belief in machinery'. Arnold, *Culture and Anarchy*, 11, 21.

6. In such a reformed-Byronic social vision (as shared by Thomas Hughes, Charles Kingsley and others) the emphasis fell more upon the need for a manly heroic temperament rather than it did upon the value of a pointedly individual healthy body. Despite the general spiritual emphasis of the early Victorians, Carlyle was no less prone in his *Past and Present* to use the metaphor of sickness and disease as a way of explaining periods of history as 'stages of growth and decay'. Even still, 'a healthy "body" cannot insure spiritual vitality' in a person or a culture, Haley, *The Healthy Body*, 62. In contrast to Matthew Arnold's summation of the Age of Pericles as the right combination of 'bodily strength and mental energy', the 'Age of Augustus could be viewed as a body without a head'. Ibid. 61. Alongside, the creation of a new 'somatic model' of the body in the public's awareness, Haley argues that there was a cognizant desire for a psychic model and a 'common knowledge [that] the mind is not simply *like* the body'. Ibid., 63.

7. Haley, 4. Citing the enormous growth in numbers of professional doctors (over 8000 entered the profession between 1801 and 1850, more 'than in all of previous history'), population, and numbers of hospitals, Haley argues that Victorians were becoming more aware of their bodies. In the mid-1820s a wave of serious epidemics began (smallpox and typhus were followed by influenza, cholera, scarlet fever and typhoid in the following two decades). Ibid., 6. The results of the epidemics, poor trade and higher prices provided shocking statistics that were used effectively by sanitary reformers in passing better hygiene laws. Ibid., 6.

8. In Bentham's day, social crises were already typically dealt with in terms of what Carlyle derisively called the 'Genius of Mechanism' upon whose 'iron back' all social burdens could seemingly be borne with ease. Bentham's ideal example of post-Enlightenment surveillance was the prison. But he had bigger fish to fry. Beyond the confines of the panopticized prison he looked towards a larger social network that would spread and amplify technology and ideas in the salvation of a damaged and threatened society. An existing dialectical view of the body as both *a* danger and *in* danger was implicit. Jeremy Bentham, *Works* (London, 1843).

9. Thomas Carlyle, 'Signs of the Times', *Scottish and Other Miscellanies*, ed. Ernest Rhys (London, 1946) 228, originally printed in *The Edinburgh Review* (1829), n. 98.

10. Dickens' use of bodily decay metaphors to describe the urban monolith are well known and can be seen not only in the so-called industrial novels such as *Hard Times* (1854) and *Little Dorrit* (1857) but also in *Bleak House* (1853) and later *Our Mutual Friend* (1866). See Berman

on Marx, *All That's Solid Melts into Air* (1988). Much earlier examples of the use of bodily disease and contagion metaphors in the works of English authors can be found in Shakespeare and Milton, Shelley and William Cobbett, as in the latter's evocative description of London as a 'Great Wen' that absorbed all the surrounding fluid of economic and social life.

11. Jackson, 3–4.
12. Haley, 12.
13. George Lewes, *Physiology of Common Life*, 2 vols (New York, 1860, 1864 [vol. 2]) 378; Lewes argued that the laws of life were crucial, and men lived in ignorance of them to their peril, bringing down upon themselves 'years of suffering, decline of powers [and] premature decay', as paraphrased in Haley, 3.
14. See Thomas Laqueur, 'Bodies, Details, and the Humanitarian Narrative', in Lynn Hunt (ed.), *The New Cultural History* (Berkeley, CA, 1989) 176–204.
15. Ibid., 204.
16. Houghton, Chapter 9, 'The Worship of Force', 198–209. In such a view, the engine of history was very important. Within the period, Charles Kingsley's Christian socialist novel *Yeast* with its young hero Lancelot and his *Westward Ho* (London, 1855), Thomas Carlyle's *Sartor Resartus* (London, 1831), and *Past and Present* (London, 1843), and the life and works of Thomas Hughes are all examples of such a strategic use of recently invented notions of the past. Carlyle saw both natural society's and the city's failings in terms of hybrid spiritual and bodily analogies. Like Carlyle and his similarly afflicted wife, Darwin, George Eliot, Tennyson, Herbert Spencer, Meredith and Ruskin were all examples of a sort of Victorian intellectual 'valetudinarianism', Haley, 13. Like many others during the middle of the century they tried numerous doctors and were able to choose from an ever expanding realm of patent medicines in pursuit of better health. See Mark Girouard's *The Return to Camelot: Chivalry and the English Gentleman* (New Haven, CT: Yale University Press, 1981); for a general examination of history as both romance and ideology, see Hobsbawm and Ranger.
17. The idea of better hygiene through more frequent bathing and the popularity of the spa grew after the middle of the century.
18. Arnold, *The Scholar Gypsy*, 203.
19. See *Locksley Hall Sixty Years After* (London, 1886).
20. Eliot (Mary Anne Evans) was married to George Lewes for many years, and she shared many interests with Herbert Spencer, who introduced her to both Lewes and her second husband.
21. William Henry Hudson, *An Outline of English Literature* (London: G. Bell & Sons, 1923) 305.
22. See Thomas Richards, *The Commodity Culture of Victorian Britain: Advertising and Spectacle, 1851–1914* (Stanford, CA, 1990).
23. For more on the history of religiosity and bodily pursuits see John M. Carter, *Medieval Games: Sports and Recreation in Feudal Society* (New York, 1992) and Dennis Brailsford, *Sport and Society: Elizabeth to Anne*

(London, 1969) particularly 76–87, 126–57 and 160–70. See also Peter Brown's study of religious attitudes to the body in late antiquity, *The Body and Society* (New York, 1988) and Catherine Gallagher and Thomas Laqueur (eds), *The Making of the Modern Body: Sexuality and Society in the Nineteenth Century* (Berkeley, CA, 1987).

24. This was also in line with the practical approach to sanitation in this period which was focused upon larger environmental issues rather than individuals. History was 'at bottom the History of the Great Men who have worked here'; see Carlyle, *On Heroes and Hero Worship* (London, 1841) 1–2. Carlyle divided the heroic into six categories: hero as divinity, as prophet, as poet, as priest, as man of letters, and as king. At least half of his treatise on the heroic was thus devoted by design to issues of the heroic as a spiritual manifestation.

25. Mort, *Dangerous Sexualities*, 163–4.

26. Dudley Sargent in the US, for example, was rare in his interest in replicating the motions of work in exercise.

27. Before Adolphe Quetelet's first major publication in 1836, the bodies of Western European non-military adults were never routinely examined. See John F. Bovard and Frederick W. Cozens, *Tests and Measurements in Physical Education, 1861–1925* (undated).

28. The connection between *demos*, status-wealth and warmaking can be seen in antiquity in the example of the Greek hoplite who fought by virtue of his free status and ability to afford the cost of arms. The same can be said of the medieval knight. The linking of exercising or training the body with that of the political and martial role of the citizen was also found in the democratic militarism of the French revolutionary government as proclaimed in Robespierre's declaration that the perfection of the physique was an essential object of education. H. De Genst, *Histoire de l'éducation physique*, vols I and II (Brussels: Maison d'édition A. De Boeck, 1947–9) vol. II, 291.

29. House of Commons (HC), British Sessional Papers (BSP), 1867, 1878 and 1901.

30. Foucault, *Discipline*, 135.

31. For example, the motion studies of Muyerbridge and Étienne Jules Marey (in 1882) were complimented by an extensive series of formal nudes done by an anonymous photographer for the French army in the 1890s. They were 'meant to study the physique of *le fantassin* – the foot soldier. In ordered postures . . . kneeling, walking, marching . . . . Here the function . . . was not to please, but to instruct', from Ben Maddow, *Nude in a Social Landscape*, in Constance Sullivan (ed.), *Nude Photographs, 1850–1980* (New York, 1980) 190. There were also related photographic collections as used by the police (the mugshot) or full nudes as part of the entering health record of American college freshmen.

32. His first work on Gymnastics (1811) was translated and distributed throughout the Western world in the nineteenth century and was often identified with the cause of freedom. For example, in the US, F. L. Jahn, *Treatise on Gymnasticks* (Northampton, MA: Simon Butler, 1828), in which the example of gymnastics in the German nation was

described as a 'powerful engine of political freedom', Jahn, iii. This interest in the German model can also be seen in the work of Dio Lewis in the US, in translations of Kloss's dumbbell instruction and Schreber's *Pangymnastikon*, included in Lewis, *The New Gymnastics* (Boston, MA: Ticknor & Fields, 1862). Lewis himself studied gymnastics in Germany and Sweden in 1856, and helped form what *Harper's Weekly* called in 1860 the 'Athletic Revival' then taking place in the US. A medical doctor and owner of the Essex Street Gym in Boston, Lewis was an important proponent of fitness in the US. This 'revival' was roughly a counterpart to the New Athleticism in Britain. Lewis was a predecessor of later physical culturists in his publication efforts. He published two short-lived journals, *Lewis' New Gymnastics and Boston Journal of Physical Culture* (1861) and *Lewis' Gymnastic Monthly and Journal of Physical Culture* (1862). He was especially significant by virtue of his inclusion of young children, women and older persons in his exercise system. American attempts to popularize exercise like those begun in Britain in the 1830s also failed; they did not reappear and become more successful until the 1860s. For a discussion of Lewis and this period in the US, see Harvey Green, *Fit for America: Health, Fitness, Sport and American Society* (New York, 1986) 181–215.

33. Modris Eksteins, *Rites of Spring: The Great War and the Birth of the Modern Age* (New York, 1990) 84.

34. For the most comprehensive overview of conventional physical education and gymnastics (apart from those such as Triat and Sandow, who are not mentioned in these works) see Genst; other useful general works on individuals important in the promotion of physical activity before the middle of the nineteenth century include Fred E. Leonard, *Pioneers of Modern Physical Training* (London, 1915) and Emmett A. Rice, *A Brief History of Physical Education* (New York, 1926).

35. Gymnastics was further encouraged by Spiess between 1833 and 1855. Earlier, John Locke emphasized the importance of physical training in *Some Thoughts on Education* (1693), as did Rousseau in his educational romance *Émile* (1762). The earliest school in Germany was founded in 1774 by Basedow, the 'Philanthropinum' at Dessau, which was open to all social classes and where bodily training was given a place from the beginning with a special teacher in charge of 'knightly exercises' (dancing, riding, fencing, and vaulting) and 'Greek gymnastics' (running, wrestling, throwing and jumping). The school closed in 1793. The first strictly private modern gymnasium was founded by Nachtegall in Copenhagen in 1799. Under the patronage of the King of Sweden, Pehr Henrik Ling opened the Royal Central Institute of Gymnastics in Stockholm in 1814. Along with Triat, the Spaniard Colonel Amoros taught gymnastics in Paris from 1817 to 1848.

36. Mosse, *Nationalism and Sexuality*, 13. The key linkage between physical training and issues of rationalizing a nation's martial manpower were extremely significant in the last century. And yet, as the later history of Imperial Germany indicates, vague rhetorical connections

made between exercise for the masses and democracy were not always the most important elements in the effective promotion of fitness or freedom.

37. See W. G. Niederland's critique of Freud's use of the Schreber case: Niederland, *The Schreber Case* (New York: Quadrangle, 1974). See also Phyllis Grosskurth, 'Freud's Favorite Paranoiac', *New York Review of Books* (18 Jan. 1990) 36–8; Morton Shatzman, *Persecution in the Family* (New York: Random, 1973); and Daniel Paul Schreber, I. Macalpine and R. A. Hunter (trans.) *Memories of My Nervous Illness* (Cambridge, MA: Harvard University Press [1903] 1988). Sigmund Freud was convinced that Schreber's son's later sensation of constriction was linked to his father's experimental use of methods to control children. Schreber's corrective approach was part of a significant strand within the modern effort to train the body. Moreover, as a response to or effect of industrialization it is interesting to note that the body was initially treated with methods like Schreber's and like those for preventing masturbation they can be easily likened to previous or contemporary techniques of torture and punishment.

38. T. A. J. Burnett, *The Rise and Fall of a Regency Dandy* (Boston, MA, 1981) 13–15.

39. None the less, from the second half of the seventeenth century onwards the tendency for public schools to become a standard phase of elite socialization was more marked, John Chandos, *Boys Together* (London, 1984) 22–3.

40. Ibid., 12.

41. Apart from these later practical curricula for physical instruction, an earlier important medical treatise by Briton Francis Fuller (1670–1706) was conversely influential in Germany. A translation of Fuller's *Medicinal Gymnastics; or a Treatise concerning the Power of Exercise with Respect to the Animal Economy, and the Great Necessity of It in the Cure of Several Distempers* (1705) was published in Germany in 1750; as described in T. D. Wood and C. L. Brownell, *Source Book in Health and Physical Education* (New York, 1925) 29.

42. Leonard, *Pioneers*, 49–51.

43. Clias went on to work in France during 1841–8. Ibid., 49–51. Before the 1850s, other foreign instructors also came to Britain, among them Carl Georgi, a graduate of the Swedish Royal Central Institute, who opened a gymnastic school in London, but by mid-century foreign methods had shown little popular effect or result in the British military.

44. Exercise was to take precedence over other forms of training; its practice was limited to a single hour a day. The manual specified that those over the age of 30 were exempt.

45. Report of the Commission appointed to Inquire into the Recruiting for the Army, British Sessional Papers (BSP), House of Commons (HC) vol. xv (1867): ix. BSP: 4. In general the primary focus of the commission was on the bodily condition of recruits at the point of enlistment. In the 'reconstructing' of the system, primacy was thus given to the medical examination of potential enlistees. The specific

objectives of the exercises were simple. They were meant to ensure that a soldier could 'cover 1000 yards or more at a rapid pace and at the end be capable of using his bayonet efficiently'.

46. Conflict in the Crimea and India inspired the formation of the Army Gymnastic Staff. Its aims focused on making the new recruit 'efficient'. Soldiers began to be judged more stringently against normal standards of appearance (through bodily measurement) and performance. The placement of the volunteer force around the same time under more tight control by the War Office (under the Volunteer Act 1863) might also be attributed to such concerns. The commercial possibilities of the volunteer movement were evidenced with founding of the *Volunteer Service Gazette*, a three penny weekly, in 1859 by Charles Templer, a barrister and captain in the Middlesex Rifle Corps. He was followed in the editorship by another volunteering barrister, Hans Busk, the author of the very popular *The Rifle and How to Use It*, a title format that was interestingly echoed in the 1894 physical culture book, *Strength and How to Obtain It*. For a closer examination of the growth of volunteering in Britain before the First World War, see Patricia Morton, 'Another Victorian Paradox: Anti-Militarism in a Jingoistic Society', *Historical Reflections/Reflexions Historique*, 8 (2) (1981): 169–89; also by Morton, 'A Military Irony: The Victorian Volunteer Movement', *Journal of the RUSI for Defence Studies*, 131 (3) (1986): 63–70; and Hugh Cunningham, *The Volunteer Force: A Social and Political History, 1859–1908* (London: Croom Helm, 1975). Apart from notions of national and racial decay, the growth of the volunteer force as largely working class in composition came about for a combination of both patriotic and recreational reasons, Cunningham, *Volunteer*: 108–9. Arguments concerning manliness and the decay of civilization as supports for conscription helped foster both motives. See Viscount Wolseley, 'War and Civilization', *United Services Magazine* (May 1897). As physical culture later demonstrated, the pleasures taken in a person's self-actualization or maintenance of respectability as a soldier comrade were not easily distinguished from one's patriotism. Clearly, the desire for 'manly' association through bodily training was integral to both.

47. Beginning around mid-century, we find the first successful linking of sport with moral improvement. In this way the elite schools' emphasis upon sports and physicality, including episodic anxieties revolving around sexuality, helped to catapult the body to the centre of late-nineteenth-century debates over maintaining the strength of the nation.

48. On American sport and fitness see Green, *Fit for America*; James C. Wharton, *Crusaders for Fitness* (Princeton, NJ, 1982); and Donald R. Mrozek, *Sport and American Mentality, 1880–1910* (Knoxville, TN, 1983). For Europe generally see also Richard Holt, *Sport and Society in Modern France* (Hamden, CT, 1980); Paul Weindling, *Health, Race and German Politics between National Unification and Nazism, 1870–1945* (Cambridge, 1989); and Jean-Paul Massicotte and Claude Lessard, *Histoire du sport de l'antiquité au XIXe siècle* (Quebec, 1984). On Europe generally, see

Eric Dunning and Norbert Elias (eds), *Quest for Excitement* (Oxford, 1986); Tony Mason, *Only a Game? Sport in the Modern World* (Cambridge, 1993); and Edward R. Tannenbaum, *1900: The Generation Before the Great War* (Garden City, NJ, 1976). On degeneracy rhetoric in the period and Max Nordau, the author of the widely translated *Degeneration* (1892), see George L. Mosse, 'Max Nordau, Liberalism and the New Jew', *Journal of Contemporary History (JCH)* (London, Newbury Park, CA, and New Delhi: SAGE), 27 (1992): 565–81; and Steven E. Ascheim, 'Max Nordau, Friedrich Nietzsche and Degeneration', *JCH* 28 (1993): 643–57. See also Françoise Baret-Ducrocq, *Pauvreté, charité et morale à Londres au XIX siècle* (Paris, 1991); Eugenio F. Biagini, *Liberty, Retrenchment and Reform: Popular Liberalism in the Age of Gladstone* (New York, 1992); Gareth Stedman Jones, *Outcast London: A Study in the Relationship between Classes in Victorian Society* (Oxford, 1984); Donald A. Mckenzie, *Statistics in Britain, 1865–1930: The Social Construction of Scientific Knowledge* (Edinburgh, 1981); and M. W. Taylor, *Man versus the State: Spencer and Late Victorian Individualism* (Oxford, 1992).

49. Richards, *Commodity Culture*, 104.

50. The introduction of the wireless, gramophone and cinema would mean even more pervasive linkages. Correspondingly, these developments contributed to a mass society ironically less easily controlled at the point of individual reception. For more on the integration of differing methods of communication and entertainment see Bailey, *Leisure and Class*; also see A. Briggs, *Mass Entertainment: The Origins of a Modern Industry* (Adelaide, 1960); and W. H. Fraser, *The Coming of the Mass Market, 1850–1914* (London, 1981).

51. A movement to limit the hours of commerce so as to provide more leisure time for workers.

52. John Lilwall, 'The Half-holiday Question Considered with Some Thoughts on the Instructive and Healthful Recreations of the Industrial Classes' (London, 1856) 6.

53. Lilwall, 50.

54. Ibid.

55. Lilwall also notes another gym having been erected in Victoria Park in the mean time and the many people who would watch the men exercising at the Duke of York's school in Chelsea on Friday afternoons: 51–2.

56. As noted in Ina Taylor, *A Woman of Contradictions: The Life of George Eliot* (New York, 1989). Bray inherited a ribbon silk weaving factory and was an early object of Mary Ann Evans' affection and intellectual admiration. He was an agnostic radical, who also founded a working-class infant school and was the author of *Address to the Working Classes on the Education of the Body* (1837), *The Education of Feelings* (1838) and *The Philosophy of Necessity, etc.* (1841). On the difficulties of the middle class in garnering working-class attention and their fear of the lower orders taking over bourgois venues, see Bailey, *Leisure and Class*; 86–7, 110–15, etc.

57. Lilwall, 19.

58. J. Hole, *The History and Management of Literary, Scientific, and Mechanics Institutes* (London, 1853): 74–6; as quoted in Bailey, *Leisure and Class*, 109–10.

59. The YMCA initially emphasized personal contact with the poor and the bridging of class divisions. It spread as far as Australia and was present in North America by 1851. Its interest in recreation did not begin until nearly ten years later. See C. Binfield, *George Williams and the YMCA: A Study in Victorian Social Attitudes* (London, 1973); Raymond Cieplik, *Physical Work and Amusements as Concerns of the Young Men's Christian Association, 1851–1884*, PhD Thesis (University of Massachusetts, 1969); and Bailey, *passim*.

60. This was also true in the US where fitness crusader Luther Gulick was successful in turning the non-denominational North American YMCAs away from their original religious orientation toward an emphasis upon his own 'body, mind and spirit' approach (his formulation) that disputed traditional body–spirit dualisms. This motto eventually became a part not only of the YMCA's logo but also of several physical culture organizations and media. Gulick argued for the rudiments of such an approach from the 1850s, but it was not until 1891 that physical education displaced evangelism in the North American context. In a general sense within the larger Anglo-American context, the YMCA tended to be confounded by its avowed dual purposes of bodily and spiritual salvation well into the post-First World War period. See Clifford Putney, 'Character Building in the YMCA, 1880–1930', *Mid-America: An Historical Review*, 73 (1) (1991): 49–70, 49, 54.

61. Haley, 205.

62. Mrozek, 224–5. In the US, this was true even for the presumed dominant class and ethnic group. In the 1880s, the rage for anything colonial and the search for one's Anglo-Saxon genealogical roots were accompanied by fears of being overwhelmed by waves of immigrants, Mrozek, Fit: 223–4. For example, fears of the rising tide of immigration and the anarchist 'Haymarket bombing' in 1886 took place amid widespread strikes beginning in the late 1870s in a supposedly classless US. The YMCA's American emphasis on white male Protestants was in some ways a response to this climate.

63. See Cunningham, *Volunteer Force*.

64. In the summer and autumn of 1884, several million persons were reported to have attended over 1000 Liberal party meetings, and an additional half million came to 200 Conservative party gatherings concerning the new franchise act. The eventual 1884 Act was the rural counterpart of the 1867 reforms which had extended the vote to the upper working classes in the cities. In effect it provided an additional 1 762 000 male votes in agricultural areas. The actual number was smaller, since the ownership of multiple properties could entitle a person to more than one vote. H. Matthew, 'Rhetoric and Politics: 1860–1950', in Matthew, *Politics and Social Change in Modern Britain* (New York, 1987) 36.

65. Report from the Commissioners 1834: XXVII, 229.

66. Of course even these other nations' vast abundances of land and population were at risk from invasion and crippling warfare. See H. J. Mackinder vs. Mahan, *Britain and the British Seas* (London, 1904) 350, referred to in Raymond Betts, *The False Dawn: European Imperialism in the Nineteenth Century* (Minneapolis, MN, 1975) 11, fn. 6; or earlier in the historian J. R. Seeley's 1881–2 lectures 'The Expansion of England'. See Seeley, 'The Concept of Empire: Burke to Attlee, 1774–1947', in Alan Bullock and F. W. Deakin (eds), *The British Political Tradition* (London, 1962) 273–6.

67. Brabazon published two books on the subject, *Prosperity or Pauperism* (London, 1888) and *Social Aims* with his wife, the Countess of Meath (London, 1893). He was also published in periodicals such as the *Nineteenth Century* and *North American Review*. Brabazon to the *Daily Chronicle* (30 December 1886).

68. Leading article in *The Scotsman* (24 September 1887), repub. in The Earl of Meath, Lord Brabazon, *Prosperity or Pauperism: Physical, Industrial and Technical Training* (London, 1888) 52.

69. This medical and moral discursive explosion was fuelled by widely discussed reports from Royal Commissions. An early example was the 'Drunken Committee', which inquired into drunkenness in 1834 and helped to foster the temperance movement. Other examples apart from Brabazon included Sir James Kay-Shuttleworth, Lord Shaftsbury, Octavia Hill, Rowntree, Booth, and Money: see John Roach, *Social Reform in England, 1780–1880* (New York: St Martin's, 1978), wherein the author refers to Seeley's *Ecce Homo* (1865) which focused on the 'person of Christ solely from the human standpoint', 9. Seeley argued that there was a special responsibility upon Christians 'to apply themselves to relieving the physical needs and distresses of their fellow creatures'; he referred to it as 'The Enthusiasm for Humanity', 9. See also Henry Mayhew, *London's Underworld*, ed. Peter Quennell (London: Bracken, 1983).

70. Ibid., 52.

71. Ibid.

72. Ibid., 56.

73. Ironically, in the following decade, the elder Gladstone would be the one who was depicted as a physical culture hero. See *Sandow's*, 1 (1).

74. The 'worthy but uninspiring' Gladstone was not destined to follow in his father's footsteps as Prime Minister. But he possessed considerable skills as a party organizer and in-fighter, and he remained a key player in the shift from an 1860s 'Gladstonian Liberalism' to the near complete reorientation of the Liberal Party in the decade of the 1890s. Though undistinguished as either a public speaker or Cabinet administrator, Gladstone later played a pivotal role as Liberal chief party whip (1899–1905). Well into the 1920s he would continue to play an important role in the wranglings between Liberal factions and the rising Labour Party as a proponent of the 'New Liberalism'. See Martin Pugh, *The Making of Modern British Politics, 1867–1939* (Oxford, 1987) 99, 118–19, 120–2, 150–1, 232.

75. Gordon was defeated and killed by the forces of the Mahdi at

Khartoum in 1885. The failed relief effort and his death received enormous press attention.

76. The models for circulating and merchandising both political ideas and new products had been established in some areas as early as the seventeenth century. See Neil McKendrick, John Brewer and J. H. Plumb, *The Birth of a Consumer Society: The Commercialization of Eighteenth Century England* (Bloomington, IN: University of Indiana Press, 1982); Peter Borsay, *The English Urban Renaissance: Culture and Society in the Provincial Town, 1660–1770* (New York: Oxford University Press, 1989); and Lorna Weatherill, *Consumer Behaviour and Material Culture in Britain, 1660–1760* (London: Routledge, 1989); for a revisionist view of modern commercialization.

77. The new union members were different from the typical skilled and politically active working man that had been the mainstay of Gladstonian Liberalism. The 'collectivist decade' of the 1880s especially found the numbers of such organizations, their membership, and resulting well-planned worker agitation on a steep and noticeable rise. By the turn of the century, friendly societies and cooperative movements formed by working people had also attained significant economic power. The new structures and organizations of mass society were in the old reformist sense impossible to control. It was under such circumstances of workers' growing success in organizing themselves amid fears of social upheaval that the NPRS was founded.

78. A. Alexander (AA) to Herbert Gladstone (HG), British Library Additional Manuscript Collection (BL Ad MS), Gladstone Papers (GP), MS 46052, f. 43.

79. *Recreation, A Monthly Record of the Society's Work*, 1 (1) [first series], George Philip & Sons (August 1886).

80. AA to HG, 21 June 1886, BL Ad MS, GP, MS 46052, ff. 154.

81. Descriptions by historians and publishers regarding readership or circulation are confusing and varied. For example, on front covers of Bernarr Macfadden's British publication *Physical Development*, 1 (3) (June 1901) and 2 (4) (Jan. 1902) a combined 'paid circulation' of 252 000 and 300 000 respectively was claimed. In editorials there were included assertions that Macfadden's two US publications had total circulations of 'nearly' 250 000. See Robert Ernst, *Weakness is a Crime: The Life of Bernarr Macfadden* (New York: Syracuse University Press, 1991) 24.

82. That is, in the rather politically neutral encouragement of sporting leagues and competitions. This occurred against a backdrop of debate over whether or not sport in general was actually helpful as a means of military training.

83. H. C. G. Matthew dates this trend as beginning in 1867 and accelerating in the 1880s, see Matthew, 'Rhetoric and Politics', 36–9.

84. In the last decade of the century further evidence of the growing popularity of exercise and its professionalization was demonstrated by a dramatic increase in interest in AGS staff vacancies. In 1894, a major building was added to the AGS school's facilities in the form of the Cranbrook gymnasium, and as the century drew to a close,

Fox and his colleagues became more interested in the Swedish system of gymnastic instruction. Up until that point, heavy weights and drill comprised most of the routine of the staff's instruction. On the eve of physical culture's début in 1897, the military began a progressive shift back toward the *pangymnastikon* of the early nineteenth century. At the same time an increasing interest in fitness on the part of the military was exemplified by the new commander Col. J. Scott Napier's building of over 80 army gyms across the country during the 1890s.

85. Earlier journals had failed repeatedly. See Budd, *Heroic Bodies*, 76–8, 80–3.

86. Ibid., 176–88.

87. In the second issue of *Recreation*, the NPRS listed 115 gyms or organizations in Great Britain and Ireland. Of the total, 37 were military ones and another 23 were YMCA clubs. Many of the other 55 were classes or activities held at sites other than gymnasiums, 1 (2) (Sept. 1886).

88. See Bailey, *Leisure and Class*, 176–88.

89. Of the 18 gyms listed (down from the 115 listed in the second issue of *Recreation*), several were classes or clubs rather than physical buildings, one was in the US, several were already existent YMCAs or public schools (such as Rugby), and one was listed twice by virtue of having both a gym and a rowing club (Exeter Hall, in Longacre). Of the total number over half (eleven) were in London proper and three in Liverpool (all three of which were associated with the Alexander brothers). Only one of those listed was an explicitly working-men's club (St Matthias's Working Men's Athletic Club, in Spital Square), and at least one was for women only ('the Ladies of the Bloomsbury Gymnastic Class'). *Gymnasium News*, 1 (12) (July 1887) (London): 185–90.

90. Ibid., 190–1.

91. B. S. Rowntree, *Poverty: A Study of Town Life* (York, 1901), as quoted in Paul Thompson, *The Edwardians: The Remaking of British Society* (London: Granada, 1977): 29–31.

92. A maximum of four for a regularly employed labourer, and possibly eight for an 'abstemious craftsman', Thompson, 30.

93. Ibid.

94. Bailey, 182–4.

95. *Physique*, published briefly in August and September 1891. *The Hygiene Advertiser: Devoted to Natural Living, Physical Culture, Health Reform, etc.* 1–19 (London, 1891–2), endured for a longer period but also failed to sustain a readership.

96. *Physique*, 2 (March 1891); and 7–8 (August–September 1891), 143–5.

97. Richard H. Heindel, *The American Impact on Great Britain: 1898–1914* (Philadelphia, PA: 1940) 24.

98. 'Terpsichorean' is taken from Terpsichore, the muse of dance and choral song.

99. *Dancing: A Journal Devoted to the Terpsichorean Art, Physical Culture and Fashionable Entertainments*, 1 (1) (1891).

2 PICTURING PHYSICAL CULTURE CONSUMERS

1. Linda Colley, *Britons: Forging the Nation, 1707–1837* (New Haven, CT: Yale University Press, 1992) 229–30.
2. Ibid., 229, *Gentleman's Magazine*, 32 (1762) 551.
3. R. Jay, *Learned Pigs and Fireproof Women* (New York, 1986) 45.
4. Topham's feats were reported in J. T. Désaguliers' *Course of Experimental Philosophy*, as noted in Edmond Desbonnet, *Les Rois de la force* (Paris: Berger-Levrault, 1901). My thanks to David Chapman for this citation.
5. Jay, *Learned Pigs*, 282–5.
6. Desbonnet.
7. By the early nineteenth century, the gardens at Vauxhall had declined in terms of royal patronage but continued to be popular among the masses. The period when the Rouselle brothers posed and competed as wrestlers was also a time when 'tumblers, rope-dancers, singers, Indian jugglers and sword-swallowers', and panorama's re-enactments of Waterloo could still be seen at Astley's Royal Amphitheatre at Lambeth and at Vauxhall. See Stella Margetson, *Leisure and Pleasure in the Nineteenth Century* (New York, 1969) 31–3.
8. The definitive classic on the Dandy is Jules Barbey D'Aurevilly's portrait of Beau Brummell, *Dandyism*, trans. Douglas Ainslie, 1845 (New York: PAJ, 1988 [1897 reprint]).
9. The dandy remained a powerful figure throughout the period and re-emerged at the end of the century as a contested though no less influential identity. The example provided by the dandy was that of the fetishization of the statuesque male poseur; an opaque artificial body underpinned by 'natural' masculine strength. Despite great efforts, its fundamentally subversive elements were never erased by Victorian culture. Today, we live in a culture in which the word 'dandy' lacks, in both discourse and practice, a substantial opposing ground of 'undandified' manliness. At a more profound level, beyond superficial judgements of cultural narcissism, corporate consumer culture seems to have made it permissible for all men to be dandies of one sort or another. For more on gender or the self as a consumer style see Alan Tomlinson (ed.), *Consumption, Identity, Style: Marketing, Meanings, and the Packaging of Pleasure* (London, 1990) 50–5; and Frank Mort, 'Boys Own? Masculinity, Style and Popular Culture', and Rowena Chapman, 'The Great Pretender: Variations on the New Man Theme', both in Rowena Chapman and Jonathan Rutherford (eds), *Male Order: Unwrapping Masculinities* (London: Lawrence & Wishart, 1988).
10. Triat's gym was eventually closed because of his habit of making it available to communist groups. For this and other activities he was arrested several times after 1870. The gym was closed in 1879, David Webster, *The Iron Game: An Illustrated History of Weightlifting* (Irvine, CA: John Geddes, 1976) 12.
11. In the Bibliothèque Nationale there are three pamphlets by Hippolyte Triat, *Au Gouvernement provisoire [Lettre demandant la création d'un*

ministère de l'éducation publique, signée Triat et Dally, 1er mars 1848] (Paris: P. Dupont, 1848); *Mémoire sur la gymnastique adressé au Conseil Municipal de Paris* (Paris: Renou et Maulde, 1872); and also with M. Dally, *Société milonienne pour l'exploitation de la gymnastique appliquée à la réhabilitation physique de l'homme, d'après la méthode de M. Triat, de Nîmes . . . Raison sociale* (Paris: A. Monair, 1847).

12. See Edwin Landseer, *Isaac Van Amburgh and his animals*, Paul Mellon Collection, Yale Center for British Art, New Haven, CT.

13. Ibid.

14. For more about the period in which Van Amburgh performed, and the era in which the circus and other popular entertainments provided a bridge between later and earlier more traditional working-class activities, see Hugh Cunningham, *Leisure in the Industrial Revolution, c. 1780–1880* (London, 1980) Chapter 1; P. N. Stearns, 'The Effort at Continuity in Working-class Culture', *Journal of Modern History*, lii (1980) 626–55; and Peter Bailey, *Leisure and Class in Victorian England: Recreation and the Contest for Control, 1830–1885* (London: Methuen, 1987).

15. *Recreation*, August 1886, n. 1: 3–4. Military leaders such as General Wolseley continued to assert specific links between defence and the degenerating bodies of workers, arguing that the problem of the unfit male was dealt with better on the continent through compulsory army training: Viscount Wolseley, later Field Marshal and Commander-in-Chief of the British Army. See Wolseley to the NPRS, War Office, 12 March 1886, 1–2, as quoted in Budd, *Heroic Bodies*, 165. In so doing, Wolseley challenged traditional sentiments against conscription that continued well into the First World War. See Edward M. Spiers, *Army and Society, 1815–1914* (London, 1980).

16. John Hargreaves, *Sport, Power and Culture: A Social and Historical Analysis of Popular Sports in Britain* (New York: St Martin's, 1986) 51.

17. Bailey, *Leisure and Class in Victorian England*, 143.

18. Richards, 105.

19. Gareth Stedman Jones, *Languages of Class: Studies in English Working Class History, 1832–1982* (Cambridge: Cambridge University Press, 1983) 207.

20. Ibid., 27–8.

21. After the turn of the century, the Seldoms were the most famous group still doing this sort of thing in England. In the 1880s, however, the poses tended to be more restrained. Along with 'La Milo', or Pansy Montague from Australia, who appeared as 'Bacchante' in 1906, the Seldoms' living statuary act showed far more flesh than would have been allowed without the white make-up. The Seldoms' work included tableaux such as 'Reaching the Winning Post', which they enacted at the London Pavilion in 1907.

22. Isenberg, *Sullivan*, 191.

23. 'It was the season for beefcake in the metropolis'. Charlie Mitchell was at the Grand Opera House, touted as 'the handsomest and most symmetrically formed man living', and the 'athletic figure' of

boxer Dominick McCaffery was listed as appearing at William's Dime Museum in the Bowery. But it was Sullivan who drew the crowds. Ibid.

24. Isenberg, 193–4.
25. Ibid., 241.
26. Ibid. From the *Pall Mall Gazette* (London), 8 Nov. 1887: 1.
27. Isenberg, *Sullivan*, 241.
28. Ibid., 242.
29. Ibid., 243–4.
30. See David Chapman, *Sandow the Magnificent: Eugen Sandow and the Beginnings of Bodybuilding* (Urbana and Chicago, IL: University of Illinois Press, 1994) 7.
31. 4 November 1889, as quoted in Gerard Nisivoccia, *Sandow the Mighty Monarch of Muscle* (Newark, NJ, 1947) 9.
32. Sandow remains an icon in today's bodybuilding culture. He can be seen for example in Charles Gaines and George Butler, *Pumping Iron: The Art and Sport of Bodybuilding* (New York: Simon, 1981) 120–1, in some of his typical poses, for example sporting a fig-leaf (*c.* 1899), and in another undated photo, seeming to support a group of fellow music hall performers, or rather '19 people and a dog', on his back, or as misidentified (as a Russian strongman) in Pronger's *Arena of Masculinity*, 169; figures 15, 16. His ideas and example continued to be influential well into the post-Second World War period. He is, perhaps, the key 'father' figure of both present-day bodybuilding entrepreneurs and members of various weightlifting associations throughout the world. See the interview with fitness publisher Joe Weider, *Interview* (September 1990) in which Sandow is mentioned.
33. He was one of over 4 million persons who emigrated from Germany to other parts of the world between 1851 and 1910. Most immigrated to North America, but there was by the time of George V's coronation in 1911 a significant German population in Britain numbering some 53 324 persons. C. Trebilcock, *The Industrialization of the Continental Powers* (1981) 310–11; *Census for England and Wales,* 1911, vol. IX (PP 1913, LXXVIII) as cited in Panikos Panayi, 'German Business Interests in Britain during the First World War', *Business History*, 32 (2) (April 1990): 244–58.
34. Atilla (1844–1924), also German, was born Louis Durlacher. The young Müller's Lutheran parents had held early hopes for his pursuit of a career in the church, but his presumed 'preaching' abilities took him elsewhere. He began a medical course in Belgium and spent what little energy he chose to devote to his studies solely on anatomy. Once in Brussels, he discovered the gymnastic school of 'Professor' Oscard Atilla and began his first money-making appearances as a strength performer in circuses and music halls in nearby Antwerp and Leyden in 1887. At the same time, they hired themselves out to train students. It was then that Müller adopted the surname of Sandow (an anglicization of his mother's maiden name of Sandov), and the first name Eugen, which he later explained was chosen as a symbol of his admiration for Francis Galton's new science of Eugenics.

35. This may have been Edward VII or the young George V. In spite of King Edward's portly bearing in later years, his upbringing was characterized by the principles of physical culture such as they existed at mid-century. The tradition of exercise was firmly established in his childhood by Prince Albert, who instructed the royal tutor Frederick W. Gibbs that the Prince and his brother be physically tired at the end of each day 'by means of riding, drill, and gymnastics'. At that time, Gibbs wrote to the King of Sardinia that whereas the Prince was a fine dancer, dancing, 'being thought rather effeminate, and insufficient to develop a manly frame', was complemented by 'a regular course of military exercises under the instruction of a Sergeant', Philip Magnus, *King Edward VII* (New York: Penguin, 1964) 24, 29 respectively. Although he was Sandow's original mentor, Atilla never approached the latter's success in publishing. His sole publication was a ghost authored book, *The Art of Weightlifting and Muscular Development . . . with Special Notes on Double Handed Lifting*, ed. Thomas Inch (London: Health Culture Publishing Co., 1903).

36. As told by Sigmund Klein in an interview published in Gaines and Butler, 110. Appropriately, the pin was composed of an image of Hercules carved in crystal and surrounded by 36 diamonds. On his deathbed at the age of 78, he was said to have clutched the stick pin tightly to his breast. Sullivan also looked backed fondly on his meeting with the Prince of Wales and was said to have been given a gift of garnets and emeralds by the future King-Emperor. Isenberg, 244.

37. In addition to training the young Sandow, Atilla also trained Louis Desbonnet, who was inspired by Triat's example. Desbonnet liquidated his family fortune and founded a physical culture school in Lille in 1885. He built a nationwide chain and became the publisher of *La Culture Physique*. Desbonnet was the author of *Les Rois de la force* and *Les Rois de la lutte*. He later published *La Force physique, culture rationelle, méthode Atilla, méthode Sandow, méthode Desbonnet, la sante par les exercises musculaires mis à la portée de tout* (Paris: Berger-Levrault, 1901) which went into its fifth edition in 1906. See examples of the Desbonnet method in William A. Ewing, *The Body: Photographs of the Human From* (London: Chronicle, 1994) 277–9.

38. As told by Klein in Gaines and Butler: 110–19.

39. The Marquis of Queensberry and Lord Clifford were in attendance at the packed house and both agreed to act as judges. On cross-class sporting relations see Wray Vamplew, 'The Sport of Kings and Commoners: the Commercialization of British Horse-racing in the Nineteenth-Century', in R. Cashman and M. McKernan (eds) *Sport in History* (Hemel Hempstead, 1979) 307–25. *Daily News*, 3 November 1889, as quoted in Webster.

40. Performances by Sullivan also had some impact on Walt Whitman's poetic descriptions of the body, see Moon, *Disseminating Whitman* (Harvard, 1992). Later American strongmen Joe Bonomo and his friend Angelo Siciliano, the latter better known as Charles Atlas, were both inspired by Sandow's image and legend. The young

Siciliano pasted a picture of Sandow on his mirror for inspiration
and was an avid reader of Macfadden's *Physical Culture* magazine.
Like Sandow, Atlas also claimed to have been inspired by the clas-
sical statuary he had seen as a boy in the Brooklyn Museum; from
Donald J. Mrozek, 'Sport in American Life: From National Health to
Personal Fulfillment, 1890–1940', in Kathryn Grover (ed.), *Fitness in
American Culture: Images of Health, Sport, and the Body, 1830–1940*
(Amherst, MA: University of Massachusetts Press, 1989) 34–7. At
the time, the model of the heroic, and the personae of the sporting
figure and the actor, might all exist within a single exemplary body.
For example, the Black boxer Peter Jackson, champion of Australia
and 'colored champion of the world', under the management of
Parson Davies of Chicago, also toured as 'Uncle Tom' in Harriet
Beecher Stowe's *Uncle Tom's Cabin* in 1894. See Billy Edwards, *The
Pugilistic Portrait Gallery* (London and Philadelphia, PA: Pugilistic
Publishing Co., 1894) 8. Also published as *Legendary Boxers of the
Golden Age of England, America, Australia, etc.*, 22.

41. Macfadden worked at the Chicago Exposition where he saw Sandow
perform. Sandow was joined by world champion boxer Jim Corbett
and the famed dancer 'Little Egypt' in his bodily displays at the
Exposition. Macfadden began publishing *Physical Development* in Britain in 1901. During the first phase of physical culture (1898–1908),
Britain was the base for strongmen entrepreneurs from several other
countries due to its publishing infrastructure and position as the
centre of the largest developed single language market in the world,
which included the empire and in some regards the US. By January
1905, Macfadden was publishing a successful rival magazine in
Britain and the US, and had produced no fewer than 14 physical
culture books. In that same period (1898–1905) a total of 44 books
related to the topic of physical culture were printed in the United
Kingdom. *English Catalogue of Books* (*ECB*), vols vi (1901) and vii
(1906).

42. Macfadden first saw Sandow while working for a friend, Alexander
Whiteley, in the midway demonstrating an exerciser, Ernst, 4–15
passim.

43. Ibid., 17.

44. As retold in Webster, 16. Sandow was in Venice during part of
that year, where he met Aubrey Hunt of the Royal Academy and
posed for a painting of a Roman gladiatorial scene. Wilhelm II was
already seated on the German imperial throne. The Crown Prince
Frederich Wilhelm is surely the intended figure, since the Villa Zirio
was his personal refuge, and because of the impossibility of the
younger Kaiser, with his injured arm, ever being able to tear a pack
of cards in two. Even if the meeting had occurred right before
Frederich Wilhelm's death, it was improbable that the latter would
have been able to deliver the 'touching speech' to Sandow that is
attributed to him, Webster, 16. The former was in residence at San
Remo as his throat cancer worsened in 1887–8. Michael Balfour, *The
Kaiser and his Times* (Boston, MA: Houghton-Mifflin, 1964) 89, 92.

See Chapman, *Sandow*, 16–19 on Hunt and the meeting with the Crown Prince.

45.   Thus, the son obeyed the leader 'from motives of affection and respect . . . the weak, because he [was] . . . strong and . . . the poor from hope of gain, because he [was] . . . rich'. From the chapter entitled 'The Lie of the Monarchy and Aristocracy', in Nordau, 88. The equivalency of right with might thus preceded the introduction of the 'supernatural' in the form of the monarchy's alliance with religion, 'A monarchy owes its existence and perpetuation to Religion', Nordau, 71. For more on atavisms and monarchial reinvigoration in relation to physical strength and militarism in this period see Arthur Waldron, 'The WarLord: Twentieth-Century Chinese Understandings of Violence, Militarism, and Imperialism', *American Historical Review* (Oct. 1991): 1073–100, especially 1075–85.

46.   Since his was not an established persona like that of a king or even a popular boxer, the distribution of Sandow's image beyond the performance venue often benefited from its referentiality to commercial products and other more traditional icons such as the king. But this worked both ways. The popular association of the figure of the monarch with a popular entertainer was also indicative of a gradual re-contextualizing of age-old symbols, for example those of 'the eagle and the sun', within a mass arena where images and enactments of celebrity were beginning to circulate more freely, Foucault, *Discipline*, 217.

47.   Muscle reading was a term coined by Dr George Beard in an article in the *Archives of Electrology and Neurology*, and further developed in articles published in the *Detroit Lancet* (1875) and *Popular Science Monthly* (Feb. 1877), and in his monograph *The Study of Trance, Muscle Reading and Allied Nervous Phenomena in Europe and America, with a letter on the moral character of trance subjects and a defense of Dr. Charcot* (New York, 1882). In these writings, Beard dealt with the technique of mind-reader Jacob Randall Brown among others; as quoted in Jay, 175. A cataleptic, Bishop, went into a 'trance' following a performance at a private New York club and was pronounced dead. Subsequently autopsied in order to tell whether his brain exhibited any physical evidence of his supposed extraordinary powers, his wife and mother accused the attending doctors of murdering the entranced bishop. No convictions resulted. But the incident played a role in producing a wave of fears over being embalmed or buried alive in the 1890s, Jay, 175.

48.   Salisbury as reproduced from the *Dart* in Edward Lawrence Levy's *Autobiography of an Athlete* (London, 1913); the Kruger cartoon was published in *Sandow's* (July 1899): 48.

49.   Both in Leicester Square. The Alhambra was remodelled as a variety house in 1882 and the Empire in 1887. In the process, the older suburban halls with their local clientele were replaced by bigger centralized theatres which put on more lavish spectacles.

50.   Charles Higham, *Ziegfeld* (Chicago, IL: Regnery, 1982).

51.   Ibid., 13.

52. Ibid.
53. On its cover, Sandow was depicted in an idealized form. *The Police Gazette: The Leading Illustrated Sporting Journal in America* (New York, Jan. 1893). Ibid., 14.
54. They also relied upon a pre-industrial view of the exoticisms of colonial and/or non-Western social orders. Stereoscopic cards of images like 'The Sultan's Favorite', no. 80, T. W. Ingersoll (1899), for example, were accompanied by texts appealing to all women's presumed taste for the luxuriant. 'Surrounded by everything that riches may buy, mistress over hordes of slaves. . . . Can she want more?' The dominant or male gaze apparent in such pictures located erotic desires for the idle female body outside and apart from the material conditions of the industrial order.
55. The figure of the performing woman, rather than a physical ideal like Sandow, was seen by Nordau as a special cause of degeneracy among upper-class men: 'when a man of rank marries beneath him, it is usually some theatrical star, circus-rider or clever adventuress . . . the woman is an abnormal being [who] . . . does not conform to the average type of humanity', she appeals to those elite males who possess a 'weak, sensual and impulsive nature', Nordau, *Conventional Lies*, 141.
56. 'Mademoiselle Arniotis: How to Succeed as a Strong Woman', *The Sketch* (27 December 1893): 491–2.
57. Ibid., 491.
58. Ibid.
59. John Stokes, *In the Nineties* (Chicago, IL: University of Chicago Press, 1989).
60. Stokes, *Nineties*, 56. Although both female and male prostitution were familiar activities in London's West End, claims about women were often based on impressionistic evidence, for example the counting of women in attendance who appeared to be of 'objectionable character', which usually meant the perception of one's being 'painted' and overdressed. Being unchaperoned was also evidence of being a possible prostitute. As Virginia Woolf noted in *The Pargiters* (published later as *The Years*), a novel of the 1880s, any unaccompanied young women was liable to suspicion, 'To be seen alone in Piccadilly was equivalent to walking up Abercorn Terrace in a dressing gown carrying a sponge', quoted in Elaine Showalter, *Sexual Anarchy: Gender and Culture at the Fin de Siècle* (New York: Viking, 1990) 119. Like boxing and racing, the music hall's carnivalesque sexualized atmosphere had its attractions for members of all classes.
61. As quoted in Mander and Mitchenson, 27.
62. See Arthur Symons in the *New Review* (Nov. 1894): 465; and Shaw, *Our Theaters in the Nineties*, 1: 86, both as quoted in Stokes, 79. Shaw decried the 'false decency' that made people ashamed of their bodies and allowed Alvin Langdon Coburn to exhibit a nude photo of himself in 1906, from 'Nude in a Social Landscape', Ben Maddow, final essay in Constance Sullivan (ed.), *Nude Photographs: 1850–1980* (New York: Harper & Row, 1980) 187. Shaw was also admired by Bernarr

Macfadden. Their friendship or meeting is mentioned in Mary Macfadden's *Dumbbells and Carrot Strips*, 70, and referred to by Hunt, in *Body Love*, 54; Hunt seems to have exaggerated the connection between Macfadden and the playwright. Ibid., 55.

63.   Stokes, 79, as quoted from D. F. Cheshire, *Music Hall in Britain* (1974) 41.

64.   Edwards, *Portrait Gallery*, 8. Edwards was the former light heavyweight champion of the world crowned in New York City in 1874.

65.   Ibid.

66.   For more on the history of the postcard, see Jeffrey Richards and E. J. Evans, *A Social History of Britain in Postcards: 1870–1930*; Aline Ripert and Claude Frere, *La Carte postale: son histoire, sa fonction sociale* (Paris: Presses universitaires de Lyons et Paris, 1983); and Barbara Jones and William Ouellette, *Erotic Postcards* (London: Macdonald & James, 1977).

67.   *The Poster and Postcard Collector*, 12 (Dec. 1903): 325. During the First World War, Germany is said to have printed 9 million postcards a month; in 1910 it is claimed that 125 million were published in France alone, George Mosse, *Fallen Soldiers* (New York: Oxford University Press, 1990) 128.

68.   The term implied an ideological and commercial cultivating of the body, and was used to encompass a broad range of phenomena relating to the popular health and fitness press. It persisted as a term for post-Second World War gay-coded muscular posing magazines. But as an ideologically defined and growing commercial movement it did not last much beyond the First World War. More on physical culture as part of a history of the representation of homoeroticism can be found in Thomas Waugh's work on the depiction of the male body from the 1860s to 1960s. Waugh describes the 'discourse of bodybuilding as a channel and incarnation – and at the same time a camouflage – of the sexualized male body', from 'Antecedents: The Physical Culture Movement of the Fin-de-siècle', unpublished paper, given at the Gay, Lesbian and Bisexual Conference (Harvard University, 1990) 1.

69.   It was probably first used in print in the 1830s. Harvey Green notes that Sandow's chief competitor, Macfadden, claimed to have coined the term, although the latter's own magazine entitled *Physical Culture* did not appear until 1899. See Green, *Fit for America*, 245.

70.   As a pejorative description of bodily practice the particular use of the term 'culture' was in line with its original etymological basis in agriculture, that is, cultivating the body, as well as its double meaning within scientific discourse: culture as both a process of artificially developing an organism, and as the end product of that same process. The notorious flexibility of the term 'culture', as elaborated upon by Arnold, and later by Eliot and Williams, was treated to myriad twists and turns within the early selling of muscular strength and beauty. On culture, see Matthew Arnold, *Culture and Anarchy* (London, 1868); T. S. Eliot, *Notes Toward a Definition of Culture* (London, 1948); and Raymond Williams, *Culture and Society* (Harmondsworth: Penguin, 1961) and *Keywords* (London: Fontana, 1976).

71. According to *ECB*, the odd tract such as *The Neglect of Physical Education* (1879) was characteristic before the 1890s. Though hardly exhaustive, the *ECB*, like *Sells Directory of Publications*, gives some indication of the growth and later wane of physical culture publications. Between January 1881 and December 1889, only three books were printed that can broadly be interpreted as being directly related to fitness. The first two, published in 1884 and 1886, were by an American, C. Betz. *ECB*, iv (1893): 49, 179; respectively, see *Betz System of Physical Culture* (1884) and *Physical Culture* (1886) both published in Kansas City. The only other listing in England was for a military manual published in 1889, *Physical Training Made Easy for New Infantry Drill*, *ECB*: 451; anonymous, Simkin (London, 1889).

72. G. Mercer Adam (ed.), *Sandow's System of Physical Training* (London: Gale & Polden, 1894) title page.

73. Within a climate of national insecurity, military publishing grew rapidly. Gale & Polden was also a major publisher of postcards, both a popular military series as well as one including some of the many images issued of Sandow. Gale & Polden's most successful series of postcards was that of the differing British regiments which continued to be published until the 1950s. Its most successful endeavour began soon after the introduction of *Sandow's*. This was *The Military Mail*, first printed in 1901, which carried on for almost 60 years and had at one point the largest military circulation in the world.

74. Adam, 14; for a further examples, see Sandow's *Strength and How to Obtain It* (London, 1897).

75. Ultimately, the army adopted a fitness programme similar to the Swedish Ling System, which focused on flexibility and gymnastic skill rather than free weight exercise. This did not prevent Sandow from making the most of his tenuous association with military training and military persons who chose to employ his methods. It was perhaps no accident that Gale & Polden highlighted the word 'physical' in the new edition of their popular military training manual (*Physical Drill: New Bayonet Exercises and Attack and Defence Made Easy*, 6th edition, March 1895). As volunteer activity increased, civilian interest in military training manuals grow alongside the appetite for physical fitness instruction.

76. See 'Mr. Gladstone as an Athlete' and its disclaimer, 'strictly speaking the title of this article is misnomer, for Mr. Gladstone was never an athlete', *Sandow's* 1 (1) (1898): 27–9. Gladstone was described similarly in *Lippincott's Magazine* by J. William White, MD, in his article 'A Physician's View of Exercise and Athletics' (undated) as quoted in *Narragansett Machine Company Catalogue*, 7; White told the story of Gladstone spending an hour in his private gymnasium on the morning he introduced the Home Rule Bill. Following a rather tortuous logic we are led to the conclusion that he was 'more athletic than an athlete', *Sandow's*, 1 (1): 27.

77. G. Mercer Adam (ed.), *Sandow's System of Physical Training* (London: Gale & Polden, 1894) title page. There may have been earlier

editions of this book. According to the *ECB*, III–VII (1874–1915), v (1898): 863; a 'new edition' under Sandow and Adam's name is listed in 1894 as *Physical Training: A Study in the Perfect Type of the Human Form*.

78. His system and its eminent portability pointed to the key factor that separated earlier attempts at fitness publishing and entrepreneurship from that after 1898. Throughout most of the nineteenth century, fitness had sometimes been connected with more cumbersome and expensive apparatus, and in any case, was usually aimed towards the middle classes who might be able to afford the parlour gymnasium or particular institutions such as schools, colleges and the military who might invest in large equipment. Ibid., 145.

79. *Sandow's*, 1 (1) (July 1898), Editorial, 'Physical Culture, What is it?': 2.

80. Ibid., 5.

81. Others were more explicit in employing Arnold's thoughts on culture and intellectual pursuits. One anonymous author, 'M.D.', applied Arnold's dictum on reading: 'with a purpose to guide it, and with system' to physical exercise, noting that the 'production of physical culture specialists' or 'to people the world with Sandows' was *not* its objective 'anymore than the object of intellectual culture is to fill it with Herbert Spencers', *Ideal Health and How to Obtain it by Physical Culture* (London, 1909) 4.

82. *Sandow's*, 1 (1) (July 1898): 5.

83. Paul Johnson, *The Birth of the Modern: World Society 1815–1830* (New York: HarperCollins, 1991): 709.

84. See Pamela Walker, *Pulling the Devil's Kingdom Down: Gender and Popular Culture in the Salvation Army, 1865–1895*, PhD Dissertation (Rutgers University, NJ, 1991); and 'I Live But Not Yet I For Christ Liveth in Me: Men and Masculinity in the Salvation Army, 1865–1890', in Michael Roper *et al.* (eds), *Manful Assertions* (London: Routledge, 1990).

85. The mean age for marriage among men in the early twentieth century was 27 for men and 25 for women, higher than at any other time in British history. Thompson, 71.

86. Thompson, 53.

87. In one sense, organized sport is different by degree rather than kind from Huizinga's notion of ideal 'play', since even in its regulation it 'remains outside the sphere of necessity', Richard Gruneau, *Class, Sports and Social Development* (Amherst, MA: University of Massachusetts Press, 1983) 40. None the less, instrumental and rationalist approaches have gone some lengths to make the 'unnecessary' a key mechanism within both capitalist consumer cultures and socialist societies. The 'relative autonomy' of cultural practice generally, suggests that 'the meanings of sports, like all cultural creations, have the capacity to be either reproductive or oppositional, repressive or liberating', 38. In this regard, just as earlier less organized forms of sport and play need to be distinguished from modern spectator sports, so does exercise need to be considered somewhat apart from other forms of 'play'. Indeed, physical culture exercise,

which involved a loss of self in the challenge and pleasure of self-perpetuation and transformation, might be read as the most necessary of acts.

88. Stokes, *Nineties, passim.*

89. The sense that such a voice and its implied panoptic vision were total in character was exacerbated by the shifting sense of time promoted by new means of technology, a sense that it was always now and that the response of the newspaper to events was immediate and complete, Altick, *Victorian People,* 96–7. See Kern, *Culture of Time,* on memory and time, 38–64; speed and simultaneity, 72–81; and the beginnings of the First World War and national consciousness, 277–86. See also Williams, *Long Revolution,* 192–206.

90. *Sandow's,* 8 (Feb. 1902), 'Hints from Sandow and Editorial Chat', 159–60.

91. *Sandow's* (27 Sept. 1906): 416.

92. Ibid.

93. See Chapman, 149–50.

94. In *Health and Vim,* 6 (11) (Nov. 1907): 595.

95. *Health and Vim,* 7 (1) (Jan. 1908): 12.

96. From George F. Bird, 'The Muscular Heroine in Fiction', *Sandow's,* 1 (4) (Oct. 1898): 249. This was a follow-up to an article in the first issue entitled 'The Muscular Hero in Fiction', *Sandow's,* 1 (1) (July 1898): 68.

97. For example, Roger Pococks' 'The White Fear' or Cutcliffe Hyne's 'The Inventor'.

98. His first attempt at fiction was serialized and then published as *The Athlete's Conquest: The Romance of an Athlete* (Physical Culture Publishing Co., 1901) Ernst, 14. *Wild Oats* is described in Clement Wood's *Bernarr Macfadden: A Study in Success* (New York: Lewis Copeland, 1929); it is resummarized in Hunt, 43–4. It was published serially in *Physical Culture* as 'Growing to Manhood in a Civilized (?) Society'. After six instalments between October 1906 and March 1907, a federal grand jury indicted Macfadden for the publication of 'obscene, lewd, and lascivious material'. A New Jersey court found that his supposed attempt at a moral tale was instead a veiled appeal to prurient tastes. He was fined $2000 and sentenced to two years in jail. The Supreme Court declined to hear Macfadden's appeal. But the prison sentence was revoked by President Taft on 18 November 1909. The fine remained in effect. See Ernst, 47–8. Later in his career, Macfadden became better known for his publication the *Daily Graphic,* a titillating mixture of photos depicting undressed women, emblazoned with shocking headlines alerting the reader to its dubious news and suggestive fiction. Ernst, 89–101; the 'Porno-Graphic' was known for its use of 'composographs', the faked picture that remains a staple of today's tabloids, 98; it was referred to by its editor Émile Gauvreau as the 'most sued paper in American journalism', 104.

99. Hunt, *Body Love,* 37–8. Sinclair was a personal friend of Macfadden's and a 'disciple' for a time. Despite his decidedly more politically

left of centre views, he wrote for Macfadden's *Physical Culture* and allowed the latter to use his name in promotions. Ibid., 29–30, 50–3.

100. He and Shaw were particularly in synch as proponents of nudism and vegetarianism, Ernst, 122. Sinclair was, like Macfadden, a crusader against venereal disease and in favour of sex education, Hunt, 52.

101. Shaw referred to Comstock as 'the celebrated Purity Witch Doctor', Ernst, 213. He was the inspirer and enforcer of the 'Comstock Act' of 1873 that prohibited the publishing and distribution of 'obscene material' (especially birth control literature) through the mail, see John D'Emilio and Estelle Freedman, *Intimate Matters: A History of Sexuality in America* (New York: Harper, 1988) *passim*. In 1905 Comstock obtained warrants for Macfadden's arrest in advance of the latter's second physical culture competition at Madison Square Garden. Posters of a man in a 'leopard skin breechcloth' and 'a dozen women in white union suits' were confiscated and Macfadden had to post bail of $1000 for his release from New York's Tenderloin police station, Ernst, 42–3. Shaw's interest in Macfadden is credible when considered alongside his fascination with the heroic T. E. Lawrence and with fascist and socialist strong-men leaders.

102. Jackson, *1890s*, 63. In the introduction for a new edition of Jackson's classic retrospective of the 1890s, Malcolm Bradbury refers to the 'quickening' or rather, the 'flowering, expression and decline of a single generation' within the space of that decade, and identifies it as a crucial trope for the twentieth century, Cresset, 1988; from the previous imprint, reissued with a new preface in 1927.

103. Ibid.

104. See Robert H. MacDonald, 'Reproducing the Middle-Class Boy: From Purity to Patriotism in the Boy's Magazines, 1892–1914', *Journal of Contemporary History*, 24 (1989): 519–39. MacDonald charts the shift from evangelical juvenile fiction to purity issues and on to a more 'practical and social' approach to young men's place in the nation and empire: 521, 524. This was a move that paralleled the trajectory of Scouting: 530–4.

105. Fitness and health publications existed as vehicles with very different trajectories for their publishers as compared to their readers who many times lived within vastly different material and ideological contexts. Nevertheless, the influence of the greater thrust of social narrative in this period upon the mass of readers cannot have been insignificant. Certainly, we can learn something from the failure of publishers to understand their readers, and in turn can relate their experience to the successes of more explicit corporatist and state methods that attempted to reform and control the consumer/citizen.

106. Nordau, 8. Shaw responded to this and specifically to Nordau's *Degeneration* in *The Sanity of Art: An Exposure of the Current Nonsense about Artists being Degenerate* (London: New Age Press, 1908), which

was first published as an essay in 1895 and then revised as a short book in the above edition.

107. He was no less harsh with respect to so-called French Naturalism or Realism, Nordau, *Conventional Lies*, 9–10. He was especially concerned with the social effect of literary models. The first chapter is entitled '*Mene, Tekel, Upharsin* (Thou art weighed in the balance and found wanting)'; from trans. note: pages unnumbered.

108. Or his novel, *A Strenuous Lover: A Romance of Natural Love's Vast Power*, 'Original Story by Bernarr Macfadden. Revised with the assistance of John R. Coryell' (New York and London: Physical Culture Publishing Co., 1904). In the latter, the hero Arthur Raymond, a woefully weak young man, overcomes his debilitation through physical culture methods. Pointedly, he does so without the help of an unsympathetically portrayed medical doctor. With his newly acquired muscles, he becomes an artist's model for 'Bernardo', a sculptor. Later he vanquishes the 'dark, handsome young' cad, Charles Morgan. Arthur's older brother is portrayed as a living metaphor for Arthur's own weakness, a kind of Hyde figure locked away as 'a hopeless maniac, confined to a padded room . . . [and] held by iron chains', 5. The poison of modern living is eradicated from his brother's body through fasting. In the end both brothers get the girl. Arthur is matched with his fellow physique model, Helen Bertram, whom he previously saved from the clutches of the unscrupulous Morgan, and former maniac Robert marries the girl next door, Amelia Winstead, who has in the mean time become a 'Physical Culture fiend'. Ibid., 458. Health and strength thus win out in Macfadden's genetically happy ending.

109. Oscar Wilde, 'The Critic as Artist'.

110. Peter Morton, *The Vital Science: Biology and the Literary Imagination, 1860–1900* (London: Unwin, 1984) 149. As demonstrated by the widespread fascination with and support of eugenicist ideas by Fabianists and others, including Shaw and Wells.

111. Ibid., 149.

112. His visits to a favourite haunt of the lower orders in Paris, the morgue, are likewise intriguing. Wilde found the waxworks horrible, and the morgue dignified by comparison. See Stokes, *Nineties*, 136–9.

113. Lovat Dickson, *H. G. Wells: His Turbulent Life and Times* (New York: Athenaeum, 1969) 41; R. Thurston Hopkins, *H. G. Wells: Personality, Character, Topography* (London: Cecil Palmer, 1922) 31.

114. Wells, *The Happy Turning: A Dream of Life* (London: Heinemann, 1945) 3.

115. As quoted in F. H. Doughty, *H. G. Wells: Educationist, A Study* (New York: Doran, 1927) 78.

116. Roslynn D. Haynes, *H. G. Wells: Discoverer of the Future; The Influence of Science on his Thought* (New York: New York University Press, 1980) 21.

117. Ibid., 21.

118. H. G. Wells, *Tono-Bungay* (London: Street & Smith, 1908) 387.
119. Ibid., 387.
120. Ibid., 168.
121. Ibid., 169.
122. Ibid., 169.
123. Ibid., 168.
124. Bladesover is the village where Wells' protagonist, the younger Ponderevo, grows up. It is described as a last vestige of a disappearing social order, and is probably patterned after Wells' birthplace at Bromley, Kent. Ibid., 8–17.
125. Tomlinson, 51.
126. *The Times*, 11 November 1891: front page advertisement; 2 May 1898: front page advertisement.
127. Viewed using a kinetoscope viewer, it was the precursor to early cinematic projection devices such as the Lumière brothers' *cinématographe* (1895) and 'Edison's Vitascope' (1896). It was invented by Thomas Armat and was yet another of the devices for which Edison took credit, David A. Cook, *A History of Narrative Film* (New York: Norton, 1981) 10–12. There are also two additional films of Sandow both copyrighted by American Mutoscope & Biograph and probably filmed around 18 December 1896; these are in the Library of Congress collection, see Kemp R. Niver and Bebe Bergsten (eds), *Early Motion Pictures: The Paper Print Collection in the Library of Congress* (Washington, DC: Library of Congress, 1985) 479, for a list of early physical culture films.
128. Cook, *Narrative Film*, 11.
129. Sandow was advertised as such in the programme for Koster and Bial's Music Hall during the 1893–4 season. This was the same theatre at which 'Edison's latest marvel', the vitascope, was premiered on 23 April 1896. Koster and Bial's was at 34th and West Broadway in New York; *Koster and Bial's Music Hall Program* (New York: Strauss and Klee, c. November–December 1893) pages unnumbered.
130. The tar-papered 'studio' within which the kinetograph was employed was likened to the 'Black Maria', a popular term for the police 'paddy wagon'. Dickson's studio was 25 ft by 30 ft and constructed on circular track for taking full advantage of the sun – its only means of lighting – through an opening in its roof, Cook, *Narrative Film*, 7. The emerging cinema depended upon existing cultural forms like the variety act or boxing match. The important basis of a developing consumer society was the 'experiencing subject' who was deemed desirous of the familiar or 'traditional' in order to make sense of such new cultural products. Miriam Hansen, 'Adventures of Goldilocks: Spectatorship, Consumerism and Public Life', *Camera Obscura* 22 (autumn 1990): 51–71. Building on her own work, and that of William Leach and Charles Musser, Hansen discusses the lack of fit between women's roles as major consumers of film products and as infrequent participants in the production of a masculine cinematic subjectivity. In her analysis she looks at some early boxing films that were presumably intended for the male gaze only.

131. Sandow's image was disseminated in the form of *cartes de visite*, postal and cigarette cards alongside a far greater number of depictions of women posed suggestively, as well as those featuring Sullivan, Corbett and others who were also known for their strength or physique.

3 SCULPTING THE HEROIC AND THE HOMOEROTIC

1. This was the same realm of monetary circulation in which 'industrial slaves', the images of physical culture models, pin-up figures and film icons also circulated. Their status as mere merchandise may be said to have been mediated only slightly by their transformation into 'living, circulating coinage', from Pierre Klossowski, 'La moneta vivente' (La monnaie vivante) Italian trans. C. Morena, *Il Piccolo Hans*, 13 (1977) 83, as quoted by Mario Perniola, 'Between Clothing and Nudity' ('Transiti – come si va pallo stesso allo stesso', Bologna, Capelli, 1985), English trans. Roger Friedman in *Zone: Fragments for a History of the Human Body, Part Two*, ed. Michel Feher *et al.* (Urzone, New York, 1989), 252.

2. As Marx noted, attaining the commodity form fundamentally promotes ease of exchange above all else. In the process, national or local characteristics are most often lost or diminished. Marx also commented on the need to distinguish within product genres, taste segments of population, and categories of nationality and gender. The desire for differentiation is in eternal opposition to the play of the elusive commodity form itself. In this dialectic, Sandow never forgot the power of emotional appeals, for example, those that played upon fears of social threats like degeneracy, or the seductive qualities of historical referents. Neither did he lose sight of the value of vivid personal examples.

3. The recognizable change was often the difference made by a bath and the donning of Salvation Army gear.

4. See Tagg, 117–52.

5. These were part of a macabre but not uncommon photographic genre in the Victorian period, usually taken so as to give the impression that the person was sleeping. They were most common during the period of the 'cased image' (1839–69) and less so later. O. Henry Mace, *Collectors' Guide to Early Photographs* (Radnor, PA: Wallace-Homestead Book Co., 1990) 40, 204. Interestingly, Roland Barthes described the photographic process itself as similar to the process of making a deathmask. See John Tagg, *The Burden of Representation: Essays on Photographies and Histories* (Amherst, MA, 1988) 1–2.

6. From which he hoped to create a 'Book of Beauty', 'such has rarely glorified the world', *Sandow's*, 4: 475.

7. *The Times*, 'Physical Culture Display', London (16 September 1901): 7.

8. Ibid.

9. The sculptures were often sold or awarded as prizes in competitions.

10. The resultingly inelegant piece was on display at the British Museum for a time. *Sandow's*, 7 (Nov. 1901) frontispiece: Sandow life-size cast statue then on display at South Kensington Museum (photo by Arthur Weston of London).

11. *Strand Magazine*, 22 (Oct. 1901): 461.

12. Ibid.

13. Ibid.

14. Ibid., 462.

15. In *Sandow's*, 8 (Jan. 1902), a new cover device was used, employing the reproduction of Sandow's head from the cast.

16. Ads for portraits of winners by Harrison and sons, 1/- each, post free 1/2, 45, St Martin's Lane, *Sandow's*, 76; Ad pages, *Sandow's*, 15 (106) (13 July 1905).

17. *Sandow's*, 8 (June 1902), photo of Fred Wells, 'A Sandow enthusiast's den' showing a young man seated with arms folded, three barbells and a wall over a fireplace decorated with a shrine of Sandow pictures and postcards, also a photo set from the competition on the back wall. Ibid., 455. See also a photo sent in of a kind of photographic shrine to physical culture and Sandow, opposite a shot of Sandow, 'A Model for Youthful Aspirants', *Sandow's*, 17 (15) (11 Oct. 1906): 460–1.

18. *Sandow's*, 17 (15) (11 Oct. 1906), cover, composite of Sandow readers.

19. Editorial, *Vim*, 2 (11) (Nov. 1904): 325.

20. This was highlighted in reference to an article by Galton in the *Daily Chronicle*, in which he complained of the difficulty of getting 'opportunities of studying the nude figures of our countryman in mass', *Sandow's* (Oct. 1903): 167–9. Galton none the less 'often watched crowds bathe, as in the Serpentine, with a critical eye, and always came to the conclusion that they were less shapely than many of the dark-coloured peoples whom I have seen', 168.

21. Ibid., 168.

22. Ibid.

23. Ibid.

24. Sarah Kent, 'Pleasure Principles', *Time Out*, London (16–22 May 1985): 14–17.

25. *Vim*, 15 December 1902.

26. See *Health and Vim*, 'Reader's Parliament' and 'Vim Parliament' (1906–11). Advertisement, 'The Great Physical Development Competition', *Health and Vim*, 7 (1) (Jan. 1908): 16.

27. *Vim* was one of the most successful and long-lived magazines of the twentieth century, changing and adapting to shifts in audience tastes and surviving well into the 1970s.

28. *Vim*, 1 (1): 1.

29. Nascent health culture entrepreneurs often linked hydropathy or other body cleansing contraptions with the Salvationists' emphasis upon frequent bathing, as did Salvation Army Captain Thomas McCallum, whose article 'Disorders of the Liver', *Vim*, 1 (6) (15 May 1903) offset a veiled testimonial noting the army's purchase of several Gem baths for use in the care of derelicts: 160–1.

30. *Vim* (15 December 1902): 2.
31. The title of a book by Macfadden, published in 1906.
32. At various times Macfadden claimed to have a combined US and British circulation of over a quarter of a million, Ernst, 24. On front covers of his British publication *Physical Development*, 1 (3) (June 1901) and 2 (4) (Jan. 1902) he claimed combined 'paid circulation' of 252 000 and 300 000 respectively. In editorials he claimed that his two US publications had total circulations of 'nearly' 250 000. Such assertions were often boldly emblazoned on the magazine's cover. His circulation claims were sometimes extrapolations of the total number of readers based on the presumption that there were five readers for each copy sold, Ernst, 24. At least eight other fitness and health magazines were published in the US around the turn of the century. Macfadden followed up *Physical Culture* (US) with *Health and Beauty* (US) and a weekly 'road to success' magazine titled *The Cry of Justice* which failed. His *Physical Development* (UK) was also one of several publications that sought to cash in on the presumed new interest in the healthy body.
33. Sandow's system in particular was recommended by many leading medical men of his day. Testimonials to the efficacy of Sandow's system were given by Sir Lauder Brunton (discoverer of blood pressure diagnostics), and over 180 other prominent physicians and surgeons. *The Power of Evidence*, 16–19.
34. Conan Doyle was of course interested in a wide variety of unusual movements and belief systems, and eventually fell prey to mediums and other charlatans of the supernatural.
35. The *Globe* was also quoted, Webster, *The Iron Game*, 345.
36. John Hargreaves, *Sport, Power and Culture: A Social and Historical Analysis of Popular Sports in Britain* (New York: St Martin's, 1986) 51.
37. Britain not only sold cloth to the world, but also was a major exporter of nude erotic photographs. 'George Cannon, William Dugdale and Henry Hayler were world leaders among the entrepreneurs of pornography'. See Ronald K. Hyam, *Empire and Sexuality: The British Experience* (Manchester University Press, 1990) 3, ff. 20. Although Hyam's approach and interpretation have been criticized, his expansive research makes his work an invaluable source of data at the very least. Hayler was perhaps the most successful and well organized pornographer of his day. During a police raid in 1874, 130 248 photographs and 5000 postcards, many of Hayler, his wife and two sons, were confiscated. Ibid.
38. Physical culture media often crossed presumed boundary lines of taste and morality; it was not until much later, and then only in the US, that any of its publishers were prosecuted under emerging pornography laws. And even then, it was in connection with 'smutty' talk about sex education and reproduction, especially that related to birth control.
39. Huardel appeared before Sir Albert de Rutzer, 5 November 1903; the case was publicized as a headline story: '27 550 POST-CARDS SEIZED' in *The Poster and Postcard Collector*, 12 (Dec. 1903): 319.

40. Ibid., 320.
41. Ibid., 348. The only magazine which publicized the case to any great extent was run by Huardel himself. *The Poster and Postcard Collector* was founded by Huardel in 1899.
42. Ibid., 349.
43. Ibid. (Sept. 1903): 222, 350–1.
44. The request for photos of physical culture children and the publication of semi-nude photos of young girls might also be read as possibly appealing to prurient tastes. See *Sandow's* (1889–1903) *passim*, and an advertisement for infants' food, depicting nude girls, reproduced from the *Graphic* (19 Dec. 1903) in Thomas Richard, *The Commodity Culture of Victorian England*, 242.
45. Despite ample evidence to the contrary, the typical understanding of fashion has been one that has exempted men from its power. For example, men were also the focus of rational dress rhetoric, since they too often wore restrictive garments like corsets in order to conform to an ideal figure. Advertisements for men's corsets were common in military publications. See Anne Hollander, *Seeing through Clothes* (New York: Avon, 1980) especially 360–2.
46. Ibid., 7.
47. *Sandow's*, 8 (March 1902): 165–72. Frontispiece: S. Sebastian 'The Christian Apollo' by Guido Reni, *Sandow's*, 8 (April 1902).
48. *Sandow's*, 8 (Jan. 1902); 'Sandow interviewed in America': 56–8.
49. Ibid., 56.
50. Ibid.
51. Ibid.
52. Ibid.
53. James Lees-Milne, *The Enigmatic Edwardian: The Life of Reginald, 2nd Viscount Esher* (London: Sidgwick & Jackson, 1988) 35.
54. An important development in Britain was the passage of the Contagious Diseases (CD) Criminal Law Amendment Act 1885, which was a telling example of the expansion of state surveillance over the body. This was matched by the 27 May Recidivist Act in France in that same year. This law helped to promote the Bertillon system (*bertillonage*) which consisted of the use of several skeletal measurements as a means of identifying criminals.
55. The larger Act, which included the Labouchère Amendment that made all homosexual acts in public or private illegal, had been meant as an answer to increasing concerns with female prostitution and fears of 'white slavery'. In a curious attempt at gender equality, the Labouchère addition evinced on the one hand a desire to correct the gender double-standard of the CD Acts of two decades earlier, which had allowed any woman to be apprehended under suspicion of soliciting. They were repealed in 1886. The earlier Acts had exempted men from those same provisions. The amendment to the law of 1885 certainly provided a corrective to the bias that Josephine Butler and others had campaigned against. By dealing implicitly with male prostitution, the result was not equality of treatment for men and women, but an overall tightening of the state's grip over the bodily

experiences of all its citizenry. The form and rationale behind the CD Acts were, like much of the discussion that fuelled physical culture, directly influenced by army statistics on venereal disease and public discourse on the 'immoral' body, particularly that of the soldier. See Edward M. Spiers, *The Army and Society, 1815–1914* (London: Longman, 1980). 'By 1862, 25 787 men, or 33 per cent of home-based troops, were hospitalized on account of venereal disease', 162. Captain Pilkington Jackson's report on the Soldier's Institutes highlighted the impression of enlisted men's immorality, and 'convinced the government and *The Times* that the soldier must be protected against his passions', note 68. See also Hyam, *Empire and Sexuality*.

56. Ed Cohen, *Talk on the Wilde Side: Toward a Genealogy of a Discourse on Male Sexualities* (London: Routledge, 1993) 195.

57. Also see Richard Ellman, 'A Victorian Love Affair', *New York Review of Books*, 24 (13) (1977): 6–10; Geoffrey Gorer, 'The British National Character in the Twentieth Century', *Annals of the American Academy of Political and Social Sciences*, 370 (March 1967): 74–81; and Nandy, *Intimate Enemy*, on Wilde as a threat to the mythos underpinning British colonialism, 43–6.

58. For more on the pervasive dialectic between the 'straight' and gay in sport, see Pronger, *The Arena of Masculinity*.

59. Wilde certainly admired young male athletes, for example, his comparison of a runner's leg to a poem, as quoted in Ellman, 183. His own sports career as an oarsman was nipped in the bud by his early dismissal from the Magdalen barge. During a visit to Harvard University, he especially enjoyed the Harvard gymnasium, and encouraged the student body to conjoin aesthetics and athletics by placing a Greek statue in the building, assuring them that there was more to the aesthetic movement than 'Kneebreeches and sunflowers'. He subsequently presented them with a plaster cast of Praxiteles, which was still in place in 1892 but has since disappeared; Richard Ellmann, *Oscar Wilde*, 39.

60. As Weeks notes, both the Empire and Alhambra theatres were also known cruising spots for male prostitutes. For more on the male side of Victorian prostitution see Weeks, *Coming Out: Homosexual Politics in Britain, from the Nineteenth Century to the Present* (London: Quartet, 1977) 37; and *Sex, Politics and Society* (New York: Longman, 1981) 113; also Rupert Croft-Cooke, *Feasting with Panthers* (London, 1967) 265; and Hyam, *Empire and Sexuality*, 67–9.

61. 'Some Types of Artist's Models', *Sandow's*, 15 (106) (13 July 1905): 90–2.

62. This meeting with Aubrey Hunt of the Royal Academy occurred as Sandow emerged from the sea at the Lido in Venice. Afterwards the artist engaged him to model for a painting of the Roman gladiatorial games. Sandow later acquired Hunt's painting and hung it on the wall of Sandow's School, St James Street, London. See Chapman, *Sandow*, 19–20.

63. For example, Winckelmann's death at the hands of a male 'hustler'.

64. See Weeks on the CD Acts 1885 pertaining to homosexuality, the

Cleveland Street male prostitution scandal (1889–90) and the Wilde trial (1895): *Sex, Politics and Society*.

65. F. W. Haslam, 'The Greek Ideal: Duty and Beauty' lecture reprinted in *Sandow's*, 103 (22 June 1905): 636–9.

66. E. K. Sedgwick, *The Epistemology of the Closet*.

67. See C. A. Tripp, *The Homosexual Matrix* (New York: Meridian, 1987), especially 'The Origins of Heterosexuality', 33–61. Sexual practices and identities linked explicitly with sexual behaviour can be understood as floating phenomena not too tightly tied to any single training process, category of readerly taste or gender identity. The double binds and contradictions pervading the contextual and circumstantial practice of gender as well as that of sexual object choice and practice result, in fact, from attempts to assert a practically impossible model of stable self-definition. Not that gendered and other identities do not work, but rather that they tend to be based upon rules and organizing principles that are easily transgressed and continually broken.

68. Jeffrey Weeks, *Sex, Politics and Society: The Regulation of Sexuality since 1800* (London: Longman, 1981) 108–17.

69. Like the Oxford *The Spirit Lamp* under Douglas's editorship and another Oxford undergraduate journal, *The Chameleon* and *The Quorum: A Magazine of Friendship*, *The Artist* catered to a homosexual readership. It was a product of the short-lived movement that preceded Wilde's trials and imprisonment; see Kains-Jackson, 'The New Chivalry', *The Artist* (April 1894), as quoted by Regina Gagnier, *Idylls of the Marketplace: Oscar Wilde and the Victorian Public* (Stanford University Press, 1986) 160; originally cited in Reade, *Sexual Heretics*, 313–19. For some additional background see Ellman, *Oscar Wilde*, 386–92, and Fussell, *The Great War and Modern Memory*.

70. See Fussell, *The Great War and Modern Memory*, 283–8, on the links between homosexual activist 'Uranian' poets of the 1890s and First World War poets. In its pure form, the ethos of the Uranians was that of chaste male love, as found in Walter Pater's essay on Johann Winckelmann (1867). Also see Timothy D'Arch Smith, *Love in Earnest* (London, 1970) and Weeks, *Coming Out*, 47–56.

71. Kains-Jackson's view evidenced an odd anti-militarism that required the existence of an actual stable military defence along with the cultural retention of some elements of an abstracted military social order. See Cecil D. Eby, *The Road to Armageddon: The Martial Spirit in English Popular Literature, 1870–1914* (Durham, NC: Duke University Press, 1987).

72. See Waugh, 'The Third Body', in Gever *et al.* (eds), *Queer Looks* (Routledge, 1993), on the use of gender paradigmatics in the construction of gay male film subjectivity and the triangle of the 'ephebe', versus the 'he-man' mediated by the invisible consumer, that of the 'desiring body of the gay producer-spectator' who was rarely visible within the frame of the photograph, 141–2.

73. Wilde's tour under the auspices originally of D'Oyly Carte's presentation of Gilbert and Sullivan's *Patience* in the US took place before

John L. Sullivan's grand eight-month tour. Michael Isenberg argues that no 'one, politician, entertainer, or other performer, had traveled America to such a degree' as Sullivan did in 1883. Isenberg, 144. In fact, Wilde's 9 January to 13 October 1882 tour throughout most of the US and parts of Canada was longer if not more extensive than Sullivan's.

74. It has been argued that it was Wilde's low level of discretion rather than his actual private pastimes that was the key to his downfall, Nandy, *Intimate Enemy*, 44. It must also be pointed out that Wilde had foolishly, if not heroically, taken on the Marquis of Queensberry, and played the part of the aggressor. After all, Wilde was a married and successful author. It would perhaps be too much to argue that his persona was so inherently radical that it could not have continued to be absorbed by the dominant order. Whatever might have happened had Wilde behaved differently is not so important as the completed trajectory of what he came to represent. It is here that his value in understanding the genesis of physical culture is most apparent.

75. This was attainable through the pursuit of Grecian or simply common-sensical ideals of moderate behaviour accompanied by vigorous exercise. Which he later came to articulate as the complete excellence of function in thought, morality and body (all equalling a kind of 'honourable' beauty).

76. With the end of the Boer war and the triumph of Mafeking, BP's heroicization provides us with a particularly useful figure in contextualizing physical culture in relation to the sexual norms of the reformed public school and British military. BP was a product of both. The YMCA and Scouting were often depicted as successful applications of 'physical culture' ideals, and there were many actual links between various physical culture magazines, clubs and the two movements.

77. Like Wilde and Sandow, he was a wunderkind of self-promotion who made the most of the expanding media circuits of the turn of the century. His entry into the military was as much a search for glory as a latter-day Christian knight as it was a pursuit of a stable income. The year 1871 had been a crucial one for BP, since it was then that purchase was abolished. For someone with his ambitions and lack of family funds Cardwell's reforms transformed the military into a vehicle for social mobility, a career no longer only for the rich but 'a proper profession for men with larger capabilities and smaller private incomes'. His chances for success were further helped by increasing fears of invasion. Chesney's *Battle of Dorking*, describing the successful invasion of Britain, was a 'runaway success'. Amid fears of not only Germany but also Russia and her intentions on the Northwest Frontier and in the eastern Mediterranean there was the more subtle threat of US industrial growth. Tim Jeal, *The Boy-Man: The Life of Lord BP* (New York: Morrow, 1990) 39.

78. BP admired the bodies and strength of 'men who are men' (thus assuming a great many men who were not men) in Canada, Norway,

Australia, South Africa, and among the hillsmen of Kashmir – also the 'well-built naked wonderfully made bodies' of men washing together during the great war. Jeal, 92. Also see Hyam, *Empire and Sexuality*, 200–11.

79. Jeal, 84.
80. Ibid., 90. Which he presumably saw at a Royal Academy painting exhibition in 1928. In 1923 and 1924 he had similarly been offended by the number of female nudes in the exhibition. Any exemplar of 'clean manliness' would certainly want to avoid such accoutrements of a dirty age, Ibid. Jeal states that clean was an adjective that BP used frequently in association with young men but never with women. Walt Whitman and T. E. Lawrence also made this linkage between young male bodies and cleanliness. Gen. Gordon was also known to wash the poor boys who were the object of his philanthropy. See Hyam on Gordon, H. M. Stanley, and Gen. Sir Hector MacDonald to name a few who shared BP's tastes, *Empire and Sexuality*, *passim*.
81. Jeal, 90–1, quoted from *Rovering to Success*, 111.
82. In 1919, he made a diary reference to A. H. Tod's collection of naked boys, 'Tod's photos of naked boys and trees etc. Excellent.' Tod was housemaster at Charterhouse, BP's alma mater. Tod's album of 'figure studies' were destroyed during the mid-1960s. Tod was a classicist and Jeal speculates that his boys may have been posing as Myron's Discobolus and throwing javelins or, in line with BP's tree reference, 'clambering among the branches like dryads', Ibid. In a later letter to Tod, BP wrote about starting a troop at Charterhouse, saying he would be coming up again to see the football and mentioned the possibility that he 'might get a further look at those wonderful photographs of yours?', Ibid. The photos have been compared by Jeal to those in publications such as *The Artist* whose illustrations and poetry appealed to men with homoerotic tastes. In the same period, Henry Scott Tuke's large paintings of naked boys were being hung in the Royal Academy. Tuke was gay, as were many of his patrons, but 'his pictures were art and therefore safe from censure', Ibid., 93. For more on homosexuality in the period see D'Arch Smith, *Love in Earnest*.
83. In a similar tone he advised Scoutmasters to encourage 'self-expression, instead of disciplining . . . by police methods of repression', from *The Scouter* (1934): 262. Jeal, 92.
84. Galton's comments on the shapelier bodies of subject peoples point to an enduring characteristic of the physical culture press in terms of its comparison-based consumerist dialogue and its own peculiar articulation of class and race as national and imperial properties in relation to bodily ideals, *Sandow's* (Oct. 1903): 168.
85. Edwardian adventure writers like 'Buchan and Sapper make their only sympathetically presented women indistinguishable from young men, slim hipped, athletically minded, and so forth'. Hyam, 85. Also see R. Osborne, *Clubland Heroes* (London, 1953): 101. For a woman to become even the temporary pseudo-hero meant in some sense becoming de-sexed. In literature, the 'heroine' was often boy-like, in-between childhood and adulthood, de-eroticized and in many

ways unwomanly. The category of the 'boy', which might also contain the pre-pubescent woman, was more in-between than 'purely' masculine. Here, the impoverished structure of binary gender roles and the fact of male dominance were underscored by the appropriation of independence, risk-taking and other qualities as strictly male well in advance of any individual's settling upon an adult gendered and sexual identity.

86. Waugh, 'Third Body', 141.

87. At British schools for young women in this period, students were certainly no less competitive than were their male counterparts. Like male public school masters, headmistresses strove to maintain what they understood to be natural gender dispositions. The very need for these dispositions' maintenance, however, pointed to the fact that the relationship of children generally to games playing was not strictly determined by such so-called natural biological categories. In practice many other factors besides the actual playing of games or taking up of exercise were at work. One of these was the continued 'cloistered' nature of women's sports as opposed to the very public enactment of men's sports. See Roberta J. Park, 'Sport, Gender and Society in a Transatlantic Perspective', *British Journal of Sport History*, 2 (1) (May 1985): 23. Also see Sheila Fletcher, 'The Making and Breaking of a Tradition: Women's Physical Education in England, 1880–1980', *British Journal of Sport History*, 2 (1) (May 1985).

88. See Park, 'Sport, Gender', 5–28; Steven A. Reiss, 'Sport and the Redefinition of American Middle-class Masculinity', *International Journal of the History of Sport*, 8 (1) (May 1991); Honey, *Tom Brown's Universe*; Mangan, *Athleticism*; and Rotundo, 'Body and Soul'. An issue that perplexed many during the age of physical culture was the possibility that 'sexual boundaries might become blurred', Park, 6. This points to the important question of how the sustained and pronounced rise in women's sporting activities during this period was explained and rationalized by a culture still riven by strict gendered codes of representation and behavior. Whereas similar qualities of self-abnegation and 'gentlemanly' sporting behavior were encouraged, the goals of headmistresses were different from those of headmasters. For boys, the moral qualities of the self-regulating gentleman were sought in the struggle of the playing field as a means of making respectable and productive men. For girls, the newly recognized needs of complete intellectual and physical development using similar if not the same methods were more consciously tied to fears of racial degeneration as considered in terms of the feminine role of reproduction. Katherine McCrone, 'Play Up! Play Up! And Play the Game! Sport at the Late Victorian Public School', *Journal of British Studies*, xxiii (2) (spring, 1984).

89. See Weeks on guardsmen as male prostitutes and the class complexities of male sexuality, 112–14.

90. *Sandow's*, 1 (July 1898): 5.

91. Ibid.

92. Ibid.

93. Ibid., 6.
94. Men were presumably attracted to physical culture as a way to be more manly, to act out 'innate' martial and associational desires. Others such as women and children were seen to be in more need of exercise in a scientific or practical sense. Female bodies were treated simultaneously as mechanisms of male power and as fleshly objects of desire. In sharp contrast, pictures of boxers or soldiers in military postcard series depicted men instrumentally as heroic and active in a manner that de-emphasized possible erotic readings. Exceptions in this period would be Baron von Gloeden's images of nude boys posed in neo-classical settings. Even these, however, when compared to his depictions of women indicate the presumption of a dominant male gaze within which boys and women are crucially constructed as 'non-men'. For more on von Gloeden, see Ulrich Pohlmann, *Wilhelm von Gloeden: Sehnsucht nach Arkadien* (Berlin: Nishen Verlag, 1987).

4 IMPERIAL MIRRORS

1. At the same moment, other reform phenomena such as Scouting, the YMCA, and Karl Fischer's *Wandervogel* began (1901–4). The greater youth movement spread throughout Germany, Switzerland and Austria during the years 1910–13. In Britain, the phenomenon was matched by similar groups such as the Boys' Brigades (1882) and the Boys' Empire League (1900).
2. As BP's ideas concerning 'real men' demonstrated, the framework of the heroic provided a symbolic basis for rationalizing not only gender ideals but also their crucial relationship to race and capital. Here, the 'common body' – one beyond all difference – had its place in appeals aimed at women. Class and race were in this respect more critical determinants of the ability to afford a certain wardrobe and a type of body, which in turn influenced gender's expression and how it would be read. A wealthy high-born woman such as Empress Elisabeth of Austria could thus become, in practice, a more exemplary consumer of transformative physical culture than could a male labourer with too many mouths to feed. Elisabeth of Austria was the epitome of a certain type of the modern female consumer. Prone to extreme diets and health cures, she had her own gymnasium and was obsessed with appearing younger than her age. She may, in fact, have been anorexic. See Edmond Taylor, *The Fall of the Dynasties: the Collapse of the Old Order, 1905–1922* (New York: Doubleday, 1963: 88–91); and Robert K. Massie, *The Last Courts of Europe: A Royal Family Album, 1860–1914* (New York: Greenwich, 1981).
3. For more on images of colonial women see Alloula Malek, *Le Harem colonial: images d'un sous-érotisme* (Paris, 1981); and Jenny Sharpe, *Allegories of Empire: The Figure of the Woman in the Colonial Text* (Minneapolis, MN, 1993).

4. As Jeal argues, BP's prejudice was based more upon gender conformity than it was upon the colour of one's skin. Thus his preoccupation with 'making men'. See Jeal, 163. In this fashion Jeal lets BP off the hook with regard to Michael Rosenthal's accusation of racism in *The Character Factory* (1988). That the founder of the Boy Scouts called Africans 'niggers' or 'savages' commented that blacks may be 'brothers, but they are certainly not men', BP, *The Downfall of Prempeh* (1896) 56–7; Jeal, 162, 611, fn. 14.

5. These included the first Boer war (1879–81), the Zulu war (1878–9) and the Egyptian campaign (1881–2).

6. Cunningham, *Volunteer*, 103–5.

7. Reader, *At Duty's Call: A Study in Obsolete Patriotism* (Manchester University Press, 1988) 10.

8. Reader, 11, as quoted from John K. Dunlop's *The Development of the British Army 1899–1914* (London: Methuen, 1938) as (5) 101. Over the 33 months of the war, 365 693 Imperial troops and 82 742 colonial soldiers served; 22 000 died in South Africa. Thomas Pakenham, *The Boer War* (New York: Random, 1979) 607.

9. At the same time, a good many upper- and middle-class men became members of the Imperial Yeomanry. Overall, the military remained suspicious of volunteers from any class; neither the working classes nor the gentlemen of the yeomanry were to prove very decisive in the Boer conflict.

10. Ten years on, at the beginning of the First World War, the circulation of small magazines and journals like those of the fitness media reached a circulation peak. It was only after the four ensuing years of conflict that the daily press became firmly established as a kind of daily necessity. The newspaper as a 'necessity' has by no means ever become such for more than a minority of the population. Still, by 1918, the average daily appetite for news had increased substantially, whereas the demand for small magazines may be said to have correspondingly declined.

11. The 1903 *Report of the Royal Commission on Physical Training (Scotland)* (republished by Sandow with his own comments as a supplement to the July 1903 issue) included a testimonial letter in support of Sandow from Col. Fox, then HM Inspector of Military Gymnasia. The report itself contained a more or less favourable assessment of the 'Sandow System' as one of six methods considered by the commission. Sandow, of course, disputed this in his accompanying critique. See *Sandow's* (July 1903); supplement 'Extracts from the Report of the Royal Commission on Physical Training (Scotland) . . . with Comments by Eugen Sandow', 24. The others were the so-called Swedish, German, Swiss, French and American systems. It was an indication of Sandow's success that his was the only system considered that was identified with an individual and viewed as *the* representative British method. As Sandow went to some pains to refute, the commission found the 'concentrated attention' required by his system, valuable as it was for adults, unsuitable for children – who were the focus of the study.

12. Such self-identification depended upon the formation of links between quite different ideologies, for example nationalism and race, within vastly different class contexts. It also relied upon the identification of 'others' as being outside the group. On nation and race as 'imagined' categories, and the articulation of feelings of community in relation to perceptions of boundaries, see Benedict Anderson, *Imagined Communities: Reflections on the Origin and Spread of Nationalism* (London: Verso, 1983) 15–16. R. Miles, 'Recent Marxist Theories of Nationalism and the Issue of Racism', *British Journal of Sociology*, 38 (1) (1987): 24–43, 26–7.

13. *Sandow's Magazine of Physical Culture*, 117 (Sept. 1905), 'The Return of Mr. Sandow', (28 Sept. 1905): 343–4. As quoted from the *Daily News*, 19 Sept. 1905. The event was also covered by the *Morning Standard* and the *Globe*.

14. *Sandow's Magazine*, 117 (Sept. 1905).

15. Newer types such as explorers and literary figures were already common by this period in the West. However, image-producing technologies such as the cinema had yet to transform or substantially alter the way in which the mass of individuals around the world saw celebrities or constructed exemplary public figures within local contexts. In this sense, Sandow was like the later cinema 'star' which synthesized the qualities of a fictional or mythic character with the figure of a real person. See James Monaco, *How to Read a Film: The Art, Technology, Language, History, and Theory of Film and Media* (New York: Oxford University Press, 1981) 220–3, for a discussion of the difference between 'actors' and 'stars', and the impact of film upon the larger phenomena of celebrity in relation to shared cultural values. See also Monaco *et al.* (eds) *Celebrity: Who Gets It, How They Use it, and Why It Works* (New York: Delta, 1978). In the interwar years such cults of celebrity remained focused mostly on white Europeans.

16. Monaco, 221–2.

17. Ibid., 345.

18. See David Chapman, Preface, *Adonis* (London: GMP: 1989).

19. *Sandow's*, 7 (August 1901): 125–6. The picture was found after the attack at Diamond Hill, 12 June 1900. The Lance-Sergeant had been advised to send the picture to the magazine by a fellow NCO, Sergeant Guy, who had once been employed as an instructor by Sandow. Ibid., 126.

20. It was reproduced again, *Sandow's* (Oct. 1904): 239; in hopes 'that if the original owner be alive he may be able to recognize the photo ... [and] we should be pleased to hear from him and substitute a later photo of Mr. Sandow for his lost treasure', 241.

21. 'Notes of the Month', *Sandow's*, 8 (Feb. 1902): 142, Boer prisoners at Diyatalawa camp are shown being led through exercises by one of their own.

22. See Geoffrey C. Ward, *The Maharajas* (Chicago, IL: Stonehenge, 1983) 122; I am grateful to S. B. Cook for bringing the latter to my attention. In Ward's *Maharajas*, Sandow is described as 'the famed American

strong man'. Although Sandow toured the US extensively, he was always domiciled in Britain. In examining the circulation of his image, the commodification of physical culture can be seen to have been international in spite of its linguistic domination by English-speaking publishers. The English language was a competing if not dominant force in India. Both Sandow's picture and the cast owned by the Gaekar were images that stood apart from any particular language or text.

23. The first photos from the Empire and Muscle contest were published in *Sandow's*, 10 (Feb. 1903).

24. As argued by Christopher P. Wilson, in 'The Rhetoric of Consumption: Mass-Market Magazines and the Demise of the Gentle Reader, 1880–1920', in Richard Wightman Fox and T. Jackson Lears (eds), *The Culture of Consumption: Critical Essays In American History, 1880–1920* (New York: Pantheon, 1983) 41–64; *McClure's* and the *Ladies Home Journal*, among other publications in the US, used a confident magazine rhetorical voice which intimated the possession of the 'inside dope', Ibid., 57. Like physical culture magazines, this and an ability to restate a thing in 'fifty different ways' (Ibid., 49) were crucial factors in the passage of the magazine product from 'an inanimate printed thing' to 'a vital need in the personal lives of its readers'. Ibid., 51. However, in physical culture media, the role of the reader as manipulated outsider looking in on 'real' life was complicated by the presence of participatory schemes and the basic instability of a still maturing mass publication market. Such contests and the submission of photos and testimonials went a little beyond the 'gossip-like intimacy' of the *Journal*. Ibid., 59. None the less, the ultimate passivity of the reader was assumed in both cases, as actual 'knowing' was always kept just out of reach. Thus the neediness of the consumer was ever highlighted over her or his promised or actual autonomy as a judge and buyer of products and services, Ibid., 63–4.

25. For example, the fact that Sandow might be mistaken as American or Swedish hints at one of many ways in which physique culture could be reshaped and appropriated to accommodate the requirements of local cultures and environments.

26. Debi, *Jibaner jharapata* [Scattered Leaves of Life], as quoted in John Rosselli, 'The Self-Image of Effeteness: Physical Education and Nationalism in Nineteenth-Century Bengal', *Past and Present*, 86 (Feb. 1980): 121–48, 123 and 127.

27. Similar sentiments were expressed by chemist and nationalist P. C. Ray. See Ashis Nandy, *The Intimate Enemy: Loss and Recovery of Self under Colonialism* (New York: Oxford University Press, 1989) 47.

28. Rosselli, 130–1. Founded by Atindranath Basu. Less politically oriented practices of body culture continued right up until independence. Sandow remained an exemplar for those such as Ramesh S. Balsekar who was posing and preaching physical culture in Bombay on the eve of the Second World War. Balsekar was a student of K. V. Iyer, of Bangalore, and Lawrence Woodford, author of *Physical Ideal-*

ism and the Art of Posing. Balsekar was not only the winner of the 'All-India Body Beautiful Competition' in 1938, but also one of Great Britain's 'ten most perfectly developed men'. See Balsekar, *Streamlines* (Bombay, 1940). For more on the longer-term tradition of sport in the subcontinent, see M. N. Pearson, 'Recreation in Mughal India', *British Journal of Sports History*, 1 (3) (Dec. 1984) 335–50.

29.   It was feared that the Viceroy's proposal for a more efficient administrative structure for the unwieldy Bengal (including nearby Bihar, Chota Nagpur and Orissa) was effectively a strategy of divide and rule which would roughly separate the territory along Muslim and Hindu lines. More restrained indigenous protests were to no avail and it was clear by the middle of 1905 that partition was unstoppable. In consequence, British goods were boycotted and violence erupted throughout newly reconstituted western Bengal. Newspapers were suppressed, editors jailed and the government began indiscriminately rounding-up possible subversives for interrogation. See Daniel Argov, *Moderates and Extremists in the Indian Nationalist Movement, 1883–1920* (London: Asia Publishing House, 1967); Leonard A. Gordon, *Bengal: The Nationalist Movement, 1874–1940* (New York: Columbia University Press, 1974); O. P. Goyal, *Studies in Modern Indian Political Thought, vol. I, The Moderates and the Extremists* (Allahabad: Kitab Mahal, 1964).

30.   *Sandow's*, 81 (19 Jan. 1905): 57.

31.   Ibid.

32.   It was also sometimes used as a proper name, a tribute to the Pahlavi speaking parthians. Ibid.

33.   Ibid.

34.   Probably not in this particular raja's case, since he was fairly frugal in his expenditure.

35.   Rosselli, *passim.*

36.   *Sandow's*, 80 (12 Jan. 1905), 'Eugen Sandow in India'; 'Following on his successful campaign in the cause of PC in South Africa (particulars in Oct. 1904 issue)': 35–7.

37.   Ibid.

38.   *Sandow's*, 124 (16 Nov. 1905), 'Physical Culture in India', 547.

39.   See J. A. Hobson, *Imperialism: A Study*, and Winfried Baumgart, *Imperialism: The Idea and Reality of British and French Colonial Expansion, 1880–1914* (Oxford University Press, 1982) 95.

40.   The instructors of his system were often former military men. However, Sandow's methods were in fact never formally adopted by the army.

41.   Ibid., 9. The *Bushido* ethic was the code adhered to by the Samurai. It was popularly presented as an Eastern counterpart to Western chivalry and as the key to Japanese military success. This was articulated in the English version of Inazo Nitobe's *Bushido: The Soul of Japan* (New York: G. P. Putnam, 1905). Nitobe's treatise was also translated into Mahratti, German, Polish and other languages besides English. According to Nitobe, it was read by Theodore Roosevelt and given to his friends: preface, v–vi.

42. E. E. Adams, 'Japanese Coal Heavers', *Vim*, 2 (11) (Nov. 1904): 333; according to Adams, they accomplished great feats of lifting by virtue of their rice diet, and were 'probably the happiest and most contented poor that one may find in the world'.
43. *Sandow's*, 8 (Feb. 1902): 223–4.
44. Ibid., 9 (Aug. 1902): 107–11.
45. Sharkey, a well-known prizefighter, the former noting afterwards, 'that is the way I threw Ajax the Policeman'. Ibid., 15 (82) (26 Jan. 1905): 98.
46. *Vim*, 4 (1) (Jan. 1905): 4, Professor V. Smith announced that the 'Anglo-Japanese Institute of Self-Defence and Physical Development will open at 3 Vernon Place, Bloomsbury', arguing that proof of Japanese wrestling's 'usefulness . . . is witnessed by the success of the Japanese arms in the present war with Russia'. A previous advertisement had been one for literature on the sport from a firm in Rochester, New York, *Vim*, 3 (12) (Dec. 1904).
47. *Sandow's*, 15 (104) (25 June 1905).
48. *Sandow's*, 15 (117) (28 Sept. 1905).
49. By Sir Ian Hamilton, mentioned in *Sandow's*, 15 (126) (30 Nov. 1905): 591.
50. For example, a favourable review of *Japanese Physical Training* in *Physical Education*, 1 (1) (Feb. 1904): 20–1; or a reprint of a MacDonald Smith article from the *Daily Mail* noting the 'Proper ideas upon the evil influence of fear' found in Japan, *Vim*: 287. See 'We have elevated sports as the Golden Calf . . . we assemble by the thousands to see athletics – not to become athletes ourselves', in 'Monthly Notes', *Physical Education*, 8; and in an editorial lamenting the 'growing love for watching, instead of playing football', *Vim*, 2 (10) (Oct. 1904): 289.
51. 'Japanese Health Culture', *Sandow's*, 17 (10) (6 Sept. 1906): 294–5, ju-jitsu ad, *Sandow's* (16 Dec. 1906): vii.
52. Webster, *Iron Game*, 345.
53. Viscount Esher, *National Strategy* (London, 1904): 6–7.
54. 'In Ancient Rome', *Health and Vim*, 6 (12) (Dec. 1907): 651–4.
55. See R. Ed. Pengelly, 'The Physical Culture of the Hebrews', *Sandow's*, 7 (Sept. 1901): 202–6, with an illustrative photo of Michelangelo's Moses, seeking to answer the question of 'how they came to have such virility'. Ibid., 206. For the Jew as 'unmanly' see Mosse, *Toward the Final Solution: A History of European Racism* (London: Shocken, 1978). The use of the Jewish example was not without its anti-semitic cast. In a related cartoon some months later, a small shirtless boy is seen with his father, the latter depicted with a hook nose and earring, complaining in a presumably 'Jewish' accent that the Sandow system made the boy grow out of his clothes too fast. See *Sandow's*, 8 (March 1902): 185. Other stories on the admirable efforts of British Jews in the field of education were also published: an article on the Jews' Free School, 'The Biggest School on Earth', *Sandow's*, 8 (June 1902): 408–12. Other articles on 'Jewish Physical Training' were published. Lower rates of infant mortality among immigrant Jewish

populations were seen by some as worthy of praise, *Sandow's*, 13 (July 1904): 32–3. See also Major W. Evans-Gordon's *The Alien Immigrant* (London: Heinemann, 1903) 11, which begins with a quote from Rosebery on the dangers of 'pauper immigration' in terms of 'degrading permanently the status and conditions of the nation', 1. Other racialist and yet liberal depictions of the Jews which described the importance of the influence of Judaic traditions could be found in books such as Arnold White's *The Modern Jew* (London: Heinemann, 1899). Notes concerning Jewish sporting activities were not uncommon, 'Notes of the Month': mention of the Jewish Athletic Association, *Sandow's*, 13 (77) (Nov. 1904): 367–8.

56.   From the *Sporting Chronicle* (5 July 1886) as quoted in Ray Jenkins, 'Salvation for the Fittest? A West African Sportsman in Britain in the New Age of Imperialism', 23, *International Journal of Sport History*, 7 (1) (May 1990): 23–60. Wharton's 'blackness' was described variously as 'gentleman of colour', 'brunette of pronounced complexion', 'by no means a representative Englishman in appearance', and later, as ' "Darkie", "Darkey", or "Duskey" Wharton', 25. He was incorrectly labelled as being born in the Caribbean when in fact he was born and raised in what is now Ghana in West Africa. Ibid.

57.   Ibid., 26.

58.   As exemplified by the experience of his contemporary, boxer Peter Jackson, 'the late nineteenth-century's most famous black athlete', 143, discrimination in the face of exceptional ability remained the rule. David K. Wiggins, 'Peter Jackson and the Elusive Heavyweight Championship: A Black Athlete's Struggle against the Late Nineteenth Century Color-Line', *Journal of Sport History*, 12 (2) (1985): 143–56.

59.   'A Word About Our Cover', *Health and Vim*, 8 (5) (May 1909): 219–20. Le Bon's and Saussure's arguments against the dangers of educating colonial subject people above their station were validated to some extent by the physical culturist's emphasis on the positive aspect of the primitive's fine 'savage' body. It was assumed by many that no amount of physical vigour could outweigh the white man's moral and intellectual superiority. For an analysis of this aspect of racial ideology both in the denigration of inferior races and in the romanticizing of the so-called 'savage's' closer harmony with nature, see Michael Adas, *Machines as the Measure of Man*, 318–42 and 392–401; conversely, the notion of the African's laziness or the superiority of whites by virtue of their better 'bodily discipline' was also asserted as an explanation of Western dominance over its colonial subjects, Ibid., 256–8.

60.   *Sandow's*, 9 (July 1902): 24–6. For a provocative ethnographic analysis of contemporary Indian wrestling as a way of life organized around the somatic experience of the competing body, see Joseph S. Alter, *The Wrestler's Body: Identity and Ideology in North India* (University of California Press, 1992).

61.   R. Hodder, *Sandow's* (Sept. 1902): 199–202.

62. *Sandow's*, 9 (Dec. 1902): 332–9.
63. *Sandow's* (Oct. 1903): 180–2 and (April 1904): 316–17.
64. 'The Artizan and Physical Culture', *Sandow's*, 1 (27 Sept. 1906) 416.
65. Ibid., 9 (Oct. 1902): 300–1.
66. Ibid., 8 (April 1902).
67. *Sandow's* (14 June 1905): 219.
68. *Sandow's*, 16 (112) (24 August 1905): 204–5, from *Daily News*.
69. *Sandow's*, 16 (16) (19 April 1906): 498–500. Attempts to promote an imperial framework based on the body were also emphasized. *Sandow's*, 15 (106) (13 July 1905), 'What is Muscle Bound?', 'Lord Rosebery on Physique': 37–8.
70. Ibid., 14 (96) (4 May 1905): 466; as found in a regular feature 'Physique and the Theatre Halls' and its description of a new arrival at the Lyceum, 'wonderful little fellow Smaun of British Burma', 22 yrs, 34 in. high and weighs 20 lb. Sing Hpoo was his surname. He performed as the 'miniature hercules'.
71. *Sandow's*, 117 (Sept. 1905), 'The Return of Mr. Sandow', (28 Sept. 1905): 343–4.
72. Ibid.
73. See Chapman, 156.
74. *Sandow's* (3 Jan. 1907): 12.
75. Ibid.
76. This was the same lack of control that was usually attributed to women. For more on shifting and contradictory British perceptions of the Irish, particularly as soldiers and administrators in relation to subaltern peoples on the subcontinent, L. P. Curtis, Jr, *Anglo-Saxons and Celts*, and S. B. Cook, *The Example of Ireland: Political and Administrative Aspects of the Imperial Relationship with British India, 1855–1922*, PhD Dissertation (Rutgers University, NJ, 1987) 35–9.
77. See Ballhatchet's study of the policies of administrators in India with regard to the 'distance' between imperial rulers and their subjects, *Race, Sex and Class Under the Raj: Imperial Attitudes and Policies and their Critics, 1793–1905* (London, 1980): 96–122.
78. *The Power of Evidence* (1919) 58.
79. In 1900 565 per thousand were under height (5 ft 6 in.) as compared to 105 per thousand in 1845. At a Manchester recruitment station in 1899, over three-quarters of 12 000 total men were rejected as 'virtual invalids', Hyam, *Empire and Sexuality*, 74. Also see Spiers.
80. H. Sidden, a newsagent in Hastings, is shown with his shop covered with *Health and Vim* posters, 8 (12) (Dec. 1909) 583.
81. *Health and Vim*, 8 (10) (Oct. 1909): 487–9.
82. Cover, *Health and Vim*, 8 (11) (Nov. 1909).
83. Hyam, 74.
84. Physique oriented discourses, varied as they were – whether referenced to personalities, the natural, the religious, or the ideas of the monarchy or the nation – might thus be viewed as part of the desire for the 'slice of eternity' Iwan Bloch described as the chimerical antidote to the upsetting 'vibrations of modernity'. As quoted by Mosse, *Nationalism and Sexuality*, 9; from Iwan Bloch, *Die Perversen*

(Berlin, undated) 28. See also Lesley A. Hall, *Hidden Anxieties: Male Sexuality, 1900–1950* (Cambridge, 1991); George L. Mosse, *Nationalism and Sexuality: Middle-Class Morality and Sexual Norms in Modern Europe* (Madison, WI, 1985); Brian Pronger, *The Arena of Masculinity: Sports, Homosexuality, and the Meaning of Sex* (New York, 1990); and Jeffrey Weeks, *Sex, Politics and Society: The Regulation of Sex since 1800* (London, 1981).

85. *Health and Vim*, 10 (6) (June 1911): 360.

86. E. Adair Impey, 'Military Training Considered as Part of General Education', *Journal of Scientific Physical Training* (Dec. 1912): 16–21; and see also June 1915 and October 1916. Its editors took an active part in the debates over compulsory military training and the importance of non-military trained physical education instructors for school children.

87. See Percy K. Rutlege, 'Purity Teaching by the Gymnastic Masters in Secondary Schools', *Journal of Scientific Physical Training*, 6 (17) (1914): 69–74. See also the earlier purity publication, *The Sentinel*, the journal for the Association for the Improvement of Public Morals, 1879–1900.

88. 'A Great Sin', *Health and Vim*, 9 (4) (April 1910): 180.

89. For example, much like similar pieces in *Health and Vim*, an anti-masturbation tract with reference to the bad morals of men in the army, 'Sex Education through the Gymnasium', also by E. Adair Impey, and a note on the published proceedings of that year's conference on Public Morals can be seen in the *Journal of Scientific Physical Training*, 3 (7) (autumn 1910): 85–90 and 112 respectively; see also Rutlege, 'Purity Teaching by the Gymnastic Masters'.

90. A purity manifesto was published in *Health and Vim*, 9 (3) (March 1910): 130–3. The editors claimed in the following issue that the badges had sold out. The cost for enrolling in the association was four shillings, which included a one shilling joining fee, one shilling for the badge, and an additional two shillings for a twelve month subscription to *Health and Vim*.

91. *Health and Vim*, 10 (4) (April 1911): 224–5.

92. 'The Ladies Pages', R. Gary, 'The Temptations of City Typists'. Ibid., 166–8. 'Danger lies not in the desire for fun, but in the way that desire is satisfied'. Ibid., 166.

93. 'Ladies Pages', 'The Slaves of the Kitchens: A Straight Talk to Girls in Service', *Health and Vim*, 10 (4) (April 1911): 231–2. Here again we can see evidence of the possibility that physical culture editors purposefully chose sex as a topic that might titillate and attract readers.

94. Advertisement for W. N. Willis' *Why Girls Go Wrong – How the White Sale Gangs Work*, *Health and Vim* publishing, 14 (156) [n. 25] (Jan. 1914): 1.

95. *Journal of Scientific Physical Training* (Oct. 1916): 57–9.

96. See Mort, *Dangerous Sexualities*. Earlier broadbased community health efforts were rooted in an 1830s and 1840s coalition between moral and medical reformers. This linkage was shattered in the acrimonious debates which resulted from the passing of the Contagious Diseases Acts in the 1860s. In those discussions the medical profes-

sions had held the upper hand. However, the Moralist cause resurfaced successfully, alongside the founding of the NPRS in the 1880s, within the Purity Movement and grew in strength before the war.

97. Ibid., 174.
98. Arnold Bennett, *Mental Efficiency and Other Hints to Men and Women* (New York: George H. Doran, 1911) 7.
99. Ibid., 8.
100. Ibid., 8.
101. Ibid., 8.
102. June 1911: 333. Like his great-great uncle, he was a younger son. The former Prince William Henry was the third son of George III. George V was the second son of Edward VII. In both cases, it was a name that had been earned through service at sea, principally in the days before advances in cold storage technology made long sea voyages more pleasurable, at least in terms of diet. He began the rigorous life of a cadet in 1877 at the age 12. As Prince George Frederick, he first went to sea as a midshipman in 1880. Until the death of his older brother Albert Victor, he spent 13 years in active naval service on 11 battleships, with brief service on the Queen's yacht and even a tour on a torpedo boat. During these tours of duty, which took him around the globe, Prince George progressed somewhat modestly to the rank of commander in 1891. After his brother's death in 1892, however, he passed quickly to the rank of captain (1893), and in the year of his father's accession (1901) was made rear-admiral. In the year before his own accession he was named Admiral of the Fleet; from Harold Nicolson, *King George V* (London: Constable, 1970) 11–13.
103. In my use of the two latter adjectives and the idea of calculation, I refer to Foucault's notion of a shift from gens and honour as the basis of society to one based on statistical approximation, with the person seen as a calculable quantity. See Foucault, *Discipline*, and T. R. Malthus, *Essay on Population*.
104. In the US, presidents from William McKinley (1897–1901) onward began to find the growing popular press open to their manipulation, and Roosevelt had made the most of this new media tool in presenting himself as the self-made manly hero, Robertson: 311–13. See Arnoldo Testi, 'The Gender of Reform Politics: Theodore Roosevelt and the Culture of Masculinity', *Journal of American History* (March 1995): 1509–33; especially the cartoon illustrations of TR giving 'Straight Talks to Effete Civilisations', *Punch* (4 May 1910) and that of the Kaiser and Roosevelt recognizing one another as 'a man of my type', *Brooklyn Eagle* (*c.* 1910): 1514, 1516.
105. As reported in *The Mirror of Life and Sport* (8 April 1911), 'His Majesty King George has conferred an unique honour upon Mr. Eugen Sandow, the world-renowned founder of scientific physical culture. Mr. Sandow just having had the honour of being appointed Professor of Scientific Physical Culture to his Majesty . . . there is no desire more dear to his Majesty's heart than to improve the conditions of life for the masses', as quoted in Webster, 22.

106. *Health and Vim*, 10 (4) (April 1911): 201.
107. *Health and Vim*, 10 (6) (June 1911): 333.
108. Ibid., 356.
109. 'Physical Pars', *Sandow's* (Oct. 1903): 199, as quoted from *Pearson's Weekly*. Sandow married an English woman in November 1889 and was probably a naturalized British citizen.
110. The greater political movement, 'National Efficiency' coincided with the birth and development of physical culture. It included various supporters from Fabian socialists to 'collectivist conservatives like Milner, Chamberlain and, peripherally, Balfour', Martin Pugh, *The Making of Modern British Politics, 1867–1939*, 5th edn (Oxford: Blackwell, 1987) 103. Both 'National Efficiency' and physical culture can be seen to have been responses to general feelings of British social decline and to specific events such as the Boer war and the report of the 1904 Inter-Departmental Committee on Physical Deterioration.
111. Bennett, 9.

5 SLAUGHTER MACHINES

1. Tony Mason, *Association Football and English Society, 1863–1915* (Brighton, 1980) 224, as quoted in Eksteins, *Rites of Spring*, 121. Also see Fussell, Ogden and Florence, *Militarism vs. Feminism*, 122; and Richards, 120–5.
2. Byron Farwell, *Eminent Victorian Soldiers* (New York: W. W. Norton, 1985), 347.
3. Mayer, *The Persistence of the Old Regime* (New York: Pantheon, 1981) 4.
4. J. B. Priestley, in Peter Vansittart, *Voices from the Great War* (New York: Watts, 1984), 21.
5. The public school/military model that underlies this is problematic in some respects. It tells us that men are a certain way, and will be led by particularly seductive ideas almost naturally to behave in an aggressive and masculine manner and that historicisms and traditions shape responses to life somewhat apart from other material changes.
6. As evidenced in his public dispatches and private diary entries, Haig frequently employed the public school language of sport. Corelli Barnett, *The Swordbearers*, 242.
7. This interpretation can be found in a variety of contemporary sources as well as historical accounts such as A. J. P. Taylor, *Europe: Grandeur and Decline* (London: Hamish Hamilton, 1967); *The Origins of the First World War* (London: Hamish Hamilton, 1963).
8. Fussell points to the importance of various poetic, journalistic and other narratives use of ideas like that of a sporting spirit in promoting a taste for war in the abstract, Fussell, *The Great War and Modern Memory* (Oxford: Oxford University Press, 1975), 25–8 and *passim*.

9. See Vansittart's inclusion of the story of the Russian woman who in giving herself to a young army officer thrusts her bare breasts up against his boots during a frenzied attack on the German embassy in Petrograd on 1 August 1914: *Voices*, 15; and Eksteins' juxtaposition of crowd scenes from Paris, Berlin, London and an apparently doctored photo from Petrograd, all from early August 1914, Modris Eksteins, *Rites of Spring*, figures 6–9, pages unnumbered.
10. Fussell, *The Great War and Modern Memory*, 292.
11. Owen was 25 when he was killed by machine-gun fire in November 1918, one week before the Armistice.
12. Owen as quoted in Fussell.
13. Ibid.
14. Paul Fussell contrasts the 'feudal language' of the public school idyll with the postwar technical and medical imagery of the machine, that is, to die is to *perish*, arms and legs are one's *limbs*, a soldier is a *warrior*, and so on, based upon the medievally inspired classicism of the public school. In fact the two coexisted before the war, and were most apparent in physical culture's combination of the mechanistic with romantic historicism, Fussell, 21–4.
15. Ibid.
16. Philip Mason, *The English Gentleman: The Rise and Fall of an Ideal* (New York: William Morrow, 1982) 23. Also see Richard Dellamora, *Masculine Desire: The Sexual Politics of Victorian Aestheticism* (Chapel Hill, NC: University of North Carolina Press, 1990) especially Chapter 10, 'Scandal and Compulsory Heterosexuality in the 1890s', and his discussion of 'dandyism' and the 'gentleman'.
17. Maurice Keen, *Chivalry* (New Haven, CT: Yale University Press, 1984) 2. In this sense, the attention to the physique that Sandow first embodied was part of what might be called a shifting chivalric paradigm. Such a paradigm's ideological flexibility, its emphasis upon bodily reformation, and the 'making' of men and women according to gendered ideals makes it useful in better understanding the breaks and continuities characterizing the move from early renaissance economic and intellectual concerns with the individual to our own present day mania for personalized fitness and self-psychologizing.
18. Other examples of chivalric based self-creation texts include Ramon Lull, *Libre de l'ordre de cavayleria*, trans. William Caxton (London, 1474). Geoffrey de Charny, *Livre de chevalerie* (fourteenth century); Castiglione, *The Courtier*, trans. Sir Thomas Hoby (London, 1561); Giovanni Della Casa, *Of the Manners and Behaviours, it behoveth a Man to use and eschewe, etc.*, trans. Robert Peterson (London, 1576); Sir William Segar, *The Book of Honor and Armes* (London, 1590) and *Honor Military and Civil* (London, 1602); Robert Ashley, *Of Honour* (c. 1596–1603); L'abbé Goussault, *Le Portrait de l'honnête homme* (Paris, 1694); and Stefano Guazzo, *Civile Conversation*, trans. George Petite (1581) and Bartholomew Young (1586). Also Thomas Deloney's *Jacke of Newbury* (1596?), *Thomas of Reading* (1597), *The Gentle Craft, Part I* (1597) and *The Gentle Craft, Part II* (1598), as discussed in Leonard

180   *Notes*

Mustazza, 'Thomas Deloney's *Jacke of Newbury*: A Horatio Alger Story
for the Sixteenth Century', *Journal of Popular Culture*, 23 (3) (1989):
165–77.

19.   See Fuller, *Training Soldiers for War* (London, 1914) 20.
20.   In a speech given in Edinburgh published in the *Fortnightly Review*
      (new series, 1898), Balfour demonstrated an interest in the deteriora-
      tion of the body and anthropometric observation. See *Sandow's*, 'The
      Premier and the Physique' (Sept. 1904).
21.   Of course, this diffusion served to transform the elite models upon
      which it was based. Thus, during the war, the gentlemanly charac-
      ter of the officer became less a 'class' definition and more a status
      attached to the profession itself. In the past, only 'gentlemen' might
      become officers. By the late nineteenth century this had changed
      enough so that to be an officer, which usually meant being a public
      school boy as well, made one a gentleman. See C. B. Otley, 'The
      Social Origins of British Army Officers', *Sociological Review*, 18 (2)
      (1970): 213–40; and Van Doorn, 35.
22.   Graham equated the 'victories of the sporting field' with the 'value
      of the bayonet charge', Graham, 2–3.
23.   William Redmond (London, 1918) 42.
24.   Maurice Baring, *Flying Corps Headquarters* (London, 1968) 57.
25.   Foucault, *Discipline*, 221.
26.   Today these values are perhaps best personified in the professional
      athlete. Despite growing participation and spectatorship by women,
      professionalized sports are still largely a process of male associa-
      tion, which express manliness and allow male spectators to vicari-
      ously define themselves as men. For an investigation of sport as a
      component of masculinity, see Eric Dunning's 'Sport as a Male Pre-
      serve: Notes on the Social Sources of Masculine Identity and its Trans-
      formations', in Eric Dunning and Norbert Elias, *Quest for Excitement*
      (Oxford University Press, 1986) 267–83. For an analysis of public
      school sports in this period see Mangan, *Athleticism*.
27.   Bertrand Russell, letter to the 'Nation' 15 August 1914, quoted in
      Vansittart, *Voices*, 29.
28.   Already by the 1870s the increase in numbers of unmarried women
      began an ascent which continued into the second half of the twen-
      tieth century. This has been explained by higher male death rates and
      their tendency to immigrate in greater numbers than females. John
      R. Gillis, *For Better, For Worse, British Marriage 1600–Present* (Oxford
      and New York, 1985) 234. More men immigrated not only because
      they were free to do so (as women were often not) but also be-
      cause of the social expectation and economic necessity of making
      money.
29.   See a laudatory note on Baden-Powell and Boy Scouts, 'Our Boys
      Corner', *Health and Vim*, 9 (7) (July 1910): 515–17; a photo of a young
      scout, Percy Tilston of Liverpool, who is keen on physical culture, 10
      (2) (Feb. 1911): 86; more compliments for the Scouts with a reference
      to a meeting between Theodore Roosevelt and their founder in 'Our
      Boys Corner', 105–7; and a photograph of Scouts and a reprint from

Headquarter's Gazette, Baden-Powell talking on purity, *Health and Vim,* 10 (5) (May 1911): 275 and 282–3 respectively.

30. *Health and Vim,* 14 (156) [n. 25] (Jan. 1914): 7 and 15 respectively.
31. *Health and Vim,* 10 (1) (Jan. 1911): 10.
32. *Health and Vim,* 14 (158) [n. 27] (March 1914): 95.
33. *Health and Vim* (Dec. 1914): 107.
34. Ibid., 109.
35. Ibid., 84.
36. Ibid., 116.
37. Ibid., 115.
38. *Health and Vim,* 14 (161) [n. 30] (June 1914): 232.
39. *Health and Vim,* 14 (163) [n. 31] (August 1914): 288.
40. *Health and Vim,* 14 (164) [n. 33] (Sept. 1914): 321.
41. *Journal of Scientific Physical Training* (Oct. 1916): 7. See also Chapman, 168–70.
42. Ex-Soldier X, *War is War* (London, 1930) 96.
43. Published 1919. Macfadden was especially adept at using the motivator of gender confusion, or fears of deviancy and degeneracy which in some ways presaged war-guilt approaches to recruitment. Macfadden, *Physical Development.*
44. *Health and Vim,* 14 (165) [n. 34] (Oct. 1914): 395.
45. *Health and Vim,* 14 (167) [n. 36] (Dec. 1914): 411.
46. Ibid., 430.
47. Ibid.
48. Ibid., 370, also 420–1; for example, the ICS War League was open to all ICS students for sixpence.
49. Ibid., 381.
50. See, for example, Boy Scouts on the cover of January 1914 of *Health and Vim* and so on to successive military covers for September, October, November and December 1914. Munitions workers were seen on covers (February 1916), as were other military and naval images until 1917 when cover pictures were discontinued.
51. At this time, Ramsay MacDonald began writing articles for its pages. *Health and Vim,* MacDonald, 'The Importance of Home Life' (March 1917) and 'New Worlds for Old' (Oct. 1918). Philip Snowden also wrote 'Education and Morality' for *Health and Vim.*
52. *Health and Vim,* 14 (165) [n. 34] (Oct. 1914): 356.
53. *Health and Vim,* 14 (166) [n. 35] (Nov. 1914): 387.
54. Ibid.
55. Ibid.
56. *Health and Vim,* 16 (187) [n. 56] (August 1916): insert.
57. *Health and Vim,* 16 (188) [n. 57] (Sept. 1916).
58. Mort, *Dangerous Sexualities,* 173.
59. Quoted in Laurence Housman (ed.), *War Letters of Fallen Englishmen* (London: Gollancz, 1930), 159. Housman was the brother of the poet A. E. Housman.
60. Captain Charles Hamilton Sorley, killed 13 October 1915; letter to his father, 15 July 1915. Ibid., 245.
61. Willis (ed.), *The Keeling Letters* (London, 1918) 145. Brooke mocked

friends who felt it their duty to civilization *not* to fight. He wrote to a French friend, 'it seemed it was going to be a serious and long business: and I felt that if we were going to turn into a military nation, and all the young men go in, I should be among them', Keynes, 618.

62. Letter to his aunt; he was killed 23 March 1918 at the age of 29. Housman, 298.

63. Daniel Pick, *War Machine: The Rationalization of Slaughter in the Modern Age* (New Haven, CT: Yale University Press, 1993) 188.

64. Charles Carrington, *A Subaltern's War* (London: P. Davies, 1929) 209.

65. Ibid., 197.

66. As quoted in Eksteins, *Rites*, 215, from Heather Robertson, *A Terrible Beauty: The Art of Canada at War* (Toronto, 1977) 92.

67. Letter to his mother, 1 June 1915, quoted in Laurence Housman (ed.), *War Letters* 74.

68. Joseph Murray, *Gallipoli As I Saw It* (London, 1965) 106–7.

69. Vera Brittain, *Testament of Youth: An Autobiographical Study of the Years 1900–1925* (London: Gollancz, 1933) 97, 374, 395, 379.

70. See Thomas W. Laqueur, 'Memory and Naming in the Great War' in John R. Gillis (ed.), *Commemorations: The Politics of National Identity* (Princeton, NJ, 1994) 150–67.

71. See Seth Koven, 'Remembering and Dismemberment: Crippled Children, Wounded Soldiers and the Great War in Britain', *American Historical Review* (Oct. 1994): 1167–202, especially 1193–200.

72. Fussell, *The Great War and Modern Memory*, 306.

73. Fussell, 303. Tuke, Walker and Scott were all painters of boys bathing in the prewar period.

74. As well as the poems of Robert Bridges and Tennyson. Ibid., 21.

75. Ibid., 276–7.

76. Adams, *The Great Adventure*.

77. Fussell, 284. Weeks, *Coming Out*, 135. Housman was a member of the Uranian British Society for the Study of Sex Psychology (BSSP).

78. Ibid., 178.

79. It may go some way in explaining the former's firm resistance to the not unusual desire to view the Scouts as militaristic or use them as an actual training arm of the military forces. See Allen Warren, 'Sir Robert Baden-Powell: The Scout Movement and Citizen Training in Great Britain', *English Historical Review*, 101 (399) 1986: 376–98.

80. Mosse, *Sexuality*, 114–15. More on the role of male desire in relation to the war can be found in Michael C. C. Adams, *The Great Adventure: Male Desire and the Coming of World War I* (Bloomington, IN: Indiana University Press, 1990). Adams attempts to revise the view of the war by looking at prewar gender distinctions as a root cause.

81. Gilbert, 'Soldier's Heart: Literary Men, Literary Women, and the Great War', *Signs* 8 (3) (1983): 443. See also Theweleit, *Male Fantasies*.

82. See Richards, *Happiest Days*, 123, and Fussell, *passim*.

83. In this sense, the public school and the military were the prototype for nineteenth-century professionalization and later male organizations of various stripes. The formation of various men's clubs and organizations and, in the US, the development of higher education along lines

similar to the public school (especially, the growth of collegiate social fraternities) and Baden-Powell's initiation of the Boy Scout movement were all examples of this influential pattern. See Burton J. Bledstein, *The Culture of Professionalism: The Middle Class and the Development of Higher Education in America* (New York and London, 1978); Rosenthal, *Character Factory* (New York, 1985); and Warren, 'Sir Robert Baden-Powell'.

84. Wilkinson, 119. For an analysis of the inadequacies of the traditional British officer class, see Tim Travers, 'The Hidden Army: Structural Problems in the British Officer Corps, 1900–1918', *Journal of Contemporary History*, 17 (3) (July 1982): 523–44. Similarly, Ogden and Florence pointed out the martial cast of the typical classical education, the emphasis on battles and Greek history's 'unending succession' of wars: *Militarism vs. Feminism*, 98.

85. *Health and Vim* (Dec. 1920): 355.

86. *Health and Vim* (Nov. 1919).

87. *ECB Index*, 1919. Gale & Polden also reprinted a new version of Sandow's *Body Building; or Man in the Making. How to Become Healthy and Strong* (originally published October 1904).

88. (New York: Romaine Pierson, 1934).

89. As befitted his emergent trade – which was a direct beneficiary of the war – he was a true social constructionist. Ibid., 37.

90. Ibid., 23, 25.

91. It was accompanied by the caption: 'Perfect harmony of form and proportion'. Ibid.

92. As quoted in Mark Seltzer, 'The Love-Master', 146, Joseph Boone and Michael Cadden (eds), *Engendering Men: The Question of Male Feminist Criticism* (London: Routledge, 1990) 140–58. Seltzer notes the 'double logic of prothesis' illustrated in Henry Ford's projection of the possibility of the preponderance of automotive production tasks (88 per cent) being accomplished by 'legless', 'one-armed' and other less than 'able-bodied' men. Seltzer, Ibid. He relates this duality, which encompasses the 'emptying out of human agency' by machine technology vs. the 'transcendence of the natural body' and an extension of human agency by the same means, to the double-bind of contemporary 'sheer culturalism'. Ibid. The latter, dependent upon a similar machine-like constructivism, seems to posit an illusory escape from the traditional nature/culture dichotomy by way of 'the elimination of the first term and the inflation of the second' without bothering to confront the differences between such intellectual binarisms: 145–6.

6   CONCLUSION

1. Advertisements for men's corsets were common in military publications. See Hollander, *Seeing through Clothes*, especially 360–2.

2. *Max Weber on Charisma and Insitution Building*, ed. S. N. Eisenstadt,

trans. H. H. Gerth and C. Wright Mills, (Chicago, IL: University of Chicago Press, 1968): 20–1.

3.   Ibid., 21.

4.   Ibid., 22–3.

5.   This is certainly an aspect of the development of fitness as an industry and cultural ideology that needs to be investigated further, that is, the links between present-day professionalism, Olympianism, and the recent proliferation of gyms, health clubs and cosmetically oriented fitness publications. See Alan M. Klein, *Little Big Men: Bodybuilding Subculture and Gender Construction* (Albany, NY: State University of New York Press, 1993).

6.   Foucault on Bentham, *Discipline*, 193–4.

7.   Mayer, *The Persistence of the Old Regime* (New York: Pantheon, 1981) 12.

8.   In contemporary representation we can see a continued use of the abstracted strong and healthy body as a seductive mediating ground that finesses and subsumes numerous questions of political and economic conflict, cultural difference and sexual and social identity. For other sociological and art historical works dealing with the mediating power of the bodily image see John Tagg, *The Burden of Representation: Essays on Photographies and Histories* (Amherst, MA: University of Massachusetts Press, 1988); Stuart Ewen, *All Consuming Images: The Politics of Style in Contemporary Culture* (New York: Basic Books, 1988); and Alan Tomlinson (ed.), *Consumption, Identity, Style: Marketing, Meanings, and the Packaging of Pleasure* (London: Routledge, 1990).

9.   Richards, *Commodity Culture*, Chapter 2, 'The Image of Victoria in the Year of Jubilee', 73–118.

10.   As with other more traditional images of popular military men or monarchs such as Queen Victoria or the Sultan of Turkey, the stage strongman's image assisted in differentiating among generic products such as soaps, beverages and tobacco. As in advertisements for tobacco using the Sultan's name or that of the then Prince of Wales, copywriters freely used the image familiarity of royalty without bothering to gain permission. It was in this period that the structure for classifying products or services as provided 'by appointment' to the British monarch began. However, as a voice of brand authority, the figure of the monarch was to recede somewhat in the initial years of the coming century as individuals like Sandow, alongside athletes and other entertainers, gradually refined the concept of the celebrated person.

11.   As time went by, Victorian advertisers began to shift from the latter to the former, Richards, 7.

12.   The consequent history of similar health entrepreneurship over the rest of the century has been characterized by more sophisticated photographic practices, more precise market targeting, and a non-political and less explicit or even negligible moral tone. However, as late as 1939, books like Bob Hoffman's *Big Arms: How to Develop Them* (York, PA: Strength & Health Pub., reprinted 1950) were offering the same formula as pre-First World War physical culture pub-

lications. *Big Arms* included a brief history of the 'movement' with reference to Greek statuary and Sandow. Hoffman was the editor of *Strength and Health*, and the author of other body culture titles such as *How to be Strong, Healthy and Happy*. (I am indebted to Charles Rosenberg for bringing Hoffman's book to my attention.)

13. See Webster, 51–4. Hadley was apparently instrumental behind the scenes in both the affairs of Macfadden and Sandow, Ibid., 52. Hackenschmidt was yet another of George Bernard Shaw's strongman 'protégés'. They debated and Shaw was intrigued by Hackenschmidt's odd theories on evolution and physics, Ibid., 54.

14. See Eksteins' discussion of Remarque and his First World War novel *All Quiet on the Western Front*, and Tannenbaum on *Sport im Bild* before the war.

15. For more on the body and sexuality and the significance of film stars such as Valentino, see Kevin White, *The First Sexual Revolution: the Emergence of Male Heterosexuality in Modern America* (New York, 1993) 19, 31, 180.

16. Fussell, 316.

17. See Emil Ludwig, *Talks with Mussolini*, trans. Eden and Cedar Paul (Boston, MA: Little, Brown, 1933) 45–6, 142–3, and Macfadden's *Physical Development: Mind, Body, Soul, Beauty, Charm and Personality* (September 1932) which includes an interview with Mussolini, and reference to 'History's Greatest Experiment in Physical Culture', Macfadden's training of 'forty Italian youths', 17.

18. Hyam, 69–71. See also Weeks, *Coming Out*, 139–50, and Mort, *Dangerous Sexualities*, 189–209.

19. The lineal descendants of these first fitness periodicals had by the 1950s become entirely composed of erotically coded photographs of the male body. See Waugh, and Mark Gabor, *The Pin-Up* (New York: Bell, 1972) 250–4. In the 1920s, nudist magazines such as *Sun and Health, Helios*, and *Gymnos* also began to employ the 'physical culture' rationale.

20. As excerpted in Arthur O. Lewis, Jr (ed.), *Of Machines and Men* (New York: Dutton, 1963) 247–59.

21. Lewis, 250.

22. Ibid., 250.

23. See Lewis Mumford, *Technics and Civilization* (New York: Harcourt, 1934); and Adas, *Machines as the Measure of Men*, Introduction, 1–16.

24. Lewis (Orwell, *Wigan Pier*) 250.

25. Mosse, *Nationalism and Sexuality*, 63–4. Historians such as George Mosse have isolated Germany as the breeding ground of a special fascist-directed trajectory of bodily rediscovery and nationalist fervour in response to the artificiality of industrial life. In Britain, where Sandow settled and became prosperous, there was perhaps less of a need to rediscover the body. Mosse, 62.

26. See Chapman, *Sandow the Magnificent*.

27. Letter to potential subscribers of *Men's Health* (Erasmus, PA, Michael Lafavore, exec. ed., 1990).

28. Ibid.

29. This was a phrase used frequently by Macfadden well into the 1930s.
30. This recent technology is a combination of holographic and computer aided design applications that use fast-drying resins to produce sculpted objects according to 3-D specifications.

Bibliography

EARLIER BOOKS, PRIVATE PAPERS, GOVERNMENT
PUBLICATIONS AND REPORTS

Adam, G. Mercer (ed.), *Sandow's System of Physical Training* (London: Gale & Polden, 1894).

Anonymous, *Physical Training: A Study in the Perfect Type of the Human Form* (London, 1901).

Arnold, Matthew, *Culture and Anarchy* (London, 1868).

Atilla (Louis Durlacher), *The Art of Weightlifting and Muscular Development . . . with Special Notes on Double Handed Lifting*, ed. Thomas Inch (London: Health Culture Publishing Co, 1903).

Baden-Powell, Robert, *The Downfall of Prempeh* (London, 1896); *Memories of India: Recollections of Soldiering and Sport* (Philadelphia, PA, 1915); *Rovering to Success* (London, 1922).

Beard, George M., *American Nervousness: Its Causes and Consequences* (New York, 1881); *Sexual Neurasthenia: Its Hygiene, Causes, Symptoms and Treatment, etc.* (New York, 1884).

Bennett, Arnold, *Mental Efficiency and Other Hints to Men and Women* (New York: George H. Doran, 1911).

Brabazon, Lord, *Prosperity or Pauperism* (London, 1888); *Social Aims* (with the Countess of Meath) (London, 1893).

Carlyle, Thomas, *Sartor Resartus* (London, 1831); *Past and Present* (London, 1843); *On Heroes and Hero Worship* (London, 1841).

Carrington, Charles, *A Subaltern's War* (London, 1929).

Castiglione, Baldassare, *The Courtier*, trans. Sir Thomas Hoby (London, [1561] 1928).

Desbonnet, L., *Les Rois de la force* and *La Force physique, culture rationelle, méthode Atilla, méthode Sandow, méthode Desbonnet, la santé par les exercises musculaires mis à la portée de tout* (Paris: Berger-Levrault, 1901, 1906).

Edwards, Billy, *The Pugulistic Portrait Gallery* (London and Philadelphia, PA: Pugilistic Publishing Co., 1894).

Elyot, Thomas, *The Gouernour*, first published as 'The Boke named the Governour', 1531 (London: Foster Watson, J. M. Dent & Sons, 1907).

The English Catalogue of Books Issued in Great Britain and Ireland and the Principal Works Published in America (ECB) vols III–VII (London: Sampson, Low, Marston & Co., 1874–1915).

Esher Papers. BL. Ad. Ms.

Esher, Viscount, *National Strategy* (London, 1904).

Evans-Gordon, Major W., *The Alien Immigrant* (London: Heinemann, 1903).

Ex-Soldier X, *War is War* (London, 1930).

Fuller, J. F. C., *Training Soldiers for War* (London, 1914).

Gerrard, James, *Face to Face with Kaiserism* (New York, 1918).

Gladstone Papers. BL. Ad. Ms.

Guazzo, Stefano, *Civile Conversation*, trans. George Petite (1581) and Bartholomew Young (1586).

House of Commons, *Parliamentary Papers*, British Sessional Papers (London: HMSO, 1867, 1876, 1878 and 1901).

Heron, Haly, *The Kayes of Counsaile: A Newe Discourse of Morall Philosophie* (London, 1579).

Hole, J., *The History and Management of Literary, Scientific, and Mechanics Institutes* (London, 1853).

Imperator et Rex, by the anonymous author of *Martyrdom of an Empress* (London, 1904).

Jackson, Holbrook, *The 1890s* (London: Cresset Library, 1988, 1st edition 1913).

Jahn, F. L., *Treatise on Gymnasticks* (Northampton, MA: Simon Butler, 1828).

Jenness, Mabel, *Physical Culture* (New York, 1891).

Koster and Bial's Music Hall Programme (New York: Strauss & Klee, c. November–December 1893: pages unnumbered).

Landseer, Edwin, *Isaac Van Amburgh and his Animals* (Paul Mellon Collection, Yale Center for British Art, New Haven, CT).

LeBon, Gustave Lois, *Psychologiques de l'évolution des peuples* (Paris, 1894); *The Psychology of the Crowd* (New York, 1896); *The Psychology of the Great War* (New York, 1917).

Le Coubertin, Baron, *Les Jeux Olympiques, 776 av. J.C.–1896* (Paris: H. Le Soudier, 1896, trans. 1966).

Leonard, F. E., *Pioneers of Modern Physical Training* (New York, 1915).

Leslie, Shane, *Men Who Were Different* (London, 1937).

Levy, E. L., *Autobiography of an Athlete* (London, 1913).

Lewis, Dio, *The New Gymnastics* (Boston, MA: Ticknor & Fields, 1862).

Lilwall, John, *The Half-holiday Question Considered with Some Thoughts* on the Instructive and Healthful Recreations of the Industrial Classes (London, 1856).

Locke, John, *Some Thoughts on Education* (1693).

Macfadden, Bernarr, *The Athlete's Conquest: The Romance of an Athlete* (London and New York: Physical Culture Publishing Co., 1901).

Mackinder, H. J., *Britain and the British Seas* (London, 1904).

Maclaren, A., *A System of Physical Education, Theoretical and Practical* (Oxford, 1869).

Mayhew, Henry, *London's Underworld*, ed. Peter Quennell (London: Bracken, 1983).

Monthly, Quarterly and Periodical Publications of the British Isles, ed. Hubert W. Peet (London: Sells World Press, 1915).

Muyerbridge, Edward, *Animal Locomotion: An Electro-Photographic Investigation of Consecutive Phases of Animal Movement 1872–1885* (University of Pennsylvania: limited subscription edition, 1888).

Narragansett Machine Company Pocket Manual; Narragansett Machine Company Catalogue of Standard, etc. (Hay-Rider Collection, John Hay Library, Brown University, 1887, 1889).

Nitobe, Inazo, *Bushido: The Soul of Japan* (New York: G. P. Putnam, 1905).

Nordau, Max, *Degeneration* (New York, 1895); *Conventional Lies* (New York, 1886).

Northcliffe Papers (1907), BL. Ad. MS. 62182 (19).

Patents for Inventions: Abridgement of Specifications, Class 132, Toys, Games, and Exercises (London: HMSO, 1893, 1898, 1903, 1922, and Subject Matter Index, 1905–10) 290–1; *Patents for Inventions, Abridgements of Specifications, Class 132, Toys, Games and Exercise, period A.D. 1889–92* (London: HMSO, printed 1898).

Redmond, William, *Trench Pictures from France* (London, 1918).

Report of the Commission appointed to Inquire into the Recruiting for the Army, British Sessional Papers (BSP), House of Commons (HC) vol. xv (1867).

Rousseau, Jean-Jacques, *The Social Contract and Discourses*, trans. G. D. H. Cole (New York: Dutton, 1950).

Rowntree, B. S., *Poverty: A Study of Town Life* (York, 1901).

Sandow, Eugen, *On Physical Training: A Study in the Perfect Type of Human Form* (New York and London, 1894); *Strength and How to Obtain it* (London, 1895, 1900, 1903, etc.); *Body Building or Man in the Making: How to Become Healthy and Strong* (London, 1904); *Strength and Health: How Disease May be Successfully Combated by*

Physical Culture (New York, 1906, 1919); *Health from Physical Culture*, Sandow's Correspondence Course (*c.* 1908); *Life is Movement: The Physical Reconstruction and Regeneration of a People* (Hertford, UK, 1919); *The Power of Evidence* (London, 1919).

Schreber, *Pangymnastikon*, in Lewis, *The New Gymnastics*.

Sell, Henry (ed.), *Sell's Dictionary of the World Press 1886* (London, 1886).

Shaw, G. B., *The Sanity of Art: An Exposure of the Current Nonsense about Artists being Degenerate* (London: New Age Press, 1908).

Simmel, George, *The Philosophy of Money* (1907, trans. London, 1978).

'The Sultan's Favourite', no. 80, T. W. Ingersoll (1899) [postcard].

Triat, Hippolyte, *Au Gouvernement provisoire [Lettre demandant la création d'un ministère de l'éducation publique, signée Triat et Dally, 1er mars 1848]* (Paris: P. Dupont, 1848); *Mémoire sur la gymnastique adressé au Conseil Municipal de Paris* (Paris: Renou et Maulde, 1872); also with M. Dally, *Société milonienne pour l'exploitation de la gymnastique appliquée à la réhabilitation physique de l'homme, d'après la méthode de M. Triat, de Nîmes . . . Raison sociale* (Paris: A. Monair, 1847).

von Schierbrand, Wolf (ed., trans.), *The Kaiser's Speeches* (New York, 1903).

Weber, Adna Ferrin, *The Growth of Cities in the Nineteenth-Century* (Ithaca, NY, 1899).

Wells, H. G., *Tono-Bungay* (London: Street & Smith, 1908); *The Happy Turning: A Dream of Life* (London: Heinemann, 1945).

White, Arnold, *The Modern Jew* (London: Heinemann, 1899).

Wile, Frederic William, *Men around the Kaiser: The Makers of Modern Germany* (New York: Bobbs-Merrill, 1913).

Willis (ed.), *The Keeling Letters* (London, 1918).

Wood, T. D. and Brownell, C. L., *Source Book in Health and Physical Education* (New York, 1925).

NEWSPAPERS AND PERIODICALS
(published in London unless otherwise noted)

Bailey's Sports and Pastimes
Boys
Daily Chronicle
Dancing: A Journal Devoted to the Terpsichorean Art, Physical Culture and Fashionable Entertainments
Evening News

Fortnightly Review
Graphic
Gymnasium News
Harts' Army List
Health and Strength
Health and Strength (US)
Health and Vim
Health Culture (US)
Journal of Scientific Physical Training
Mind and Body (US)
Morning Standard
Nineteenth Century
North American Review (US)
Physical Culture (Macfadden, US)
Physical Development
Physical Education
Physique
Public School Magazine
Recreation: A Monthly Record of the Society's Work [first series]
Sandow's Magazine of Physical Culture
Sandow's Magazine (Boston, MA)
Strand Magazine
The Empire Review
The Gymnasium
The Health Magazine (Baltimore, MD)
The Hygiene Advertiser: Devoted to Natural Living, Physical Culture, Health Reform, etc.
The Poster and Postcard Collector
The Times
True Story (US)
United Services Magazine
Vim Magazine: A Monthly Magazine for the Encouragement of Physical and Mental Culture

LATER AND CURRENT BOOKS

Adas, Michael, *Machines as the Measure of Men: Science, Technology, and Ideologies of Western Dominance* (New York: Cornell University Press, 1990).

Agnew, Jean-Christophe, *Worlds Apart: The Market and the Theatre in*

Anglo-American Thought, 1550–1750 (Cambridge: Cambridge University Press, 1987).

Alford, B. W. E., *W. D. and H. O. Wills and the Development of the U.K. Tobacco Industry, 1786–1965* (London: Methuen, 1973).

Altick, Richard D., *Victorian People and Ideas* (New York, 1973); *Deadly Encounters: Two Victorian Sensations* (Philadelphia, PA: University of Pennsylvania Press, 1986).

Anderson, Benedict, *Reflections on the Origin and Spread of Nationalism* (London: Verso, 1983).

Annan, Noel, *The Headmaster: Roxburgh of Stowe and his Influence on English Education* (New York: Shocken, 1966).

Apadurai, Arjun (ed.), *The Social Life of Things* (Cambridge: Cambridge University Press, 1986).

Argov, Daniel, *Moderates and Extremists in the Indian Nationalist Movement, 1883–1920* (London: Asia Publishing House, 1967).

Auerbach, Nina, *Private Theatricals: The Lives of the Victorians* (Cambridge, MA: Harvard University Press, 1990).

Bailey, Peter, *Leisure and Class in Victorian England: Recreation and the Contest for Control, 1830–1885* (London: Methuen, 1987); Bailey (ed.), *Music Hall: The Business of Pleasure* (Buckingham: Open University Books, 1986).

Balfour, Michael, *The Kaiser and his Times* (Boston, MA: Houghton-Mifflin, 1964).

Ballhatchet, Kenneth, *Race, Sex and Class Under the Raj: Imperial Attitudes and Policies and their Critics, 1793–1905* (London: St Martin's, 1980).

Baring, Maurice, *Flying Corps Headquarters* (London, 1968).

Barker-Benfield, G. J., *Horrors of the Half-Known Life: Male Attitudes Toward Women and Sexuality in Nineteenth Century America* (New York: Harper, 1976).

Barnett, Correlli, *Britain and her Army 1509–1970: A Military, Political and Social Survey* (London: Allen Lane, 1970).

Baumgart, Winfried, *Imperialism: The Idea and Reality of British and French Colonial Expansion, 1880–1914* (Oxford: Oxford University Press, 1982).

Beloff, Max, *Imperial Sunset, V. I: Britain's Liberal Empire, 1897–1921* (New York: Knopf, 1970).

Berman, Marshall, *All That is Solid Melts into Air: The Experience of Modernity* (New York: Penguin, 1988).

Best, Geoffrey, *Mid-Victorian Britain, 1815–70* (Glasgow: Fontana/Collins, 1982).

Betts, Raymond, *The False Dawn: European Imperialism in the Nineteenth Century* (Minneapolis, MN: University of Minnesota, 1975).

Binfield, C., *George Williams and the YMCA: A Study in Victorian Social Attitudes* (London, 1973).

Binkley, Robert C., *Realism and Nationalism* (New York and London, 1941).

Bledstein, Burton J., *The Culture of Professionalism: The Middle Class and the Development of Higher Education in America* (New York: Norton, 1978).

Bloch, Marc, *The Royal Touch: Sacred Monarchy and Scrofula in England and France*, trans. J. E. Anderson (London: Routledge, 1973).

Boff, Vic, *You Can Be Physically Perfect, Powerfully Strong* (New York: Arco, 1975).

Boone, Joseph and Cadden, Michael (eds), *Engendering Men: The Question of Male Feminist Criticism* (London: Routledge, 1990).

Borsay, Peter, *The English Urban Renaissance: Culture and Society in the Provincial Town, 1660–1770* (New York: Oxford University Press, 1989).

Briggs, Asa, *A Social History of England* (New York: Viking, 1983); *Mass Entertainment: The Origins of a Modern Industry* (Adelaide, 1960).

Brittain, Vera, *Testament of Youth: An Autobiographical Study of the Years 1900–1925* (London: Gollancz, 1933).

Budd, Michael A., *Heroic Bodies: Physical Culture and the Pursuit of the Perfected Self, 1898–1918*, PhD dissertation (Rutgers University, NJ, 1992).

Bullock, Alan and Deakin, F. W. (eds), *The British Political Tradition*, book 6 (London, 1962).

Burke, Peter, *Popular Culture in Early Modern Europe* (New York, 1978).

Burnett, T. A. J., *The Rise and Fall of a Regency Dandy* (Boston, MA: Atlantic, 1981).

Butler, Judith, *Bodies that Matter: On the Discursive Limits of 'Sex'* (New York and London: Routledge, 1993).

Campbell, A. E., *Great Britain and the U.S., 1895–1903* (London: Longman, 1960).

Campbell, Charles S., *The United States and Great Britain: 1783–1900* (New York: Wiley, 1974).

Cantelon, Hart and Holland, Robert (eds), *Leisure, Sport, and Working-Class Cultures: Theory and History* (Toronto: Garamond Press, 1988).

Cash, Thomas F. and Pruzinsky, Thomas (eds), *Body Images: Development, Deviance and Change* (New York and London: Guilford Press, 1990).

Chambers, Iain, *Popular Culture: The Metropolitan Experience* (London and New York: Methuen, 1986).

Chandos, John, *Boys Together* (London: Yale University Press, 1984).

Chapman, David L., *Sandow the Magnificent* (Urbana and Chicago, IL: University of Illinois Press, 1994).

Chapman, David, Preface, *Adonis* (London: GMP, 1989).

Chapman, Rowena and Rutherford, Jonathan (eds), *Male Order: Unwrapping Masculinities* (London: Lawrence & Wishart, 1988).

Cheshire, D. F., *Music Hall in Britain* (Newton Abbot, 1974).

Chesney's Battle of Dorking (New York: Putnam, nd).

Cieplik, Raymond, *Physical Work and Amusements as Concerns of the Young Men's Christian Association, 1851–1884*, PhD Dissertation (University of Massachusetts, 1969).

Clark, Kenneth, *The Nude: A Study in Ideal Form* (Princeton, NJ: Princeton University Press, 1972).

Clatterbaugh, Kenneth, *Contemporary Perspectives on Masculinity: Men, Women, and Politics in Modern Society* (Boulder and San Francisco, CA, and Oxford: Westview, 1990).

Cook, David A., *A History of Narrative Film* (New York: Norton, 1981).

Cook, S. B., *The Example of Ireland: Political and Administrative Aspects of the Imperial Relationship, British India, 1855–1922*, PhD Dissertation (Rutgers University, NJ, 1987).

Croft-Cooke, Rupert, *Feasting with Panthers: A New Consideration of Some Late Victorian Writers* (New York: Holt, Rinehart & Winston, 1967).

Cunningham, Hugh, *The Volunteer Force: A Social and Political History, 1859–1908* (London: Croom Helm, 1975); *The Working-Class in England, 1875–1914*, ed. John Benson (London: Croom Helm, 1975) 133–64; *Leisure in the Industrial Revolution, c. 1780–1880* (London: St Martin's, 1980).

D'Arch Smith, Thomas, *Love in Earnest* (London, 1970).

Debord, Guy, *Society of the Spectacle* (Detroit, MI: Black and Red, 1977).

De Genst, H., *Histoire de l'éducation physique*, vols I and II (Brussels: Maison d'édition A. De Boeck, 1947–9).

Dickson, Lovat, *H. G. Wells: His Turbulent Life and Times* (New York: Atheneum, 1969).

Dinnage, Rosemary, *Annie Besant* (London, 1986).

Dinwiddy, J. R., *From Luddism to the First Reform Bill: Reform in England 1810–1832* (Oxford: Basil Blackwell, 1986).

Doughty, F. H., *H. G. Wells: Educationist, A Study* (New York: Doran, 1927).

Drescher, S., *Political Symbolism in Modern Europe* (New Brunswick, NJ: Transaction, 1982).

Dunlop, John K., *The Development of the British Army 1899–1914* (London: Methuen, 1938).

Dunning, Eric and Elias, Norbert (eds), *Quest for Excitement* (Oxford: Oxford University Press, 1986).

Eksteins, Modris, *Rites of Spring: The Great War and the Birth of the Modern Age* (New York: Anchor, 1990) 84.

Elias, Norbert, *Power and Civility: The Civilizing Process, II*, trans. Edmund Jephcott 1939 (New York: Pantheon, 1982).

Ellman, Richard, *Oscar Wilde* (New York: Knopf, 1988).

Engels, Friedrich and Marx, Karl, *The Communist Manifesto* (New York: Bantam, 1992).

Ernst, Robert, *Weakness is a Crime: The Life of Bernarr Macfadden* (New York: Syracuse University Press, 1991) 17.

Ewen, Stuart, *All Consuming Images: The Politics of Style in Contemporary Culture* (New York: Basic Books, 1988).

Eyck, Erich, *Bismark and the German Empire* (New York: Norton, 1950).

Fallon, Michael and Saunders, Jim, *Muscle Building for Beginners* (New York: Arco, 1960).

Farwell, Byron, *Eminent Victorian Soldiers* (New York: Norton, 1985); *For Queen and Country* (London: Allen Lane, 1983); *Mr. Kipling's Army* (New York: Norton, 1981).

Feher, Michel, *et al.* (eds), *Zone: Fragments for a History of the Human Body* (New York: Urzone, MIT, 1989).

Foucault, Michel, *Discipline and Punish: The Birth of the Prison*, trans. Alan Sheridan (New York: Vintage-Random, 1979).

Fox, Richard Wightman and Lears, T. Jackson (eds), *The Culture of Consumption: Critical Essays in American History, 1880–1920* (New York: Pantheon, 1983).

Fraser, W. Hamish, *The Coming of the Mass Market, 1850–1914* (Hamden, CT: Archon, 1981).

Fulford, Roger, *George the Fourth* (New York: Putnam, 1935).

Fussell, Paul, *The Great War and Modern Memory* (New York: Oxford University Press, 1975).

Gagnier, Regenia, *Idylls of the Marketplace: Oscar Wilde and the Victorian Public* (Stanford, CA: Stanford University Press, 1986).

Gaines, Charles and Butler, George, *Pumping Iron: The Art and Sport of Bodybuilding* (New York: Simon, 1981).

Gallagher, C. and Laqueur, T. (eds), *Society in the Nineteenth Century* (Berkeley, CA: University of California Press, 1987).

Garrard, Mary D., *Artemisia Gentileschi: The Image of the Female Hero in Italian Baroque Art* (Princeton, NJ: Princeton University Press, 1989).

Gawer, Herman and Michelman, Herbert, *Body Control: How to Build Up, Reduce or Strengthen Any Part of Your Body* (New York: Crown, 1950).

Gever, Martha, Greyson, John, and Parmar, Pratibha (eds), *Queer Looks: Perspectives on Lesbian and Gay Film and Video* (New York and London: Routledge, 1993).

Gillis, John R., *For Better, For Worse, British Marriage 1600–Present* (Oxford and New York: Oxford University Press, 1985); (ed.), *Commemorations: The Politics of National Identity* (Princeton, NJ: Princeton University Press, 1994).

Girouard, M., *The Return to Camelot: Chivalry and the English Gentleman* (New Haven, CT: Yale University Press, 1981).

Gledhill, Christine (ed.), *Stardom: Industry of Desire* (London: Routledge, 1991).

Gordon, Leonard A., *Bengal: The Nationalist Movement, 1874–1940* (New York: Columbia University Press, 1974).

Gorn, Elliott J., *The Manly Art* (New York: Cornell University Press, 1986).

Goyal, O. P., *Studies in Modern Indian Political Thought, vol. I, The Moderates and the Extremists* (Allahabad: Kitab Mahal, 1964).

Green, Harvey, *Fit for America: Health, Fitness, Sport and American Society* (New York: Pantheon, 1986).

Gretton, R. H., *A Modern History of the English People* (London: G. Richards, 1913).

Grover, Kathryn (ed.), *Fitness in American Culture: Images of Health, Sport, and the Body, 1830–1940* (Amherst, MA: University of Massachusetts Press, 1989).

Gruneau, Richard, *Class, Sports and Social Development* (Amherst, MA: University of Massachusetts Press, 1983).

Haley, Bruce, *The Healthy Body and Victorian Culture* (Cambridge, MA: Harvard University Press, 1978).

Hall, Lesley A., *Hidden Anxieties: Male Sexuality, 1900–1950* (Cambridge: Polity, 1991).

Haraway, Donna, *Cyborgs, Simians and Women* (New York: Routledge, 1991).

Hargreaves, John, *Sport, Power and Culture: A Social and Historical Analysis of Popular Sports in Britain* (New York: St Martin's, 1986).

Harvey, A. D., *Collision of Empires: Britain in Three World Wars, 1793–1945* (London and Rio Grande: Hambledon Press, 1992).

Haynes, Roslynn D., *H. G. Wells, Discoverer of the Future: The Influence of Science on his Thought* (New York University Press, 1980).

Heindel, Richard Heathcote, *The American Impact on Great Britain: 1898–1914* (Philadelphia, PA: University of Pennsylvania Press, 1940).

Higgins, Patrick (ed.), *A Queer Reader* (London: Fourth Estate, 1993).

Higham, Charles, *Ziegfeld* (Chicago: Regnery, 1982).

Hobsbawm, Eric, *Labouring Men: Studies in the Histories of Labour* (New York: Basic, 1964).

Hobsbawm, Eric and Ranger, Terrance (eds), *The Invention of Tradition* (Cambridge: Cambridge University Press, 1983).

Hoffman, Bob, *Big Arms: How to Develop Them* (York, PA: Strength & Health Publishing Co., 1950).

Hollander, Anne, *Seeing Through Clothes* (New York: Avon, 1980).

Holroyd, Michael, *Bernard Shaw, vol. 3, The Lure of Fantasy, 1918–1950* (London: Chatto, 1991).

Honey, J. R. de S., *Tom Brown's Universe: The Development of the English Public School in the 19th Century* (New York: Quadrangle, 1977).

Hopkins, R. Thurston, *H. G. Wells: Personality, Character, Topography* (London: Cecil Palmer, 1922).

Houghton, Walter E., *The Victorian Frame of Mind, 1830–1870* (New Haven, CT: Yale University Press, 1957).

Hudson, William Henry, *An Outline of English Literature* (London: G. Bell & Sons, 1923).

Hull, Isabel, *The Entourage of Kaiser Wilhelm II* (New York: Cambridge University Press, 1982).

Hunt, Lynn (ed.), *The New Cultural History* (Berkeley: University of California Press, 1989).

Hunt, Lynn (ed.), *Eroticism and the Body Politic* (Baltimore, MD: Johns Hopkins University Press, 1991).

Hunt, William R., *Body Love: The Amazing Career of Bernarr Macfadden* (Ohio: Bowling Green State Popular Press, 1989).

Inches, Howard V. H., *Brother, Heal Thyself* (Cleveland, OH: Phoenix Press, 1938).

Isenberg, Michael, *John L. Sullivan and his America* (Urbana, IL: University of Illinois Press, 1988).

James, Robert Rhodes, *The British Revolution, 1880–1939* (New York: Knopf, 1977).

Jay, R., *Learned Pigs and Fireproof Women* (New York: Villard, 1986).

Jeal, Tim, *The Boy-Man, the Life of Lord Baden-Powell* (New York: Morrow, 1990).

Jeffords, Susan, *Hard Bodies: Hollywood Masculinity in the Reagan Era* (New Brunswick, NJ: Rutgers University Press, 1994).

Jehlen, Myra, *American Incarnation: The Individual, the Nation, and the Continent* (Cambridge, MA: Harvard University Press, 1987).

Jermey, David J. (ed.), *Dictionary of Business Biography: 1860–1980* (London: Butterworths, 1985).

Johnson, Don Hanlon, *Body: Recovering our Sensual Wisdom* (Berkeley, CA: North Atlantic Books and Somatic Resources, 1992).

Johnson, Paul, *The Birth of the Modern: World Society 1815–1830* (New York: Harper/Collins, 1991).

Jones, Barbara, and Ouellette, William, *Erotic Postcards* (London: Macdonald & James, 1977).

Jordan, Thomas E., *Victorian Childhood: Themes and Variations* (Albany, NJ: State University of New York Press, 1987).

Kantorowicz, Ernst H., *The King's Two Bodies: A Study in Mediaeval Political Theology* (Princeton, NJ: Princeton University Press, 1957).

Kaplan, Joel H. and Stowell, Sheila, *Theatre and Fashion: Oscar Wilde to the Suffragettes* (New York: Cambridge University Press, 1994).

Keen, Maurice, *Chivalry* (New Haven, CT: Yale University Press, 1984).

Kelley, Veronica and Von Mucke, Dorothea E., *Body and Text in the Eighteenth Century* (Stanford, CA: Stanford University Press, 1994).

Kendrick, Walter, *The Secret Museum: Pornography in Modern Culture* (New York: Viking, 1987).

Kern, Stephen, *The Culture of Time and Space, 1880–1918* (Cambridge, MA: Harvard University Press, 1983); *Anatomy and Destiny: A Cultural History of the Human Body* (Indianapolis, IN: Bobbs-Merrill, 1975).

Klein, Alan M., *Little Big Men: Bodybuilding Subculture and Gender Construction* (Albany, NY: State University of New York Press, 1993).

Kohut, Thomas A., *Wilhelm II and the Germans: A Study in Leadership* (Oxford: Oxford University Press, 1991).

Landes, David, *Prometheus Unbound: Technological Change and Industrial Development in Western Europe from 1750 to the Present* (Cambridge: Cambridge University Press, 1969).

Laqueur, T., *Making Sex: Body and Gender from the Greeks to Freud* (Cambridge, MA: Harvard University Press, 1990).

Le Brun, Annie, *Sade: A Sudden Abyss*, trans. Camille Naish (San Francisco: City Lights Books, 1990).

Leder, Drew, *The Absent Body* (Chicago, IL: University of Chicago Press, 1990).

Lees-Milne, James, *The Enigmatic Edwardian: The Life of Reginald, 2nd Viscount Esher* (London: Sidgwick, 1988).

Lewis, Arthur O. jr (ed.), *Of Machines and Men* (New York: Dutton, 1963).

Lipovetsky, Gilles, *The Empire of Fashion: Dressing Modern Democracy* (Princeton, NJ: Princeton University Press, 1994).

Longford, Elizabeth, *Queen Victoria* (New York: Harper, 1965).

Lukacs, John, *Outgrowing Democracy: A History of the U.S. in the 20th Century* (Garden City, NJ: Doubleday, 1984).

Mace, O. Henry, *Collectors' Guide to Early Photographs* (Radnor, PA: Wallace-Homestead, 1990).

Macfadden, Mary and Gauvreau, Emile, *Dumbbells and Carrot Strips: The Story of Bernarr Macfadden* (New York: Henry Holt, 1953).

Mack, M. P., *Jeremy Bentham: An Odyssey of Ideas 1748–1792* (New York: Columbia University Press, 1963).

Macleod, David I., *Building Character in the American Boy* (Madison, WI: University of Wisconsin Press, 1983).

Magnus, Philip, *Gladstone* (London: John Murray, 1978).

Mandell, Richard D., *The First Modern Olympics* (Berkeley, CA: University of California Press, 1976).

Mander, Raymond and Mitchenson, J., *British Music Hall* (London: London House & Maxwell, 1965).

Mangan, J. A., *Athleticism in the Victorian and Edwardian Public School* (Cambridge: Cambridge University Press, 1981).

Mangan, J. A. and Walvin, James (eds), *Manliness and Morality: Middle-Class Masculinity in Britain and America 1800–1940* (New York: St Martin's Press, 1987).

Margetson, Stella, *Leisure and Pleasure in the Nineteenth-Century* (New York: Coward-McCann, 1969).

Markovich, Alexander, *The Publishing Empire of Bernarr Macfadden*, MA thesis (University of Missouri at Columbia, 1958).

Marsh, Peter (ed.), *The Conscience of the Victorian State* (New York: Syracuse University Press, 1979).

Marx, Karl, *Grundrisse: Foundations of the Critique of Political Economy* (New York: Vintage, 1973).

Mason, Philip, *The English Gentleman: The Rise and Fall of an Ideal* (New York: Morrow, 1982).

Mason, Tony, *Association Football and English Society, 1863–1915* (Brighton, 1980); *Sport in Britain: A Social History* (New York: Cambridge University Press, 1989).

Mayer, Arno, *The Persistence of the Old Regime* (New York: Pantheon, 1981).

McKendrick, Neil, Brewer, John, and Plumb, J. H., *The Birth of a Consumer Society: The Commercialization of Eighteenth Century England* (Bloomington, IN: University of Indiana Press, 1982).

Monaco, James, *How to Read a Film: The Art, Technology, Language, History, and Theory of Film and Media* (New York: Oxford University Press, 1981).

Monaco, James, et al. (eds), *Celebrity: Who Gets It, How They Use it, and Why It Works* (New York: Delta, 1978).

Moon, Michael, *Disseminating Whitman: Revision and Corporeality in 'Leaves of Grass'* (Cambridge, MA: Harvard University Press, 1992).

Moorhouse, Geoffrey, *India Britannica* (London: Paladin, 1984).

Morton, Peter, *The Vital Science: Biology and the Literary Imagination, 1860–1900* (London: Unwin, 1984).

Mosse, George, *Fallen Soldiers: Reshaping the Memory of the World Wars* (New York: Oxford University Press, 1990); *Nationalism and Sexuality: Middle-Class Morality and Sexual Norms in Modern Europe* (Madison, WI: University of Wisconsin Press, 1985).

Mrozek, Donald, *Sport and American Mentality, 1880–1920* (Knoxville, TN: University of Tennesee Press, 1983).

Mumford, Lewis, *Technics and Civilization* (New York: Harcourt, 1934).

Murray, Joseph, *Gallipoli As I Saw It* (London: W. Kimber, 1965).

Musser, Charles, *Resisting Images: Essays on Cinema and History* (Philadelphia, PA: Temple University Press, 1990); *Before the Nickelodeon: Edwin S. Porter and the Edison Manufacturing Co.* (Berkeley, CA: University of California Press, 1991); *High-class Moving Pictures: Lyman H. Howe and the Forgotten Era of the Traveling Exhibition, 1880–1920* (Princeton, NJ: Princeton University Press, 1991).

Nandy, Ashis, *The Intimate Enemy: Loss and Recovery of Self Under Colonialism* (New York: Oxford University Press, 1989).

Nicolson, Harold, *King George V* (London: Constable, 1970).

Niederland, W. G., *The Schreber Case* (New York: Quadrangle, 1974).

Nisivoccia, Gerard, *Sandow the Mighty Monarch of Muscle* (Newark, NJ, 1947).

Niver, Kemp R. and Bergsten, Bebe (eds), *Early Motion Pictures: The Paper Print Collection in the Library of Congress* (Washington, DC: Library of Congress, 1985).

O'Connell, Robert L., *Of Arms and Men: A History of War, Weapons and Aggression* (Oxford: Oxford University Press, 1989).

Osborne, R., *Clubland Heroes* (London: Constable, 1953).

Owens, Craig, *Beyond Recognition: Representation, Power and Culture*, ed. S. Bryson, B. Kruger, L. Tillman and J. Weinstock (Berkeley, CA: University of California Press, 1992).

Pakenham, Thomas, *The Boer War* (New York: Random, 1979).

Pakenham, Valerie, *Out in the Noonday Sun: Edwardians in the Tropics* (New York: Random House, 1985).

Panikkar, K. M., *Asia and Western Dominance: A Survey of the Vasco De Gama Epoch of Asian History, 1498–1945* (London: Unwin, 1959).

Penley, Constance and Ross, Andrew (eds), *Technoculture* (Minneapolis, MN: University of Minnesota Press, 1991).

Pick, Daniel, *Faces of Degeneration: A European Disorder, c. 1848– c. 1918* (Cambridge and New York: Cambridge University Press, 1989); *War Machine: The Rationalisation of Slaughter in the Modern Age* (New Haven, CT, and London: Yale University Press, 1993).

Pike, E. Royston, *Human Documents of the Industrial Revolution in Britain* (London: George Allen & Unwin, 1966).

Pohlmann, Ulrich, *Wilhelm von Gloeden: Sehnsucht nach Arkadien* (Berlin: Nishen Verlag, 1987).

Polhemus, Ted (ed.), *The Body Reader: Social Aspects of the Human Body* (New York: Pantheon, 1978).

Pollard, Sidney, *A History of Labour in Sheffield* (Liverpool: Liverpool University Press, 1959); *The Development of the British Economy, 1914–1950* (London: Edward Arnold, 1962); *European Economic Integration, 1815–1970* (London: Thames & Hudson, 1974).

Porter, Roy, *Health for Sale: Quackery in England, 1660–1850* (New York: Manchester University Press, 1989).

Proctor, Robert N., *Racial Hygiene: Medicine Under the Nazis* (Cambridge, MA, and London: Harvard University Press, 1988).

Pugh, Martin, *The Making of Modern British Politics, 1867–1939*, 5th edn (Oxford: Blackwell, 1987).

Raknem, Ingvald, *H. G. Wells and his Critics* (Trondheim, Norway: George Allen & Unwin, 1962).

Read, Benedict, *Victorian Sculpture* (New Haven, CT, and London: Yale University Press, 1982).

Reader, W. J., *At Duty's Call: A Study in Obsolete Patriotism* (Manchester: Manchester University Press, 1988).

Reid, J. C., *Bucks and Bruisers: Pierce Egan and Regency England* (London: Routledge, 1971).

Rhodes, Robert James, *Rosebery: A Biography of Archibald Philip, Fifth Earl of Rosebery* (New York: Macmillan, 1963).

Richards, Jeffrey, *Happiest Days: The Public Schools in English Fiction* (Manchester: Manchester University Press, 1988); Richards, J. and Evans, E. J., *A Social History of Britain in Postcards: 1870–1930* (New York and London: Longman, 1980).

Richards, Thomas, *The Commodity Culture of Victorian England: Advertising and Spectacle, 1851–1914* (Stanford, CA: Stanford University Press, 1990).

Ripert, Aline, and Frère, Claude, *La Carte postale: son histoire, sa fonction sociale* (Paris: Presses universitaires de Lyons et Paris, 1983).

Roach, John, *Social Reform in England, 1780–1880* (New York: St Martin's, 1978).

Roditi, Edouard, *Oscar Wilde* (New York: New Directions, 1947).

Rodney, Walter, *How Europe Underdeveloped Africa* (Washington: Howard University Press, 1982).

Roebuck, Janet, *The Making of Modern English Society from 1850* (London: Routledge, 1973).

Rohl, John C. G. and Sombart, Nicolaus, *Kaiser Wilhelm II: New Interpretations* (Cambridge: Cambridge University Press, 1982).

Roper, Michael *et al.* (eds), *Manful Assertions* (London: Routledge, 1990).

Rosenthal, Michael, *The Character Factory: Baden-Powell and the Origins of the Boy Scout Movement* (New York: Pantheon, 1986).

Sands, Mollie, *The Eighteenth-Century Pleasure Gardens of Marylebone, 1737–1777* (London: Society for Theatre Research, 1987).

Sappington, Rodney and Stallings, Tyler (eds), *Uncontrollable Bodies: Testimonies of Identity and Culture* (Seattle, WA: Bay Press, 1994).

Schlereth, Thomas J., *Victorian America: Transformations in Everyday Life, 1876–1915* (New York: Harper, 1991).

Sedgwick, Eve Kosovsky, *Epistemology of the Closet* (Berkeley, CA: University of California Press, 1990).

Senelick, Laurence, *et al.*, *British Music-Hall, 1840–1923* (Hamden, CT: Archon, 1981).

Shatzman, M., *Persecution in the Family* (New York: Random, 1973).

Showalter, Elaine, *The Female Malady: Women, Madness, and English Culture, 1830–1980* (New York: Pantheon, 1985); *Sexual Anarchy: Gender and Culture at the Fin de Siècle* (New York: Viking, 1990).

Sinfield, Alan, *The Wilde Century: Effeminacy, Oscar Wilde and the Queer Moment* (New York: Columbia University Press, 1994).

Smart, C. M. jr, *Muscular Churches: Ecclesiastical Architecture of the High Victorian Period* (Fayetteville, AR, and London: University of Arkansas Press, 1989).

Spiers, Edward M., *The Army and Society, 1815–1914* (London: Longman, 1980).

Stansell, Christine, *City of Women: Sex and Class in New York, 1789–1860* (New York: Knopf, 1986).

Stansky, Peter (ed.), *The Victorian Revolution* (New York: New Viewpoints, 1973); *England Since 1867: Continuity and Change* (New York: Harcourt, 1973).

Stedman Jones, Gareth, *Languages of Class: Studies in English Working Class History, 1832–1982* (Cambridge: Cambridge University Press, 1983).

Steedman, Carolyn, *et al.*, *Language, Gender and Childhood* (London: Routledge, 1985).

Steiner, Werner, *Kulturfahrplan*, trans. Bernard Grun (New York: Simon, 1979).

Stokes, John, *In the Nineties* (Chicago, IL: University of Chicago Press, 1989).

Suleiman, Susan Rubin (ed.), *The Female Body in Western Culture: Contemporary Perspectives* (Cambridge, MA, and London: Harvard University Press, 1985).

Sullivan, Constance (ed.), *Nude Photographs: 1850–1980* (New York: Harper & Row, 1980).

Synnot, Anthony, *The Body Social: Symbolism, Self and Society* (London: Routledge, 1993).

Tagg, John, *The Burden of Representation: Essays on Photographies and Histories* (Amherst, MA: University of Massachusetts Press, 1988).

Tannenbaum, Edward R., *1900: The Generation before the Great War* (Garden City, NJ: Anchor Press/Doubleday, 1976).

Teich, Mikulás and Porter, Roy (eds), *Fin de Siècle and its Legacy* (New York: Cambridge University Press, 1990).

Thompson, Paul, *The Edwardians: The Remaking of British Society* (London: Granada, 1977).

Tomlinson, Alan (ed.), *Consumption, Identity, Style: Marketing, Meanings, and the Packaging of Pleasure* (London: Routledge, 1990).

van Doorn, Jacques, *The Soldier and Social Change* (London, 1975).

Vansittart, Peter, *Voices from the Great War* (New York: Watts, 1989).

Vernant, Jean-Pierre, *Mortals and Immortals*, ed. I. Zeitlin (Princeton, NJ: Princeton University Press, 1991).

Walkowitz, Judith, *Prostitution and Victorian Society: Women, Class and the State* (New York: Cambridge University Press, 1980).

Ward, Geoffrey C., *The Maharajas* (Chicago, IL: Stonehenge, 1983).

Watney, Simon, *Policing Desire: AIDS, Pornography, and the Media* (Minneapolis, MN: University of Minnesota Press, 1987).

Waugh, Clifford J., *Bernarr Macfadden: The Muscular Prophet*, PhD Dissertation (Buffalo, NY: State University of New York, 1979).

Weatherill, Lorna, *Consumer Behaviour and Material Culture in Britain, 1660–1760* (London: Routledge, 1989).

Webster, David, *The Iron Game: An Illustrated History of Weightlifting* (Irvine, CA: John Geddes, 1976).

Weeks, Jeffrey, *Coming Out: Homosexual Politics in Britain, from the Nineteenth Century to the Present* (London: Quartet, 1977); *Sex, Politics and Society: The Regulation of Sexuality since 1800* (New York: Longman, 1981).

Weiner, Martin J., *English Culture and the Decline of the Industrial Spirit, 1850–1980* (Cambridge: Cambridge University Press, 1981).

White, Arnold, *The Modern Jew* (London: Heinemann, 1899).

White, Kevin, *The First Sexual Revolution: The Emergence of Male Heterosexuality in Modern America* (New York and London: New York University Press, 1993).

Whorton, James, *Crusaders for Fitness: The History of American Health Reformers* (Princeton, NJ: Princeton University Press, 1982).

Wilkinson, Rupert, *The Prefects, British Leadership and the Public School Tradition* (London: Oxford University Press, 1964); *American Tough: The Tough-guy Tradition and American Character* (Westport, CT: Greenwood, 1984); *Governing Elites: Studies in Training and Selection* (New York: Oxford University Press, 1969).

Williams, Eric, *Capitalism and Slavery* (University of North Carolina Press, 1944).

Williams, Raymond, *Culture and Society* (Harmondsworth: Penguin, 1961); *Keywords* (London: Fontana, 1976); *The Long Revolution* (New York: Columbia University Press, 1961).

Wohl, Anthony S. (ed.), *The Victorian Family: Structure and Stresses* (New York: St Martin's Press, 1978).

Woods, Gregory, *Articulate Flesh: Male Homo-Eroticism and Modern Poetry* (New Haven, CT, and London: Yale University Press, 1987).

Zuboff, Shoshana, *In the Age of the Smart Machine: The Future of Work and Power* (New York: Basic Books, 1988).

CURRENT ARTICLES

Annan, Noel, 'In Bed with the Victorians', *New York Review of Books* (20 Nov. 1986).

Bogacz, Ted, 'War Neurosis and Cultural Change in England, 1914–22', *Journal of Contemporary History* (London: SAGE) 24 (2) (April 1989): 227–56.

Bonfante, Larissa, 'The Naked Greek', *Archaeology* (Sept./Oct. 1990): 28–35.

Brantlinger, Patrick, 'Mass Media and Culture in *fin-de-siècle* Europe', in Teich and Porter (eds), *Fin de Siècle and its Legacy* (1990).

Cecil, Lamar, 'History as Family Chronicle: Kaiser Wilhelm II and the Dynastic Roots of the Anglo-German Antagonism', in Rohl and Sombart (eds), *Kaiser Wilhelm II* (Cambridge: Cambridge University Press, 1982).

Cell, John, 'The Imperial Conscience', in Marsh (ed.), *The Conscience of the Victorian State* (1979).

Chapman, Rowena, 'The Great Pretender: Variations on the New Man Theme', in Chapman and Rutherford (eds), *Male Order* (1988).

Dubbert, Joe L., 'Progressivism and the Masculinity Crisis', *Psychoanalytic Review*, 61 (1974): 443–55.

Dunning, Eric, 'Sport as a Male Preserve: Notes on the Social Sources of Masculine Identity and its Transformations', in Dunning and Elias (eds), *Quest for Excitement* (1986).

Eichberg, Henning, 'The Enclosure of the Body – On the Historical Relativity of "Health", "Nature" and the Environment of Sport', *Journal of Contemporary History*, 21 (1986): 99–121.

Ellman, Richard, 'A Victorian Love Affair', *New York Review of Books*, 24 (13) (1977): 6–10.

Fine, Ben and Leopold, Ellen, 'Consumerism in the Industrial Revolution', *Social History*, 15 (2) (May 1990).

Fletcher, Sheila, 'The Making and Breaking of a Tradition: Women's Physical Education in England, 1880–1980', *British Journal of Sport History*, 2 (1) (May 1985).

Gilbert, Sandra, 'Soldier's Heart: Literary Men, Literary Women, and the Great War', *Signs*, 8 (3) (1983).

Gorer, Geoffrey, 'The British National Character in the Twentieth Century', *Annals of the American Academy of Political and Social Sciences*, 370 (March 1967): 74–81.

Grosskurth, Phyllis, 'Freud's Favorite Paranoiac', *New York Review of Books* (18 Jan. 1990): 36–8.

Hansen, Miriam, 'Adventures of Goldilocks: Spectatorship, Consumerism and Public Life', *Camera Obscura*, 22 (Autumn 1990): 51–71.

Hunt, Lynn, 'The Many Bodies of Marie Antoinette', in Hunt (ed.), *Eroticism and the Body Politic* (1991).

Hutton, Patrick H., 'The Foucault Phenomenon and Contemporary French Historiography', *Historical Reflections/Relexions Historique*, 17 (1) (1991): 77–102.

Hyam, Ronald, 'Empire and Sexual Opportunity', *Journal of Imperial and Commonwealth History*, xiv (2) (Jan. 1986): 34–90.

Jenkins, Ray, 'Salvation for the Fittest? A West African Sportsman in Britain in the New Age of Imperialism', *International Journal of Sport History*, 7 (1) (May 1990): 23–60.

Johnson, Richard, 'Educational Policy and Social Control in Early Victorian England', in Stansky (ed.), *The Victorian Revolution* (1973).

Kent, Sarah, 'Pleasure Principles', *Time Out* London (16–22 May 1985): 14–17.

Klossowski, Pierre, 'La moneta vivente' (La monnaie vivante), Italian trans. C. Morena, *Il Piccolo Hans*, 13 (1977).

Koven, Seth, 'Remembering and Dismemberment: Crippled Children, Wounded Soldiers and the Great War in Britain', *American Historical Review* (October 1994): 1167–202.

Laqueur, Thomas, 'Bodies, Details, and the Humanitarian Narrative', in Lynn Hunt (ed.), *The New Cultural History* (Berkeley: University of California Press, 1989); 'Memory and Naming in the Great War', in Gillis (ed.), *Commemorations: The Politics of National Identity* (1994).

MacDonald, Robert H., 'Reproducing the Middle-Class Boy: From Purity to Patriotism in the Boy's Magazines, 1892–1914', *Journal of Contemporary History* (London: SAGE) 24 (1989): 519–39.

Maddow, Ben, 'Nude in a Social Landscape', in Sullivan (ed.), *Nude Photographs* (1980).

Matthew, H. C. G., 'Rhetoric and Politics in Britain, 1860–1950', in *Politics and Social Change in Modern Britain* (New York: St Martin's, 1987).

McCrone, K., 'Play Up! Play Up! And Play the Game! Sport at the Late Victorian Public School', *Journal of British Studies*, xxiii (2) (1984): 127–8.

Mckendrick, Neil (*et al.*), 'Commercialization of Fashion', in *The Birth of a Consumer Society: The Commercialization of Eighteenth-Century England* (London: Europa, 1982).

Miles, R., 'Recent Marxist Theories of Nationalism and the Issue of Racism', *British Journal of Scoiology*, 38 (1): 24–43.

Mort, Frank, 'Health and Hygiene: The Edwardian State and Medico-Moral Politics', in *The Edwardian Era* (London: V & A Museum, 1987); 'Boys Own? Masculinity, Style and Popular Culture', in Chapman and Rutherford (eds), *Male Order* (1988).

Morton, Patricia, 'Another Victorian Paradox: Anti-Militarism in a Jingoistic Society', *Historical Reflections/Reflexions Historique*, 8 (2) (1981): 169–89; 'A Military Irony: the Victorian Volunteer Movement', *Journal of the RUSI for Defence Studies*, 131 (3) (1986): 63–70.

Mrozek, Donald J., 'Sport in American Life: From National Health to Personal Fulfillment, 1890–1940', in Grover (ed.), *Fitness in American Culture* (1989).

Mulvey, Laura, 'Visual Pleasure and Narrative Cinema' *Screen*, 3 (autumn 1975): 6–18.

Mustazza, Leonard, 'Thomas Deloney's *Jacke of Newbury*: A Horatio Alger Story for the Sixteenth Century', *Journal of Popular Culture*, 23 (3) (1989): 165–77.

Nye, Robert A., 'Degeneration and the Medical Model of Cultural Crisis in the French *Belle Époque*', in S. Drescher (ed.), *Political Symbolism in Modern Europe* (New Brunswick, NJ: Transaction, 1982).

Otley, C. B., 'The Social Origins of British Army Officers', *Sociological Review*, 18 (2) (1970): 213–40.

Panayi, Panikos, 'German Business Interests in Britain during the First World War', *Business History*, 32 (2) (1990): 244–58.

Park, Roberta J., 'Sport, Gender and Society in a Transatlantic Perspective', *British Journal of Sport History*, 2 (1) (1985): 5–28.

Pivato, Stefano, 'The Bicycle as a Political Symbol: Italy, 1885–1955', *International Journal of the History of Sport*, 7 (2) (1990).

Pointon, Marcia, 'Liberty on the Barricades: Women, Politics, and Sexuality in Delacroix', in Reynolds (ed.), *Women, State and Revolution* (1986).

Potts, Alex, 'Beautiful Bodies and Dying Heroes', *History Workshop*, 30 (autumn 1990): 1–21.

Putney, Clifford, 'Character Building in the YMCA, 1880–1930', *Mid-America: An Historical Review*, 73 (1) (Jan. 1991): 49–70.

Reiss, Steven A., 'Sport and the Redefinition of American Middle-class Masculinity', *International Journal of the History of Sport*, 8 (1) (1991).

Rosselli, John, 'The Self-Image of Effeteness: Physical Education and Nationalism in Nineteenth-Century Bengal', *Past and Present*, 86 (Feb. 1980): 121–48.

Rotundo, Antony E., 'Body and Soul: Changing Ideals of American Middle Class Manhood, 1770–1920', *Journal of Social History*, 16 (4) (1983): 23–38.

Sedgwick, Eve Kosovsky, 'Homophobia, Misogyny, Capital: The Example of *Our Mutual Friend*', *Raritan*, 2 (3) (1983): 144–8.

Seltzer, Mark, 'The Love-Master', in Boone and Cadden (eds), *Engendering Men* (1990).

Sobieszek, Robert, 'Reflections on the Nude Photograph', in Sullivan (ed.), *Nude Photographs* (1980).

Sombart, Nicholas, 'The Kaiser in his Epoch: Some Reflections on Wilhelmine Society, Sexuality and Culture', in Rohl, John C. G. and Sombart, Nicolaus (eds), *Kaiser Wilhelm II* (Cambridge: Cambridge University Press, 1982).

Stansky, Peter, 'Lyttleton and Thring: A Study in 19th Century Education', in Stansky (ed.), *The Victorian Revolution* (1973).

Stearns, P. N., 'The Effort at Continunity in Working-class Culture', *Journal of Modern History*, lii (1980): 626–55.

Stedman Jones, Gareth, 'Working-Class Culture and Working-Class Politics in London, 1870–1900', *Journal of Social History* (summer 1974).

Stoianovich, Traian, 'Gender and Family: Myth, Models and Ideologies', *The History Teacher*, 15 (1) (Nov. 1981): 67–117.

Taft, William H., 'Bernarr Macfadden', *Missouri Historical Review*, 63 (1) (1968).

Travers, Tim, 'The Hidden Army: Structural Problems in British Officer Corps, 1900–1918', *Journal of Contemporary History*, 17 (3) (1982): 523–44.

Trumbach, Randolph, 'London's Sodomites: Homosexual Behavior and Western Culture in the 18th Century', *Journal of Social History*, 11 (1) (1977).

Vamplew, Wray, 'The Sport of Kings and Commoners: the Commercialization of British Horse-racing in the Nineteenth-Century', in Cashman and McKernan, *Sport in History* (1979).

Waldron, Arthur, 'The WarLord: Twentieth-Century Chinese Understandings of Violence, Militarism, and Imperialism', *American Historical Review* (Oct. 1991): 1073–100.

Walker, Pamela, ' "I Live But Not Yet I for Christ Liveth In Me": Men and Masculinity in the Salvation Army, 1865–1890', in Roper et al. (eds), *Manful Assertions* (1991).

Waugh, Thomas, 'The Third Body: Patterns in the Construction of the Subject in Gay, Male Narrative Film', in Gever, Greyson, Parmar (eds), *Queer Looks: Perspectives on Lesbian and Gay Film and Video* (London: Routledge, 1993).

Weeks, Jeffrey, 'Inverts, Perverts and Mary-Annes: Male Prostitution and the Regulation of Homosexuality in the Nineteenth and Early Twentieth Centuries', *Journal of Homosexuality*, 6 (1/2) (1980/81).

Wiggins, David K., 'Peter Jackson and the Elusive Heavyweight Championship: A Black Athlete's Struggle against the Late Nineteenth Century Color-Line', *Journal of Sport History*, 12 (2)/(1985): 143–68.

Wilson, Christopher P., 'The Rhetoric of Consumption: Mass-Market Magazines and the Demise of the Gentle Reader, 1880–1920', in Fox and Lears (eds), *The Culture of Consumption* (1983).

Yagoda, Ben, 'The True Story of Bernarr Macfadden', *American Heritage* (Dec. 1981).

Index